Globalization and Social Change in Contemporary Japan

JAPANESE SOCIETY SERIES

General Editor: Yoshio Sugimoto

Lives of Young Koreans in Japan
Yasunori Fukuoka

Globalization and Social Change in Contemporary Japan
J.S. Eades Tom Gill Harumi Befu

Globalization and Social Change in Contemporary Japan

Edited by

J.S. Eades Tom Gill Harumi Befu

Trans Pacific Press

Melbourne

First published in 2000 by
Trans Pacific Press
PO Box 120, Rosanna, Melbourne, Victoria 3084, Australia
Telephone: +61 3 9459 3021
Fax: +61 3 9457 5923
E-mail: enquiries@transpacificpress.com
Website: http://www.transpacificpress.com

Reprinted 2005

Set in CJR Times New Roman by digital environs Melbourne
enquiries@digitalenvirons.com

Printed in Melbourne by Brown Prior Anderson

Distributed in North America by
International Specialized Book Services, Inc.
5804 NE Hassalo Street
Portland, Oregon 97213-3644
USA
Telephone: +1 800 944 6190 (toll free)
Fax: +1 503 280 3644
E-mail: orders@isbs.com
Website: http://www.isbs.com

ISSN 1443–9670 (Japanese Society Series)
ISBN 1–876843–01–2

National Library of Australia Cataloging in Publication Data

Globalization and social change in contemporary Japan

Bibliography
Includes index
ISBN 1 876843 01 2

1. Globalization. 2. Japan – Social aspects. 3. Japan – Social life and customs – 20th century. 4. Japan – Social conditions – 20th century. 5. Japan – Religious life and customs. I. Befu, Harumi, 1930–. II. Eades, J. S., 1945–. III. Gill, Tom, 1960–. (Series: Japanese society series; v.2).

952.033

British Library Cataloging in Publication Data

A catalogue record for this book is available from the British Library.

US Library of Congress Cataloging in Publication Data

Contents

Tables

Figures

Preface

The idea for this book arose from a symposium on 'Recent Social and Cultural Change in Japan,' organized by Harumi Befu and Tom Gill at Kyoto Bunkyo University on March 14–15, 1998. The intention of the symposium was to provide a forum in which the increasing number of Anglophone scholars working and carrying out long-term research in Japan could meet and talk about their ongoing interests. We would like here to thank the Kyoto Bunkyo University Institute for Cultural and Human Research for funding the event. Following its success, two similar meetings have been held, organized by David Slater and John Clammer at Sophia University in Tokyo in 1999, and by John Mock at the University of Minnesota campus in Akita in 2000.

The introductory literature survey by Eades and the chapters by Befu, Möhwald, McVeigh, Davis, Herbert, Riessland, and Clammer all started life as presentations at the 1998 Kyoto meeting. These papers covered such a broad cross-section of life in contemporary Japan that it was not long before the idea took shape of using them as the basis of a more inclusive book around the themes of changing Japan and globalization. Gradually the coverage was extended through the inclusion of additional papers covering Japanese capitalism overseas (Sedgwick), women and the Japanese labor market (Bishop), the structure of casual labor (Gill), and changes in traditional craft industries (Eades, Eades, Nishiyama, and Yanase).

The editing of the book has been complicated by the fact that all three of us have been on the move over the last few months: Tom Gill from Kyoto Bunkyo University to the University of Tokyo, Harumi Befu from Kyoto Bunkyo University to the Humboldt University in Berlin, and Jerry Eades from Shiga University in Hikone to Ritsumeikan Asia Pacific University in Beppu. The editorial work had to be fitted in around these movements, and the final order of names is actually a measure of the relative time available to each of us over this rather difficult period. We are grateful to Yoshio Sugimoto of Trans Pacific Press for his agreement to include the book in his Japanese Society Series and for his advice and support in the preparation of the final version. We also wish him every success in his efforts to globalize the speed and efficiency which are the norm in contemporary Japanese publishing, but which are all too often lacking elsewhere.

Japanese words have been transcribed in the conventional Hepburn system, with long 'o' and 'u' represented by 'ō' and 'ū' respectively. Generally Japanese names have been given in the usual Japanese order, with family names first. The main exception is that of Japanese names in the Table of Contents and chapter headings, where the western order has been retained to avoid confusion in citations.

The Editors
July 2000

1 Introduction: Globalization and Social Change in Contemporary Japan

Jerry Eades

Japan in the 1990s

In his review of Japanese anthropology up to the start of the 1990s, Kelly (1991) focused on a number of trends typical of the period: the deconstruction of anthropological theory, the increasing interplay between anthropology and history, and the increasing tendency of anthropologists to concentrate on regional issues in Japan rather than general theory. After reviewing the increasingly problematic attempts to grapple with broad, general concepts such as 'culture' and 'personality' within the Japanese context, he moved on to consider specific areas of Japanese life that had become major foci of research. These included: changing forms of the family and relations between the generations; the anthropology of work and the workplace, including both large corporations and smaller types of enterprises; education; gender and patriarchy; life in the large cities and the outlying regions; festivals, heritage, and cultural tourism; law and social control; stratification and the status of minorities; religion; and the anthropology of medicine and healing.

A decade later, this list of topics is still a reasonably accurate guide to research on Japan, even though there has been a boom in some other types of studies, such as popular culture. Apart from the monumental attempt to comprehend the nature of 'Japanese civilization' in comparative perspective by Eisenstadt (1996), most scholars have adopted a much more delimited focus. But even though there has been continuity in the subjects of research, there has been a dramatic change in the context within which this research has been carried out. After the preceding decades of rapidly increasing prosperity, the 1990s turned out to be a particularly turbulent period in Japanese history. This began with the collapse of the 'bubble economy,' which triggered collapses on the stock market and in land prices (Wood 1993, 1994; Katz 1998). This in turn threw the entire financial sector into confusion, with the failure of major banks and securities firms. In 1993 the Liberal Democratic Party, which had held power since 1955, was replaced by a coalition of seven smaller parties (Schlesinger 1997: part 4; Curtis 1999: 99–136). It was soon back in power, but in the meantime the map of Japanese politics had been redrawn through a change in the electoral system that the coalition had introduced. In early 1995 the devastating Kobe earthquake (Terry 1998) was followed by the sarin gas attack by members of Aum Shinrikyō, an apocalyptic religious cult, on the Tokyo subway system (Kaplan and Marshall 1996; Brackett 1996; Reader 1996). These events were not only shattering in themselves, but their inept handling by the government, the bureaucracy, and the police further undermined public trust in the government and administrative system.[1] Since then, the media have become increasingly vociferous in pushing for change. New scandals involving politicians, bureaucrats, and the police are coming to light almost daily, accompanied by scenes on television of investigators removing cartons of seized documents from offices, and suspects photographed in the back seats of police cars after their arrests. Demands for reform are almost universal – even if agreement on the content of these reforms is much more difficult to achieve.

Underlying these changes are processes which are less dramatic but of fundamental importance in understanding change within Japan. One of the measures of the success of Japanese economic development has been the enormously increased life expectancy of its older citizens. But this has been accompanied by a collapse in the birthrate, now one of the lowest in the world (Jolivet 1997). There is much discussion in the media of the problems of the aging society, and the declining percentage of the population who are economically active and able to support those who are not. The situation is most acute in the towns and villages in the outlying areas of the country (e.g. Traphagen 2000), where mayors and bureaucrats are racking their brains to find ways of reviving the local economy in places where many of the young people have left for the larger cities. Meanwhile the government has to grapple with the problems of the costs of medical, welfare, and pension systems that were set up on the basis of a very different demographic structure. Also related is the debate over the reasons why women are having so few children. Factors frequently cited include the pressures of the education system, which the mother usually has to bear on her own, and the continued prevalence of overtime working, which means that fathers have little time to spend with their families. At the same time, the Japanese 'salaryman' himself is increasingly seen as something of an endangered species, with falling job security, rising unemployment, and the off-shoring of much of Japan's industrial production. Even though for the longer term the United Nations is predicting that Japan will eventually have to import millions of foreign workers to make up for the shortage of labor, the present problem is that of finding jobs for the high school and university graduates moving into the labor market. Had not Japan's birthrate fallen so low so quickly, the unemployment problem might by now have been even worse.

Research in the social sciences, including sociology and social and cultural anthropology, has reflected these trends. Increasingly this research has taken on significance for public policy, and even for politics. Studies of the family merge with studies of the problems of housing (Brown 1996), relations between the generations (Kaplan et al. 1998), and the problems of old people, especially in smaller towns and villages with high rates of out-migration (Traphagen 2000). Studies of the expansion of Tokyo and the other large cities (e.g. Fujita and Hill eds 1993; Dearing 1995; Tabb 1995: Chapter 7; Karan and Stapleton eds 1997; Cybriwsky 1998; Eades 1999: xiii–xxxvi) merge with critiques of planning, pollution, and the 'construction state' (McCormack 1996: 25–77; Kidder 1997; Broadbent 1998). Studies of work have focused not only on salarymen and women (Lam 1992; Kriska 1997), factory workers (Roberts 1994; Turner 1995), and small businesses (Kondo 1990; Whittaker 1997; Roberson 1998), but also on immigrant workers (Weiner 1994; Komai 1995; Herbert 1996a; Ventura 1992), and casual day laborers (Fowler 1996; Stevens 1997; Gill 1999, forthcoming 2001, see also Chapter 8). Studies of education, from pre-school to colleges (e.g. Peak 1991; Lewis 1995; McVeigh 1997; Benjamin 1997; Rohlen and LeTendre eds 1998) merge with calls for educational reform at all levels (Schoppa 1991; McVeigh 1998b: 124–79; Okano and Tsuchiya 1999: 194–237). In the same way, studies of minorities such as the resident Koreans (Weiner, 1994; Ryang 1997; Fukuoka 2000), Burakumin (Neary 1997, see also Chapter 7), and migrant workers from overseas (Weiner ed. 1997) are closely linked to calls for a reduction in discrimination and the liberalization of immigration policy to help offset the declining birthrate (Komai 1995; Shimada 1994; Mori 1997). Studies of popular culture (Martinez ed. 1998; Treat ed. 1996) are now closely linked with the world of business, whether through advertising companies (Moeran 1996a, 1995b), shopping (Clammer 1997; MacPherson ed. 1998), the pursuit of leisure (Linhart and Früstück eds 1998), or the massive international tourist industry with its burgeoning resorts and theme parks (Havens 1994; Bryman 1995; Raz 1999). Even in the study of religion the most dramatic event of the decade, the Aum Shinrikyō affair, has led to intense soul-searching and analysis of the causes of the alienation that led some of Japan's best and brightest into the arms of a seemingly irrational and bizarre cult.

As these issues have unfolded, the broader trends highlighted by Kelly have also continued. The growing rapprochement between anthropology, sociology, and history has meant that disciplinary boundaries are largely irrelevant in much of the best research being carried out on Japan. The contents of introductory surveys from the point of view of the three disciplines increasingly overlap (cf. Hendry 1995; Sugimoto 1997; Waswo 1998), and the stuff of history has become the research material of anthropology (Yoneyama 1999) or *vice versa* (Gordon ed. 1993). And while many of the classic issues in the anthropology of Japan have been put onto the back burner, other concerns which are shared with sister disciplines have come to the fore – including that of globalization.

Globalization and the 'information society'

'Globalization' became one of the most fashionable buzzwords in the social sciences of the 1990s, even though, as Bauman points out, 'the more experiences [these words] pretend to make transparent, the more they themselves become opaque' (Bauman 1998: 1). Generally the word has been used to refer broadly to one or other of two processes. The first is that of the globalization of the world economy: the increasing dominance of the multinational companies at the expense of the nation-state, the speeding up of flows of capital both within and across international boundaries, and the consequent movement of labor across the globe (Castells 1996: Chapter 3; Tabb, 1995: Chapter 10). The second is that of the global diffusion and 'creolization' of cultural forms and meanings (Hannerz 1992: 264–69), manifested in phenomena such as the 'McDonaldization' of eating habits (cf. Watson ed. 1997), the proliferation of theme parks, or the popularity of international brand name goods. These two levels of reality are increasingly mediated by information technology, especially the Internet.

One of the best accounts of these processes together with the global context in which they are taking place is that of Manuel Castells in his recent trilogy, *The Information Age* (Castells 1996, 1997, 1998). His basic position can be summarized as follows: advanced industrial countries are moving from economies based on manufacturing and industry to economies based on the production, manipulation, and dissemination of information (Castells 1996: Chapters 1–2). The effects of this transformation are to be seen throughout the world, not only in the regions that dominate the information technology industry, but also those that are excluded from it – because of the increasing polarization of the rich, who have access to this technology, and the poor, who do not.

Some of the most obvious effects of this transition are to be seen in the labor markets of the advanced countries, with the growth of the financial services industry in the 'global cities' (cf. Sassen 1991), the collapse of more traditional forms of production, and the replacement of full-time male employment by lower-paid and more casual female employment. The nature of work itself is changing with the rise of the 'network enterprise' (Castells 1996: Chapters 3–4). There are also cultural effects: the 'shrinking' of space and time by information technology means that we experience the world differently (Castells 1996: Chapters 5–7).

These changes are in turn having a knock-on effect on the family and social organization. The 'patriarchal' families headed by male primary breadwinners which used to be the norm are now in a minority, thanks to the frequency of divorce, an increasing reluctance to marry, and the increasing popularity of homosexual and other alternative lifestyles (Castells 1997: Chapter 4). 'Traditional' sex roles are seen as under threat, and attempts to shore them up are reflected in the popularity of fundamentalist versions of Christianity and Islam, with their instant moralities and their strong patriarchal role models (Castells 1997: 12–27). Religious, ethnic, and national identities provide anchors for people trying to organize their lives in the post-industrial, globalized world, as do social movements, including various forms of environmentalism (Castells 1997: Chapters 1–3). Meanwhile the position of the nation-state itself is being undermined, as it becomes increasingly unable to control the multinationals and the international flows of capital in the 'global casino' of the currency markets (Castells 1997: Chapter 5). In the major democracies, the media increasingly influence the nature of politics, with their insatiable thirst for marketable information, however trivial (Castells 1997: Chapter 6). As the fortunes of nation-states decline, with those of the Soviet Union collapsing completely (Castells 1998: Chapter 1), those of regional organizations, led by the European Union, are on the rise (Castells 1998: Chapter 5), as nation-states trade a degree of autonomy for longer-term stability.

This is leading to profound changes in regions like East Asia, where the 'economic miracles' of the last few decades were generally based on an alliance between strong 'developmental states' and local capital (Castells 1998: Chapter 4; cf. Johnson 1995). The question for the future is whether the states of the region can retain control of the development process in the face of the forces that these economic miracles have unleashed. Meanwhile the areas excluded from access to new technology face very different problems: these include not only regions such as much of Africa and the former Soviet Union, but also the poorer areas of the advanced capitalist countries, such as the inner city ghettoes and casual laborer quarters (Castells 1998: Chapters 1–2).

Social change in Japan

Some elements of Castells' model are very suggestive in the case of Japan. From the mid-1950s to the early 1970s, Japan experienced its own period of high-speed growth (Tabb 1995: Chapter 4), based at least in part on the activities of the 'developmental state,' itself the subject of considerable debate (Johnson 1982, 1995; Calder 1993). These in turn produced a knock-on effect in the other countries of East and Southeast Asia as high levels of growth spread: first to Korea, Hong Kong, Taiwan, and Singapore, and later to coastal China and southeast Asia, including Thailand, Malaysia, and parts of Indonesia (Overholt 1993; Chan 1993; Tipton 1998; Thompson ed. 1998). Now they are even affecting inland China and Vietnam. In most of these instances, high-speed growth was associated with an influx of Japanese technology, capital, and personnel, as the larger Japanese companies looked for cheaper labor and new markets abroad. Meanwhile they were also setting up factories in Europe and North America, in order to penetrate these markets further and to reduce the chronic Japanese balance of payments surplus.

As Harumi Befu shows in Chapter 2, this is only the latest phase in Japanese expansion abroad. The first phase actually took place as long ago as the sixteenth century, but came to a halt when the country closed up during the Tokugawa period. By the time Japan was forced to open up again by the Americans in 1853, it found that it had fallen way behind the West, especially in the development of military hardware, and it attempted to catch up (Morris-Suzuki 1994).

It soon did so, thanks to the 'Meiji oligarchs,' the remarkable group of political leaders who led the country after the Meiji restoration in 1868. In the process they transformed themselves into dedicated followers of Western fashion.[2] The pace of change was breathtaking. By 1895, the Japanese were able to defeat China and take over Taiwan, and in 1904–5 they went to war with the Russians, and sank the Russian fleet. So began a second period of Japanese expansionism, which only ended with their defeat in 1945. This period took the Japanese as far afield as Latin America, the United States, the islands of the South Pacific, Korea, Manchuria, and coastal China.[3] With the end of the Pacific War most of the overseas Japanese nationals in Asia, some six million in all, were repatriated to Japan, though many also perished on the way. In the case of Manchuria, for instance, Japanese emigration continued almost until the end of the War, promoted by a bureaucratic machine that refused to stop. The migrants were subsequently abandoned by the retreating Japanese army as it withdrew to safety. A third of them died, through starvation, suicide, or at the hands of the local Chinese and the invading Soviet army (Young, 1998: 399–411).

The global expansion of Japanese capital in the post-war period is the third phase of Japanese expansion abroad. Corporate employees make up a large part of this new wave of Japanese migrants, but as Befu shows there are other categories of people involved as well: post-war economic migrants; the 'war brides' and others who have married foreigners; migrants setting up businesses to provide retail, restaurant, and other services to Japanese company employees living abroad; people who are simply fed up with life in Japan; and high school or university dropouts in search of a good time.

One of these groups is examined in greater detail by Mitchell Sedgwick in Chapter 3, which is based on fieldwork among Japanese company employees based in France. This shows well not only the complex chains of supply and command which globalization entails, but also the varying success with which Japanese employees adapt to the local culture and working environment outside Japan. These adaptations and the ways in which they are negotiated provide the real substance of the processes of globalization and 'internationalization' (another popular buzzword in Japan), as the employees attempt to communicate with those around them using a mélange of spoken languages and rapidly scribbled diagrams to get their points across. The result of the Japanese adaptation to life in France is a cultural hybrid, rather than a simple transplantation of 'the Japanese system.'

Chapter 4, by Ulrich Möhwald, provides a different perspective on the impact of these changes on society in Japan, drawing on the voluminous statistics on attitudes and value change collected by Japanese government organizations and others since the late 1950s. Möhwald argues that during the period of high-speed growth in the 1960s and 1970s, the process of social change could generally be seen in terms of a transition from 'traditional' to 'modern' society. From the early 1980s onwards, however, there was increasing differentiation and fragmentation of the Japanese 'value universe,' and the situation had become even more fluid by the start of the 1990s. Increasing affluence has resulted in the development of a significant number of young people largely concerned with personal pleasure and enjoyment (something also discussed in Chapter 12, by Clammer), though at the expense of commitment and meaningful links with the rest of the community. Attitudes toward work have also changed, and it is no longer regarded as the sole *raison d'être* in the way that it once was. Hence the calls from the Right for greater discipline and a return to 'traditional values.'

The 'informational economy,' however, requires creativity and initiative rather than discipline, and the educational system has long been under attack for failing to foster them. The response from government has been a series of proposals for reform, even though the direction and details of reform are bitterly contested, as Brian McVeigh explains in Chapter 5. Historically, there have only been two periods of rapid reform in Japanese education: during the Meiji period, and again during the American Occupation at the end of the Second World War.[4] Otherwise changes have been slow and piecemeal. In McVeigh's view, most educational 'reform' initiatives in Japan are actually attempts by the state and capitalist interests to shore up the status quo – by maintaining the levels of literacy and mathematical skills required to keep the economy going, together with a 'correct' sense of what it means to be Japanese. Education therefore involves not only the acquisition of the knowledge and skills required by the economy, but also a degree of indoctrination. This is achieved through a system of 'strategic schooling' monitored and implemented by the Monbushō (the Japanese Ministry of Education), its agencies, and the individual schools under their control. The subtext is the maintenance of 'traditional morality' in the form of hierarchy, loyalty, obedience, and diligence, as prescribed in the Imperial Rescript on Education of 1890 (Beauchamp and Vardaman eds 1994: 37–38). This was formally repealed after 1945, but is still much admired by more conservative reformers. (Their priorities perhaps help explain why, despite the sense of economic crisis in 1999, Japanese legislators chose to spend so much time and effort in making the national flag and national anthem official.) The result is that, despite the criticisms of Japan's educational system and the various calls for 'reform,' the changes implemented have actually achieved little.

Another area where would-be reforms have so far produced disappointing results is in the position of women in the labor market, an issue examined by Beverley Bishop in Chapter 6. This is another area in which the literature of the 1990s is particularly rich.[5] As Bishop notes, the Japanese economic recession of the 1990s was especially severe for the employees of smaller companies, which traditionally employ a large proportion of women on low wages. Even women who worked for the larger companies have generally been treated as marginal within them, on the assumption that they will probably leave when they get married. Despite a series of legal rulings in favor of women employees, the equal opportunities legislation enacted in 1986, and the increasing number of women entering employment (due partly to the demographic factors mentioned above), many of them still experience working conditions and job security inferior to those of their male colleagues with similar educational qualifications. Despite the formal moves toward equality, the increasingly fierce competition resulting from globalization has led to the increasing casualization of labor as employers have attempted to cut costs, a trend further exacerbated in some industries by processes of deregulation – and women are especially prone to casualization. Bishop's conclusion is that many informal obstacles to women's advancement still remain, and that women therefore bear a disproportionate part of the costs of the globalization process.

Chapter 7, by John Davis, examines another case of marginality, that of the Burakumin, who have traditionally been excluded from mainstream Japanese society because of their association with 'polluting' occupations, such as the trades in meat and leather. Thanks to an increasing number of studies of this and other disadvantaged groups within Japanese society, such as the Ainu, the Okinawans, and the Koreans, the idea of Japan as a racially and socially homogeneous society is no longer taken very seriously.[6]

The distinction between the Burakumin and the rest of the population arose early on. Despite the formal abolition of status categories during the Meiji period, discrimination against the Burakumin continued, and their economic position was actually made worse by the loss of their monopoly over certain industries. Growing militancy led to the formation of the Buraku Liberation

League. In the 1960s the government passed a package of special measures aimed at the redevelopment of *buraku* communities and the prevention of discrimination (cf. Neary 1997: 51–52). According to Davis, these have resulted in reduced levels of Burakumin poverty and the creation of communities with access to facilities on average at least as good as those of the rest of the population. Increasing mobility across *buraku* community boundaries has been matched by increasing entry into higher education, and the geographical and social boundaries between the Burakumin and the rest of Japanese society have become progressively blurred. Davis argues that the notion that the Burakumin community has distinct boundaries ignores the historically arbitrary nature of *buraku* identity, and the ways in which meanings and public perceptions have changed over time. Ironically, even though the notion of Japan as a 'homogeneous society' is under attack from social scientists, Burakumin activists have found it useful in arguing that they are no different from other Japanese. Davis's material is therefore theoretically important, not only within the context of Japan, but for the study of minorities in general and the ways in which social boundaries are perceived and conceptualized.

Yet another type of marginality is dealt with in Chapter 8 by Tom Gill, on the changing position of the casual labor force in the larger cities of Japan during the long economic recession of the 1990s.[7] Over the years the job security of the employees of the larger Japanese companies has been underwritten by the inferior working conditions to be found further down the job hierarchy, both among casual workers and employees of the smaller firms that make up the majority of Japanese enterprises.

Gill describes a particular concentration of casual workers in the construction industry. Even though construction contracts are allocated to large, nationally known corporations, much of the actual work is subcontracted to local companies that hire their labor from the *yoseba*, the casual laborer quarters of the larger cities. The best known of these are San'ya in Tokyo (cf. Fowler 1996), Kotobuki in Yokohama (cf. Stevens 1997), and Kamagasaki in Osaka. The labor is hired by street-corner brokers called *tehaishi*, some of whom specialize in the recruitment of Korean, Chinese, and Filipino migrants. In addition to low pay, these workers also experience poor housing conditions, low job security, and inadequate protection and compensation in the case of the industrial accidents that are frequent in this kind of work.

One response to the increasing pressures on the labor market in the 1990s has been the rise of the *ninpudashi*, a boarding house system whose owners provide employers with labor, while providing the workers themselves with work opportunities, loans, accommodation, meals, and transportation. The *ninpudashi* system has long been common in the industrial cities of northern Kyushu, where a similar system used to operate in the steel industry. Wages are paid to the *ninpudashi* rather than the workers, and they deduct the cost of their own services before passing the money on to the workers. In practice, therefore, the system can be highly exploitative, as the workers may see very little of the money they earn and can even build up large debts to the *ninpudashi*.

Gill argues that the rise of the *ninpudashi* followed the end of the bubble economy and the subsequent fall in the demand for casual labor. Many of the workers left the casual sector, and the average age of those remaining increased rapidly. A growing number who are unable to find work have joined the ranks of the homeless in the parks and railway stations of the major cities. In order to stay in work, others have moved into the orbit of the *ninpudashi*. Even though city governments have responded to the problems of laborers by easing access to welfare payments, the *yoseba* of the major cities have become shadows of their former selves, while the *ninpudashi* survive and flourish, largely because they represent a more efficient system of worker exploitation.

The list of supporting characters in Gill's paper includes the *yakuza*, the Japanese gangsters, who also play a role in the construction industry, setting up dummy companies which skim off part of the profits, in addition to controlling labor recruitment. They also form the subject of Chapter 9 by Wolfgang Herbert, who looks at the ways in which they have been affected by government attempts to restrict and control their activities, particularly the legislation of 1992 targeted at the *yakuza* bosses and their sources of income.

However, the strategy of the authorities in practice has been to control the activities of these groups rather than to eliminate them altogether. Previous attempts at control have been counter-productive: on each occasion, the *yakuza* have managed to adapt to the new situation, retaining and consolidating their strength and influence. Despite official condemnation, the *yakuza* remain a powerful institution in Japanese society (Kaplan and Dubro 1986; Seymour 1996), providing goods and services in the sex, money-lending, and illegal drug industries, together with an alternative career structure for the socially disadvantaged. Because of the shortage of lawyers and the slow pace of court proceedings, many mainstream organizations in Japanese society have traditionally relied on the *yakuza* to perform a variety of roles, such as strike breaking, the control of political extremists, the eviction of unwanted tenants from land, or the management of shareholders' meetings.

The *yakuza* reacted swiftly to the 1992 legislation, transforming their groups into joint stock companies, and removing the gang insignia displayed inside and outside their offices in some cases. Fraternization with the police was curtailed, and 'under-performing' members of the gangs were pushed out. Gang bosses economized on their lavish lifestyles. Ironically the *yakuza*, who once evicted tenants on behalf of landlords, are now disrupting attempts by landowners to auction land that the *yakuza* themselves occupy. The *yakuza* have also become involved in debt collection, as well as robbery (an activity which they used to despise), and smuggling migrant workers into Japan. Despite these adaptations they are still on the defensive, according to Herbert: recruitment has become more difficult and the average age of gang members is rising. In the final analysis, however, it is unclear whether they have been affected more seriously by the legislation or by the economic recession.

Chapter 10, by Carla and Jerry Eades, Nishiyama Yuriko and Yanase Hiroko, deals with the effects of recession and globalization on another section of the workforce, the traditional craftsmen who produce the Buddhist altars (*butsudan*) still to be found in many Japanese houses.[8] *Butsudan* are interesting for a number of reasons apart from their use in household ritual: they embody traditional craftsmanship of the highest order, and they are also extremely expensive. In production areas such as Hikone, near Kyoto, where the research was carried out, they form an important part of the local economy. Demand for them has been affected by a number of factors over the years, such as changes in lifestyles and the decline in the birthrate. Although caring for the family *butsudan* was traditionally a responsibility passed on to the eldest son, in many cases it is no longer clear which member of the family will eventually inherit it, or indeed whether they will have a suitable space in their house where they can put it. Despite this, Hikone makers have continued to produce and market large *butsudan* using traditional techniques, despite a decline in recent years both in the number of new recruits to the industry, and in the amount of work available.

The larger *butsudan* companies in the city are attempting to cope with changes in the market in a number of ways. Even though their advertising depends heavily on images of 'Japanese tradition,' they have become increasingly dependent on cheaper techniques and on components manufactured abroad, at first in Korea and Taiwan, and more recently in mainland China and Vietnam. The Ministry of International Trade and Industry (MITI) attempts to maintain traditional production techniques and standards, both through the designation of production areas, and through an inspection system that guarantees the quality of materials and craftsmanship in the more expensive items. However, this system does not cover the cheaper end of the market. The local *butsudan* association is made up of both merchants and craftsmen, but the interests of these two groups are diverging as a result of the economic recession: while the merchants expand their imports, claiming that it is difficult to find skilled labor locally, the local craftsmen are increasingly underemployed. While it is probable that the production of *butsudan* in Japan will be kept alive by wealthier clients for whom the quality of the goods is more important than the price, future demand may be too small to sustain the existing number of production areas. And even though the industry's publicity will continue to stress the importance of its 'tradition,' the goods themselves will increasingly be produced abroad or by using non-traditional techniques.

Religion and ritual provide a link with Chapter 11 by Andreas Riessland, who considers the activities of groups of *yamabushi*, mountain ascetics who practice a religion known as Shugendō, combining elements of Buddhism and Japanese folk religion. Despite the esoteric nature of the religion, the basis of the dispute he describes is a fairly typical one in contemporary Japan: a plan for the construction of a new road to provide access for tourists.

On Mount Haguro in northern Japan there are actually two groups of *yamabushi*, Buddhist and Shintō, a division that dates back to the start of the Meiji period, when Shugendō was purged and reorganized by the national government. For many years the groups coexisted peacefully, even though each claimed to be the true heir of the Shugendō tradition. However, at the time of Riessland's research, the latent rivalry had been brought into the open by the issue of the new road. One of the purposes was to improve access to the Shintō shrine, but it was feared by the Buddhists that it would pass near their own temple and disrupt the rituals taking place there. It was therefore interpreted as a ploy by the Shintō group to increase its own affluence at the expense of the Buddhists.

Riessland attributes this resurgence of conflict to the changes that have taken place in the composition of the two groups since earlier research on the area in the 1960s. Not only has the number of participants risen, but many of them now come from outside the area. This means there is less need to avoid the kind of confrontation that would disrupt social relations within the Mount Haguro region itself, and conflict is therefore expressed more openly. The split also reflects the difference between the esoteric Buddhists and the more worldly managers of the Shintō shrine, who are eager to promote the local tourist trade. The local community also benefits considerably from this trade – and so its residents are generally unwilling to assist the Buddhists in protesting against the construction of the road, even though they are sympathetic to their cause.

The last chapter in the volume, by John Clammer, draws together many of the theoretical strands in the other chapters, providing both a critique of the contemporary anthropology of Japan and some possible starting points for future development. He argues that at the moment there is little consensus on how to interpret Japanese society, but that many classical approaches fail to capture the changes which are taking place, including globalization, the increasing heterogeneity of Japanese society, and the rise of consumerism. He suggests that the beginnings of an alternative approach may be visible in attempts to bring together social and cultural theory, and in the increasing body of work being published on Japanese consumption and popular culture. His prime focus is on the emotions, which, he argues, cannot be understood in purely biological terms: the discussion has to be expanded to include everyday economic activity, and particularly consumption,[9] given that the subjective side of Japanese life is largely constructed in relation to material things.

As an example, he cites the proliferation of popular magazines aimed at particular subgroups of the population, containing detailed advice on the latest consumer products and the ways in which they should be consumed. He quotes Michel Maffesoli's suggestion that advanced capitalist society is structured around 'neo-tribes' of people sharing a particular type of consumption. The state also plays its part, for instance through its control of the education system (as discussed by McVeigh) and the pharmaceutical industry (as in the long delay in legalizing the contraceptive pill). Patterns of protest and social movements in Japan also have their own characteristics: many of them focus on 'nostalgia,' which therefore provides the basis for a critique of modernity. In other words, what Clammer argues is that the analysis of Japanese society and its institutions should be pursued at the 'levels of the deep grammars of life, and not simply through the study of macro-economic change or of particular institutions and activities...taken in isolation.'

This is advice that would appear to have been heeded already in the other contributions to this volume, all of which deal in some way with the relationship between the globalizing Japanese economy and the subjective experiences of contemporary Japanese. Obvious examples are transformation of the values and attitudes of the Japanese executives in France and of the young people in Japan; the anger of individual women or casual laborers over their working conditions; the attempts of the Monbushō to instill officially defined attitudes to the state along with the skills required by the economy; the attempts by the Hikone *butsudan* makers to maintain pride in their work in the face of imports and globalization; the increasing perception by the Burakumin that they are not a 'minority' requiring special treatment; and the commoditization of ritual and religion in the form of the '*yamabushi* experience' being marketed to the pilgrims and tourists on Mount Haguro. These accounts of social change in contemporary Japan thus bridge the gap between the economic and cultural dimensions of the globalization process, showing how the dialectic between them is working out in the lives of their subjects as they move into the twenty-first century.

2 Globalization as Human Dispersal: From the Perspective of Japan

Harumi Befu

'Globalization' as a term reminds most readers of capitalist globalization, what with IBM, Sony, Coca Cola, etc., covering the globe.[1] Human dispersal, however, is also part and parcel of globalization, even preceding economic globalization of the kind that most people think about. In fact, one may say that human history is the history of the dispersal of the species, starting with the original spreading 'out of Africa,' antedating capitalist globalization by millennia.

More recently human movement has been accelerated by the availability of cheaper, faster, and more convenient means of transportation, thanks to the success of industrial capitalism. Thus human dispersal and globalization based on efforts to accumulate capital, especially in the form of industrial capitalism, have been closely intertwined, at least during the last five hundred years. In the following, then, I would like to trace Japanese globalization in the form of human dispersal historically, locating it within the context of the country's attempts at capital accumulation.

Most theorists, e.g. Wallerstein (1974), acknowledge that globalization – at least its Western version – began in the fifteenth century. Yet most of them in practice merely examine present-day processes of globalization. If it is a *process* – as it most certainly is – then locating it historically is mandatory if it is to be fully understood. This chapter re-formulates Japan's modern history in this spirit, using globalization as its key operational construct. I revisit Japanese history and re-frame it in terms of human dispersal within the global context.

Japan's initial efforts to globalize were made between the fifteenth and seventeenth centuries. These efforts were interrupted during the Tokugawa period (1600–1867), only to be resumed once more in the middle of the nineteenth century. This second period of globalization lasted until 1945, when Japan lost the Pacific War and was forced to give up all its colonies and occupied territories: the Japanese in these colonies and areas were repatriated, almost completely reversing the process of dispersal throughout Asia. The third period started after the war and still continues.

Japan's initial globalization

If Western globalization began toward the end of the fifteenth century, then Japan's globalization may also be said to have begun at about that time. Attempts to expand its territory began with the ill-fated invasions of Korea in 1592–93 and 1597–98 by the armies of Toyotomi Hideyoshi. Unlike the Western powers invading Africa and the Americas during this period, which faced technologically less advanced enemies, Japan was confronted with a formidable enemy roughly equal in technological capability, and was eventually forced to return home defeated. Thus Japan failed in its initial territorial and political expansion. Nonetheless, its efforts were similar to those of the Western powers to acquire other territories.

In addition, by the fifteenth century, Japanese pirates were already trafficking along the coasts of East and Southeast Asia (Ishihara 1964). One may wonder whether it is legitimate to refer to pirates as evidence of external movements and expansion. However, in terms of the pillage and violence they wrought on the inhabitants of their destinations, the early colonizing Spanish and Portuguese soldiers and sailors were little different from pirates, the only real difference being whether or not such activities were sanctioned by their own states.

By the sixteenth century, Japanese ships were frequenting China and Southeast Asia, carrying silver, swords, and other goods for trade. From 1604 to 1635, as many as 341 foreign trade permits called *shuinjō* were issued by the Tokugawa government to 106 individuals. These Japanese traders were engaged in capital accumulation just like their European counterparts. The merchants of Sakai, near Osaka, who amassed wealth through trading with Southeast Asia in those days were the Japanese equivalents of those of Venice and Genoa.

With these Japanese ships going back and forth, Japanese communities sprang up all over Southeast Asia. Some of these

'Japan towns' had populations running into the thousands. Manila in the Philippines, Ayuttaya in Siam, and Hoian in Vietnam still retain memories, if not remnants, of Japanese residents of bygone days. Ayuttaya is associated with the legendary hero, Yamada Nagamasa, who helped the Siamese King defeat his enemies, just as Manila is associated with the devout Christian, Kakayama Ukon (Ohno 1997: 60–67).

All this expansion of Japanese trading and the movement of the Japanese overseas came to an abrupt halt in the 1630s due to the prohibition of overseas trade – except by a few Dutch and Chinese merchants. Even they were only allowed to trade through Nagasaki, and only on a scale that was too small to result in significant capital accumulation in Japan. The Tokugawa government also issued a total ban on overseas travel and prohibited the Japanese then living in Southeast Asian towns from returning to Japan. This seclusion policy was of course motivated by the government's fear of excessive missionary activities by the Jesuits, which it felt could lead to eventual colonization of Japan by the European powers. The first stages of the colonization of the Philippines showed how this could happen.

This was the first real 'civilizational clash' between Japan and the West in Huntington's terms (1996), whereby the civilization of Europe threatened the integrity of that of Japan. Japan protected itself through the almost total elimination of the Christians in Japan, foreigners as well as Japanese (except those who went into hiding), and by sealing itself off from European incursions. Japan's globalization was thus interrupted for over two hundred years, a crucial setback. Europe continued its global expansion, and by the time Japan was able to resume its own efforts in the mid-nineteenth century, most of the territories available for colonization had already been taken by the European powers.

The second globalization initiative

Territorial expansion

Japan resumed its push for territorial and demographic expansion in the Meiji period (1868–1912), as soon as the Tokugawa regime was toppled. The new leaders established a nation-state with a modern government along European lines, and with aspirations for a colonial empire. Thus in the second year of the Meiji period (1869), there was already a proposal to invade Korea on the cabinet agenda, spearheaded by Saigō Takamori, Itagaki Taisuke, and Etō Shimpei. They were concerned with the problem of the disgruntled former samurai, many of whom were unemployed as well as having lost their former status. It was only the intervention of Iwakura Tomomi, then on a mission to America and Europe, which prevented this invasion. As a consolation, as it were, these erstwhile samurai were allowed to vent their discontent by invading Taiwan in 1874, after some Okinawans who had been ship-wrecked there were killed by Taiwanese aborigines in 1871. Their hopes of establishing a military garrison were, however, foiled when the Japanese and Chinese governments signed an accord, under which China paid an indemnity to Japan. As a result, Japan's acquisition of Taiwan and Korea was to be postponed for a few decades. Taiwan was acquired in 1895 as a result of the Sino-Japanese war, and Korea followed in 1905 through a series of conniving diplomatic and military maneuvers.

In the meantime, Japan established its hegemony over Hokkaido and the Ryukyu Islands by subjugating the Ainu and Okinawans. The Japanese government made these peoples subjects of Japan and proceeded to convert them into Japanese citizens, complete with pledges of loyalty to the Japanese Emperor and Japanese state.

From the start of the twentieth century, Japan accelerated its territorial expansion in Northeast, East, and Southeast Asia, as well as in Oceania. By 1945 much of East Asia was under Japanese colonial or military control. Through the late nineteenth and early twentieth centuries, Japan exploited the territories under its control as a source of capital. The details of this territorial expansion, military invasion, and exploitation of human and natural resources are well known and need not detain us here, inasmuch as they are not the central subjects of this paper.

Some might argue that this was not 'global' in the true sense of the term. But neither was the 'global' expansion of most of the European powers, since they also acquired control only of geographically delimited segments of the globe. The United Kingdom, with its claim to be the empire 'on which the sun never sets,' was the only power that came near to achieving a truly global presence. 'Globalization' is a goal, an ultimately desirable state, which no power has achieved but which all globalizing powers strive for. In this sense, it may be said that Japan was trying to globalize just as much as the European powers.

Human dispersal

While Japan contemplated expanding its territories through the invasion of Korea from the early years of the Meiji period, emigrant laborers had already left Japan for the Kingdom of Hawaii in 1868, the first year of the Meiji Emperor (*Meiji gannen*, from which they became known as *gannen-mono*), thus resuming the process of human dispersal which had been interrupted in the seventeenth century. After that, the dispersal of the Japanese through emigration continued into the post-war era. They moved not only to North and South America, but also to Southeast Asia, continental Asia, Taiwan, Sakhalin, and Micronesia. This dispersal was in large measure a state policy, in part to alleviate the domestic population problem and in part to establish ethnic Japanese institutions in the colonized and occupied territories.

The story of Japanese migration to North America is relatively well known, and migration there by Japanese began earlier than to South America.[2] The earliest Japanese emigrants to the countries of Latin America date from just before the turn of the century and the decades which followed.[3] Altogether Japan sent 244,334 emigrants to Latin America before 1945. Now there are more *Nikkei* (people of Japanese origin, i.e. Japanese emigrants and their descendants) in Latin America than in North America. In the last few decades, Nikkei from Latin America who have come to Japan to work as migrant workers (*dekasegi*) have been much discussed in the media. They are wrongly described as 'returning to Japan' or 'making a U-turn to Japan.' Unless the reference is to the *issei* or first-generation migrants from Japan, they are neither returning nor making a U-turn. Virtually all of the Latin Americans in Japan are Latin American-born second- and third-generation Japanese residents: *Nisei* and *Sansei*. They are Latin Americans who come to Japan to work, and their identity is different from that of the Japanese, despite their descent.

We are well aware of this emigration to North and South America because of the large number of Nikkei still living there. In total, however, more Japanese left for various parts of Asia and Micronesia during this second wave of human dispersal than for North America (including Hawaii) and South America put together. As of 1935 some 636,000 Japanese were living in Asia and Micronesia, compared with 373,000 in North and South America (Konno and Fujisaki 1996: 258–59). But this movement of Japanese to Asia and Micronesia is now all but forgotten because most of those who went there either died there or returned to Japan at the end of the Pacific War. Most of those who returned have now also died. Thus the Japanese diaspora in these parts of the world is now just history, a thing of the past forgotten by most Japanese, and living only in the memory of a few.

This fact should not deter us from appreciating the reality of the massive dispersal of the Japanese around Asia that took place during this period. Even before the end of the last century – about the same time that the Japanese were leaving for South America – Japanese emigrants were already going to the Philippines, primarily as construction workers to help build roads in Luzon and Mindanao. During the First World War, emigration to Mindanao increased greatly as demand increased for local products. Some 20,000 Japanese lived in Davao at that time. Japanese newspaper publishers, Shintō shrines, Buddhist temples, schools, hotels, clubhouses, and other institutions flourished to the extent that it was dubbed a 'Little Japan' (Ohno 1997: 281–282). Like most emigrants to North and South America, these construction workers did not initially plan to stay in the Philippines very long. But eventually most of them ended up staying and marrying local women. When the Pacific War began and the Japanese army invaded the Philippines, they were recruited by the Japanese army to take part in the war effort. This meant, first, that they took part in the infamous atrocities against the local people by the Japanese forces; and second, that many of them fled along with other Japanese soldiers from the advancing Allied forces into the jungle and mountains in the closing stages of the War (Konno and Fujisaki 1996: 43–164; Ohno 1991, 1997).

The media have given wide publicity to the 'comfort women' that the Japanese government and the Japanese military recruited from the colonies and occupied areas. But we should not overlook the earlier phenomenon of the *Japanese* comfort women. From the early part of the century, they were recruited (or in many cases simply kidnapped) to be sent to various parts of Southeast Asia, mainly from the southern regions of rural Japan (Konno and Fujisaki 1996: 26–29, 193–197). They were assigned to – and confined in – brothels to satisfy the sexual desire of Japanese men, both civilian and military, settled or stationed in the area, or passing through it. Their conditions are graphically depicted in Yamazaki Tomoko's account, *Sandakan Brothel No.8* (1999). In Singapore, which was a major hub for Japanese trading, there were already nearly 900 prostitutes reported just before the turn of the century (Konno and Fujisaki 1996: 26). Similar prostitution quarters were known in Sumatra, Borneo, Malaya, Batavia (Jakarta), and elsewhere throughout Southeast Asia. The foundations of Japan's southern expansion were laid, in part, on the untold misery that these women suffered.

Emigrants also went in large numbers to Micronesia upon its acquisition by Japan as a League of Nations trust territory after Germany lost its colonies as a result of its defeat in the First World War. At their peak the Japanese workers on some islands far outnumbered the local populations. Here again, as in the Philippines, many Japanese men married local women, producing offspring with Japanese names. Fortunately the Japanese treatment of the local populations was relatively benign, and most of Micronesia escaped becoming a Second World War battlefield, relieving the Japanese there from the hardships that their brothers and sisters in the Philippines had to endure. Again, the Japanese there had to be repatriated in 1945, but many left their children behind. These offspring with Japanese names are Nikkei of Japanese descent, just like the Nikkei in North and South America, including Hawaii, who are also known as *Hapa*.

As soon as Japan began to acquire colonies – Taiwan in the Sino-Japanese war of 1894–95, Sakhalin Island as a result of the Russo-Japanese war of 1904–05, and Korea in 1905 through a rather dubious treaty – these colonies began to be peopled by the Japanese, a good portion of them sent by the Japanese government. Japanese dispersal also took place in areas occupied by the Japanese army, including Manchuria, where they established a puppet government, coastal China, and insular and continental Southeast Asia. Some went as farmers, as in Manchuria, recruited from eastern and northern Japan through the enticement of the Japanese government, only to be betrayed and to suffer unimaginable hardship at the end of the War. Others went as wealthy capitalists and exploited the local people for personal gain. By 1945 millions of Japanese were residing over a vast expanse of Asia. Even the coastal cities of Siberia had Japanese communities with thousands of residents.

Ultimately all this territorial expansion and human dispersal were closely linked with Japan's efforts at capital accumulation through the exploitation of its colonized and occupied territories. Resource-poor Japan felt that it needed to secure territories rich in resources in order for its own capitalism to flourish. Such colonial exploitation followed the pattern long pursued by the Western empires. Japan, however, confronted the Western empires in the competition for resources and was resoundingly defeated in the Second World War. This was the second clash between the Japanese and Western civilizations.

After its defeat in the War, all the Japanese in the countries of Asia and the Pacific, both military and civilians, were supposed to be repatriated under the terms of the surrender. As a result some six million Japanese returned to Japan from all over Asia, including the former colonies of Sakhalin, Korea, Taiwan, and the Pacific. But what is not adequately understood is that not all the Japanese were repatriated. For varied and complex reasons unknown numbers of them – running into thousands, or perhaps even tens of thousands – stayed behind. The so-called 'orphaned' Japanese who were left behind by their fleeing parents in China are well known through the media. Less well-known are the servicemen in Thailand, the Malay Peninsula, and Indonesia who fled from their units and remained behind, unwilling or unable to re-join the other troops after surrender. More than 1,000 soldiers are said to have remained in Indonesia and over 700 in Vietnam. Many of them participated in the independence movements of these countries, playing significant roles as military experts. In Vietnam these Japanese, like other minorities, were labeled 'New Vietnamese,' thus gaining a legitimate status in society (Furuta 1998: 173).

In the Philippines, some civilian Japanese were prevented from being repatriated for a variety of reasons; others were repatriated but found life in Japan intolerable and returned to the Philippines. After the War, many of these Japanese Filipinos had to go into hiding or change their names, in order to escape violence at the hands of local Filipinos in retaliation for their own mistreatment of the local people. Even now most Japanese Filipinos suffer from extreme economic deprivation. The Japanese government extended little help to them until recently, but it has now begun to take a more positive attitude toward the problem by recognizing their Japanese citizenship and granting them the benefits they deserve (Ohno 1991: 286–322).

The third globalization initiative

After the war, Japan's globalization resumed yet again, as it had done previously during the Meiji period. Between the first and the second initiatives some 230 years elapsed, during which traces of Japanese settlements overseas were all but obliterated, affording no continuity from the first to the second periods. This was not the case in the transition between the second and the third initiatives. First, a large number of Nikkei had remained overseas, not only in North and South America, but also in Asia, though in much smaller numbers. Second, the break between the second and the third periods was brief. The war ended in 1945 and the repatriation of Japanese from overseas began immediately, but did not end until several years later. Meanwhile, Japanese migration was already starting anew, from the 1950s onwards. The continuity between the second and third periods is thus important in understanding the more recent dispersal of the Japanese.

By 1994, 699,895 Japanese citizens were living abroad on a long-term or permanent basis, an increase of 201 percent since 1969. This figure obviously does not include those who lost or gave up Japanese citizenship in order to become naturalized citizens of the countries in which they now reside. Nor does it include descendants of emigrants in North and South America and elsewhere, who are foreign citizens, numbering about two million (Sōmuchō Gyōsei Kansatsu-kyoku ed. 1995: 5). But these Japanese residents abroad are not all of one type; rather, they can be categorized into several different types, as described below.

1 Post-war emigrants

Japanese dispersal after the war began with an emigration program to Brazil in 1952 sponsored by the Japanese government, resuming an earlier program which had been interrupted by the war years.

The Japanese economy was devastated by the war, and could ill-afford to feed its population, especially when millions returned from abroad and burdened the already weakened country. The government figured that it needed to rid itself of excess population. Emigration was a quick-fix answer to this serious problem, and the Foreign Ministry announced a series of emigration plans to help cope with it. The 1958 plan, for example, envisaged the emigration of 101,000 Japanese over five years. The first group of emigrants had left already for the Dominican Republic, in 1956. What awaited them there was nothing short of total disaster (Konno and Fujisaki 1994: 284–332).

In 1973 a ship called the *Nippon-maru* took the last group of emigrants to South America and the emigration program officially ended. This post-war emigration resulted in the formation of communities distinct from their pre-war counterparts for a number of reasons. A similar phenomenon was observed when Japanese began to arrive in the United States after the war, especially on the West Coast where large Nikkei concentrations were found. For one thing, these newcomers were relatively young, being in their twenties and thirties when they migrated. Their age-mates in North and South America from the pre-war period were *Nisei* (second generation migrants) who were more comfortable in English, Portuguese, or Spanish than in Japanese, and their identity was definitely American or Latin American rather than Japanese. These communication and cultural barriers created a social gulf between the two groups. Yet the *issei*, the first generation migrants with whom the newcomers could converse in Japanese, were much older, closer to their parents' generation. The *issei* had endured hardship because of abject poverty and the War in a way totally unknown to the newcomers, making it difficult for them to see things in the same way or to form strong bonds easily. Thus the post-war immigrants tended to form their own communities, though they certainly maintained a close relationship with those of the pre-war Nikkei.

Whether we are dealing with the pre-war or the post-war emigration programs, we must note the callousness with which the Japanese government handled them. The saying, *imin wa kimin* ('emigrants are outcasts') applies well here. For the government, emigration policy was first and foremost a policy to solve the nation's population problem. Both in the late Meiji and the early post-war periods, Japan was suffering from a population that could not be supported, especially in the rural areas. The government's primary task was to rid itself of the excess population, and this being the case, it did not matter much what happened to them after they left Japan. As a result, the government officials in charge hardly investigated the destinations where emigrants were to settle, and cared little whether these destinations could provide sufficient resources for the emigrants to survive, let alone improve their living conditions. Emigration companies gave emigrants blatantly false promises. This was as true of the emigration programs to South America before and after the war as it was in the case of pre-war and wartime Manchuria. The Japanese government should be held squarely responsible for its callous neglect of its own citizens.

In the 1970s, when Japan achieved an initial degree of affluence, the Ministry of Foreign Affairs began a program of encouraging the resettlement of elderly people overseas, especially in the third world, with the claim that retired Japanese should be able to make a comfortable living there with their pensions because of the differences in living costs. This program was criticized from its inception on the grounds that the government was trying to rid itself of its welfare burden by exporting economically useless and medically costly elder citizens. Critics likened it a modern version of *ubasuteyama* – the legendary mountain where old women were abandoned. How these elderly Japanese were expected to solve obvious problems like learning a foreign language, let alone adjusting to an unfamiliar culture, apparently never entered the minds of the officials designing the program which, needless to say, folded within a few years.

2 'War brides' and international marriages

Other Japanese also began to move to and live in foreign countries after the war, though not as 'immigrants' in the conventional sense. One such group was composed of the so-called 'war brides.' This phenomenon was associated with the relative poverty and economic deprivation among the Japanese, especially in the early post-war years. Many women who worked on and around military bases came into contact with foreign servicemen and ended up marrying them. Some had unrealistic dreams of obtaining economic security and a better lifestyle in the countries of their husbands, only to be rudely awakened by unexpected problems, such as the inevitable culture shock, the husband's low socio-economic status, and the problem of mastering a new language and learning to live with the husband's kin. Most of them married Americans, and as a result most of these Japanese women became scattered throughout the United States where their husbands settled, rather than moving into areas with high concentrations of Nikkei, or others of Japanese descent. This hampered their adaptation to the U.S., since they could not take advantage of the existing Nikkei community for help. Those who married Australians and others whose husbands' homelands did not have any Nikkei populations to speak of suffered similar problems.

Recently these 'war brides' have organized themselves into an international group, and hold periodic conventions (Aoki 1997). Thus after fifty years they still maintain their identities as 'war brides' and think of themselves as a distinct category of Nikkei.

Although the marriages of the war brides were indeed international, the phrase 'international marriages' usually refers to later, non-military marriages between Japanese and foreigners, of which there have been a steadily increasing number during the last three decades. Contrary to what is often assumed, the majority of these marriages are between Japanese men and Asian women (cf. Ma 1996). However, in marriages between Japanese and 'Caucasian' foreigners (from Europe or North America) this trend is reversed, and the majority of the marriages are between Japanese women and foreign men.[4] Like the war brides, these women often move eventually to their husbands' countries. Thus they are scattered all over North America, Europe, and elsewhere. Except for those living in Japan, they do not form a sociological group, as they do not have ways of contacting or communicating with one another – though the coming of the electronic age may well change all this.

3 Multinational expatriates and their families

Japan's exports of industrial products and capital investment overseas began in earnest in the 1960s. Currently, direct Japanese investment can be seen in over 100 countries, and the total amount invested is second only to that of the United States. As of 1995, 17,015 Japanese enterprises were operating throughout the world as separate legal entities, of which 7,643 were in Asia, 4,086 in North America, and 3,407 in Europe. They employed 2,867,959 local employees and 50,657 Japanese expatriates, generally known as *chūzai'in* (*Shūkan Tōyō Keizai* ed. 1996).

The scattering of these business expatriates and their families throughout the world constitutes by far the most important type of dispersal of Japanese nationals in the post-war period, in terms of the economy. Now there are a number of Japanese communities abroad with several thousand residents or more, composed primarily of business expatriates and their families as the core, plus other Japanese who either service the business community or are 'hangers-on.' Such communities are found in cities such as Beijing, Taipei, Seoul, Hong Kong, Bangkok, Singapore, Sidney, Los Angeles, San Francisco, New York, London, Paris, and Dusseldorf, and a full range of Japanese enterprises provides them with services as described below. The major characteristics of such communities include the use of the Japanese language as the exclusive mode of communication, and the organization of the community on the basis of Japanese cultural values (Befu and Stalker 1996).

In those areas of the world where Nikkei have remained from before the war – most notably in North and South America, but also in Asia – old-timer Nikkei and newcomers remain socially somewhat separate. In North America, at the time when Japanese businessmen and their families began to arrive in significant numbers, the old-time Nikkei community consisted mostly of *nisei* and *sansei*, second- and third-generation migrants who spoke Japanese at best only with difficulty and who were largely Americanized in terms of culture and identity. In the early days,

Japanese business expatriates as newcomers relied on old-time Nikkei for guidance and advice, and the Nikkei were glad to help the newcomers as fellow Japanese.

The North American Nikkei were useful for the newly arriving Japanese multinationals in another way. When Japanese products were exported to the United States, they were widely marketed on the West Coast, where Nikkei populations were most heavily concentrated. Nikkei were the first to buy these Japanese products, at a time when the prevailing view of Japanese goods in the United States was still that they were cheap and of poor quality. Indeed, Japanese cars of the early 1960s were small and flimsily made, and could not be compared with the massive American cars. It took the second oil shock to turn the tide. In the meantime, the Nikkei accounted for a share of the sales of Japanese cars in the United States that was disproportionately large in terms of their population.

A third way in which the North American Nikkei contributed to the advance of Japanese business is that many Nikkei were hired by these companies locally. Because of their relative familiarity with the Japanese language and culture, in addition to their ethnic affinity with the Japanese expatriates, Nikkei were welcomed in Japanese multinationals and played an important role as cultural brokers between expatriates and non-Nikkei local employees, who had little understanding or appreciation of Japan. This role, to be sure, sometimes backfired because of misunder-standing between the business expatriates and Nikkei hired locally. The expatriates sometimes expected the Nikkei to understand Japanese behavior and thinking to a far greater extent than they actually did, simply because they looked like Japanese and had Japanese surnames. This sort of misunderstanding created unnecessary animosity between expatriates and Nikkei and led to further separation of their respective communities.

As time went by, and as the newcomers acquired sufficient numbers to form their own communities, the two groups drifted more and more apart. The fact that in the expatriate community English is shunned for communication, while in the Nikkei community Japanese is hardly used, is itself enough to separate the two groups. Secondly, the attitude of many expatriates, that their inordinately high salaries plus generous fringe benefits give them a position of superiority, prevents them from befriending the

Nikkei and instead alienates them. Thirdly, the prejudice against emigrants and their descendants as 'outcasts' also contributes to the expatriates' haughty attitude toward the Nikkei and the consequent separation between the two communities. A limited relationship does remain, to be sure. For example, many Nikkei are still hired locally by Japanese multinationals and work for expatriate bosses. Also, some expatriates have Nikkei friends and maintain personal relationships individually or through their families. However, the two communities remain basically distinct: the social contacts of most expatriates and their families are within their own group, as are those of most Nikkei.

4 The 'service' community

As the expatriate community began to grow, Japanese from Japan began to establish businesses to cater to it, such as travel agencies, real estate agencies, restaurants (some complete with *karaoke* facilities), beauty parlors, food stores, bookstores, and gift shops. These businesses were needed by the expatriate community because many of its members spoke little of the local language, especially in non-English-speaking countries, and trusted Japanese more than locals for no better reason than sheer prejudice. The larger the expatriate community, the more complete the range of Japanese services became. The Los Angeles expatriate community, for instance, boasts Japanese real estate agents, attorneys, physicians, employment agencies, used car dealers, and even car repair garages where Japanese is regularly spoken.

As the expatriate community thus began to depend on these Japanese services, it relied less and less on the Nikkei community, which is another reason why the two became more and more isolated from each other in North America. At the same time, we should note that business expatriates and their families on the one hand, and those servicing them on the other, also constitute distinct communities. Even though they are all Japanese from Japan, the reality is that members of these groups have vastly different careers, work patterns, lifestyles, and even worldviews. First of all expatriates are sent from their home offices in Japan, and are expected to be reassigned in a finite number of years, usually between three and five, whereas most of those servicing them have no definite plans of returning to Japan. Many of the latter hold permanent residency (known as the 'green card' in the United States). Because the business expatriates plan to return to Japan eventually, they plan their children's education accordingly – by sending them to the local Japanese school, if there is one. In any case, they try to provide an education equivalent to the curriculum in Japan so that the children can re-enroll in other Japanese schools or will be eligible to take the entrance examinations for educational institutions in Japan. The Japanese school becomes the hub of activity for the expatriate community. Those in service businesses, on the other hand, have no definite plans to return and mostly send their children to the local schools. Their lives revolve around a totally different educational environment.

Also, business expatriates are all organized in the local Japanese chamber of commerce or similar organizations for the promotion of Japanese business. The activities of these organizations carry over into family life, so that their families are also in a tightly knit and sometimes even oppressive social system. Where there is a Japanese diplomatic office, the chief diplomat plays a pivotal role in this expatriate community. The Japanese servicing the expatriate community are generally oblivious to such activities or disdain to participate in them. Lastly, business expatriates see themselves as members of a wider Japanese elite, and tend to look down on service providers, while the latter are well aware of this condescension.

Whether within the business expatriate community or the service community, newcomers from Japan have a greatly reduced need to learn the local language or adapt to the local culture, except in a few transactions such as renting a house, dealing with the landlord, or buying a car – though even these can often be done within the Japanese community. The existing Japanese community is ready to receive them through institutions such as Japanese associations, 'newcomers' clubs, bridge clubs, and golf and baseball tournaments.

In the initial stages of globalization, Japanese businessmen going abroad to establish offices and plants were forced to learn the local language or speak English, which also serves as a *lingua franca* to varying degrees in non-English speaking countries. Their families, too, had to adapt to local customs and blend into the local community. Since no Japanese schools were available, children had to be sent to the local schools, unless they were left back in Japan or sent to an international school. These options were often taken by parents unwilling to send their children to local schools, particularly in those countries where the local language was not one of the major European languages, such as English, French, or German. Even in these countries, Japanese schools are now established whenever there are enough children to form them, and the preponderant tendency is to send children to these rather than local schools. Thus, the need for local adaptation has decreased as time has gone by and as the Japanese community has developed more and more self-sufficiency.

Although there is no space to explore this further here, other globalizing countries, such as the United States, Great Britain, Germany, and France, also follow a roughly similar pattern. Many of the so-called international schools are actually taught in English, following curricula adopted in one or other of the English-speaking countries. The Alliance Française operates in most parts of the world where a large concentration of French nationals is found, and Germans have similar institutions. The expatriate population of a given country, whether Japanese, American, French, or German, tends to form its own community. Thus economic globalization may send people far afield, but those sent abroad do not necessarily become adapted to the local scene or become 'cosmopolitanized' in the sense in which Hannerz (1990) defines the term. This is not to say that some of the expatriates do not develop close relationships with the local population and with expatriates from other lands; indeed a few do (as described in the next chapter by Sedgwick). But there is a danger in assuming that this is the general trend simply because 'the world' is globalizing, or because economic globalization is equated with the cosmopolitanization of the participants in the globalizing process. We need to differentiate between economic and institutional globalization on the one hand, and the adaptations made by participants in this economic and institutional process on the other.

5 Those who forsake Japan

Starting in the 1960s but increasing in numbers since the 1970s, a new type of emigrant has been leaving Japan. As Ishitoya says, these people do not leave because they are poor, or because they want to become rich abroad – if they only want to make money, they can do it much more easily in Japan (Ishitoya 1991: 9). Yet most of these Japanese are happy that they left Japan and with the work they are doing now. It is these Japanese who make up a large part of the rank and file of the 'service community.'

They leave for a number of reasons, including dissatisfaction with their situation in Japan. A major factor for women is clearly discrimination in the workplace, as described by Bishop in Chapter 6. Some realize that this exists while they are still in school, even before they start their first jobs, while others quickly become disillusioned with the lack of opportunities once they start working. Japanese society has also traditionally been unkind to individuals perceived as marginal, such as divorcees, Burakumin (as discussed by Davis in Chapter 7), and Korean residents (Ryang 1997; Fukuoka 2000). For many businessmen and scholars, disillusionment at not being able to realize their full potential, or dissatisfaction with the excessive demands placed on them at work, are important factors leading them to resign and leave Japan. Another common pattern is for business expatriates abroad to become enamored with the country to which they are assigned, as in some of the cases described by Sedgwick in Chapter 3. Some may eventually decide to resign from their company and stay abroad, either starting their own businesses (such as Japanese import-export firms) using networks and contacts they cultivated in their previous jobs, or being hired locally by another Japanese company. In spite of the considerable reduction in pay and benefits that this may involve, they prefer a life abroad to being sent back to Japan.

Another group of Japanese who are now living abroad leave Japan without any strong motive to establish a life elsewhere. They leave the country because they are curious about exotic places or because they are bored with life in Japan. It is important to stress their adventurous spirit, and their willingness to face the unknown and take risks with their lives. A generation ago, such souls were rare. Those were the days when the Japanese tended to travel in the comfort and security of organized tour groups, easily recognized by the group flags carried by the tour guides. More recently, many younger Japanese have traveled alone. It is these independent-minded young people who find something irresistibly attractive about life overseas, like the Japanese women in Bali described by Yamashita (1999: 137–58), and end up staying there. This 'something' may well be romance, but it is more likely to be a job, or a society and culture which suits them.

Whatever the motivation for leaving Japan to live abroad, there is no question that this group is riding the tide of Japan's economic success. It is only because of the strong yen that they can save up enough funds, even only working part-time, to travel abroad and stay there long enough to become established.

Many of these people, especially the women, leave Japan relatively young, though some do not realize their ambition until middle age. In 1995–96, NHK broadcast a program featuring women who had been working abroad, and this was summarized in a two-volume publication, *Umi no Mukō de Kurashite Mireba* (How about living abroad?) (*Umi no Mukō de Kurashite Mireba* Program Staff et al. eds 1996a, 1996b). Most of these women were still in their twenties and thirties. One may well argue that NHK intentionally picked young women for the program, and this may well be true. We have no accurate statistics on Japanese leaving Japan to settle and work more or less permanently overseas. But other sources – none, to be sure, intended to be statistically representative – also suggest that those who have been leaving Japan to settle and live abroad in the last two or three decades are on the whole young men and women (Ishitoya 1991; Yanagihara 1994).

These young people featured in the above NHK program and in Ishitoya's aptly titled *Nihon o Suteta Nihonjin* ('The Japanese who abandoned Japan') (Ishitoya 1991) actually live rather modest lives abroad. They are content with an income that is far less than equivalent earnings in Japan in most cases, and is not particularly high even by local standards. Many of them live in modest accommodation, which some even share to save money. It is clear that they are not after money or wealth, although some are extremely successful. Rather, they are seeking a life that brings them satisfaction – a satisfaction that they could not find in Japan. Not all of them succeed, to be sure; but most of them find life more fulfilling overseas than in Japan.

Many examples of those who have deserted Japan for a new and more meaningful life in the United States are to be found in

Lighthouse, a monthly Japanese-language magazine catering to Japanese residents of the greater Los Angeles metropolitan area, which features profiles of recent immigrants. We have no precise idea of how many Japanese of this sort are pursuing careers outside Japan. There have never been any surveys, though it appears that this is a common phenomenon, and there are probably thousands of Japanese living overseas who fall into this category.

Even though Ishitoya (1991: 10) believes that the recent exodus of Japanese to the United States is unique, other reports seem to suggest otherwise: Japanese are leaving for many other parts of the world as well. Satō (1993) reports a number of cases in Australia. Their motives may be different, but sometimes it is a matter of chance whether they go to California or Turkey. When a future life course is wide open, chance plays a much more important role than when it is pre-determined, as it is for many people pursuing careers in Japan.

6 The drifters

The last category of Japanese living in foreign countries consists mainly of young people of college age who have started leaving Japan only in the last ten years or so, though it also includes older men and women who left Japan rather aimlessly or out of boredom. Many of the younger Japanese in this category are formally still studying, but they differ from the more serious college students who go abroad to acquire skills leading to a professional career, and who tend to enroll in well-known schools like Harvard, Oxbridge, or the Sorbonne.

These less serious students have generally been less successful in education in Japan. Their parents are wealthy enough to send them to Tokyo, and to pay for room and board in addition to paying college fees if they can get into college, but they generally cannot. The parents calculate that sending their children abroad for schooling is not much more expensive, and so they enroll them in institutions for which a student visa can be obtained, such as community colleges in North America or language schools. Other parents simply ship their children off to foreign countries to prevent them from being a burden and a nuisance around the house on a day-to-day basis. They cannot escape social censure if their child is staying home and not going to school or working, but if the child is abroad, no one cares.

Once abroad, however, these young women and men are generally not serious about studying, even if they are on student visas. Some go to America to find sexual adventure, as widely publicized in Ieda's *Ierō Kyabu* (Yellow Cab) (1991), a sensationalist work of 'non-fiction' which went through thirty-two printings in four years, though its claims about 'wild' Japanese girls appear to have been grossly exaggerated. At any rate young Japanese in this category are supported by remittances from their parents and need not worry about supporting themselves. They often get into trouble with the law, for example by overstaying their visas or working without working visas, typically in Japanese establishments such as restaurants. If discovered, they are summarily deported.

Some go to countries like Australia where the 'working holiday' system is in place. Satō (1993) says that the favorite work for these students is also waiting in Japanese restaurants, since the knowledge of the local language and the skills required are minimal. Despite the rosy picture drawn by some of the working holiday participants (e.g. Yamamoto 1985), Satō also notes that these younger people are often seen as irresponsible, quitting work on the slightest excuse or with no excuse at all. They have a reputation for being disrespectful to home-stay families, leaving their apartments without paying the rent, and being a burden on others without thinking anything of it. Most of them are hangers-on on the fringes of the Japanese-speaking community, if there is one, because of their lack of language competence. If there isn't one, they hang around almost exclusively with each other, depriving themselves of the opportunity to learn the local language.

According to old-timers, these young people are the antithesis of the hard-working, serious, law-abiding Nikkei of previous times, and they complain about them. At the 1998 convention of the Overseas Nikkei Association in Tokyo, where a Foreign Ministry representative was present to hear requests from Nikkei communities overseas, the American and Canadian delegations duly registered these complaints: they claimed that the drifters were tarnishing the reputation that the Japanese had worked hard to build up, and they asked if the Japanese government could do something about them. Of course, nothing effective can be done about them, and no doubt the young people will continue to concern the old-timers.

Conclusion

In historicizing Japan's globalization in terms of the dispersal of its population, we have defined three major periods. The first period of dispersal was preceded by a period of exploration and piracy along the Chinese coast, followed by trade with China and Southeast Asia. Even though the merchants were successful, the Tokugawa government closed the country up in order to avoid a 'clash of civilizations' between Japan and the Christian West. It is interesting to speculate what might have happened if the country had remained open – either Japan itself might have been colonized, as the shogunate dreaded, or Japanese trade might have spread as far as South Asia and the Middle East.

Japan's second attempt at global expansion followed the Western model of territorial expansion. Here, human dispersal had two motives. One was to solve the problem of overpopulation, and the second was to establish Japanese ethnic institutions in the colonies and occupied territories. By the end of the Second World War, over six million Japanese were living outside Japan proper, but most of those in Asia had to be repatriated.

In the third period of global expansion, after the end of the Pacific War, we have distinguished several different types of dispersal: 'war brides,' emigrants to South and North America, partners in international marriages, multinational business expatriates and their families, service providers for expatriate communities, and those who abandoned Japan because of discontent, failure, or boredom. These groups are distributed in different ways, and some of them, such as business expatriates, form their own communities while others do not. Thus one may recognize several types of Nikkei community abroad in a particular locale, and different mixes of communities in different regions. In North America one finds the largest number of different types of communities, even though post-war immigrants are much fewer than in South America.

What does the future hold? Given that the Japanese economy is likely to stay comparatively strong in the medium term, Japanese business expatriate communities are here to stay and, if anything, are likely to develop in areas where we still do not find them in significant numbers, such as in China, South Asia, and the Middle East. Service communities are also likely to appear and develop along with them. A growing number of Japanese are likely to abandon Japan, given the slow pace with which Japan is reforming its social structure to accommodate women, individualists, and marginal populations. The population of dropouts will probably also increase, given the trends in personal values noted by Möhwald in Chapter 4. Many of those leaving are highly trained, including graduates of top universities who could contribute much to Japanese society if they were to stay. Because of the vast differences between these recent migrants and their predecessors in terms of life situations, education, socio-economic status, etc., the recent migrants are reluctant to be called *imin* (migrants), which in Japanese connotes those who move due to economic hardship and settle elsewhere as laborers.

For those who are not as lucky or resourceful in securing professional positions, at least in areas with large Japanese communities, many employment opportunities are available simply because they are endowed with Japanese cultural capital. Japanese supermarkets and travel agencies, hotels serving Japanese tourists, gift shops for Japanese travelers, restaurants, and medical facilities all require Japanese-speaking personnel in various capacities. In Los Angeles and London demand for them is so great that there are even employment agencies specializing in placing Japanese-speaking workers.

An interesting and even ironic consequence here is that these individuals who leave Japan for reasons of discontentment end up contributing to Japan's economic growth in one way or another, directly or indirectly, as local employees for Japanese multinationals, or by running their own agencies linking Japan with the countries where they live. Most of them maintain a relatively positive attitude toward Japan, or at least recognize its merits, while being critical of the specific structural or cultural problems, which caused them to leave the country. In addition, these new migrants tend to return to Japan every few years, in contrast to earlier periods when returning was a major undertaking which migrants could afford only a few times during their lives, if at all.

One might entertain the hypothesis that Japanese society is able to retain its relatively conservative social structure and value system because the very people who suffer most from these institutions and could challenge them tend to leave. Instead of expending their energy on cultural and social reform, they exit the system, leaving it unchanged. If all those who left Japan because of dissatisfaction had stayed there, working and fighting to change the system, Japanese society might have realized change faster than it has done.

Despite two major interruptions, the Japanese are now dispersing more extensively, and in greater variety than ever before. The last stage of Japanese dispersal has been greatly enhanced by Japan's advanced industrial capitalism. But this Japanese diaspora needs to be compared and contrasted with those of other peoples around the world in order to arrive at a comprehensive understanding of the global human diaspora. This is our next task.

3 The Globalizations of Japanese Managers

Mitchell W. Sedgwick

Five rooms with five views (in a foreign factory)

At 7:45 a.m., at a subsidiary of a Japanese consumer electronics firm in rural northwest France, I am writing at a desk in a communal office surrounded by meeting rooms and semi-private managers' offices. In one office four Japanese engineers huddle over a faxed message that was waiting for them when they arrived this morning at 7:30. They are distraught to learn that according to the R&D (research and development) division in Chiba, Japan, their new chemical formulation – the basis of the newest version of their consumer product – is out of specification in three of seven key parameters. Their in-house quality assurance results, in hand for the last two weeks, had shown a tendency toward 'spec out' in only one parameter. The fax is brief, written in rather *teinei* (formal) Japanese. The chief engineer, Katai-san, is soon on the phone to Chiba, requesting a detailed report and his colleagues' *fiiringu* (feelings) concerning a revised schedule to move this new formulation into production. On the wall is a company poster with the letters 'C' and 'S' in giant ink brush strokes, proclaiming the importance of 'Customer Satisfaction.'

At 8:30 the French *directeur général* hurries in from the front parking lot, reserved for general managers and above, to make a call he had arranged to his product division's Chief of Parts Purchasing at Tokyo headquarters. Yesterday afternoon the French *directeur* received a solid semi-annual price from the Chinese firm that currently supplies 40 percent of the plastic cases for his product. The price is 8 percent lower than his other suppliers, all Japanese firms. In highly accented English, he tells 'Tokyo' that he wants to increase his Chinese share to 70 percent. A long and largely friendly discussion takes place during which he explains, 'After 10 years of production we have just broken even for the first time due to enormous efforts to cut costs. We want to extend these efforts to our case suppliers.' Three weeks later he is informed that he may increase his Chinese supply to 55 percent. He tells me he is pleased, saying he expected less. He comments in his lilting, southern French, 'This sort of internal supply relationship between "Tokyo" and its subcontractors in Japan is part of our cost of doing business.' Later in our conversation he notes in an ironic tone, 'Now that we are in the black we have to pay a higher proportion of general advertising costs to the Europe Office.' Lining the walls of the hallway that approaches his private office are oversized copies of advertisements for company products that are currently appearing in over 85 European magazines, accompanied by a television campaign that, it is estimated, is viewed by at least 16 million European households daily.

Satō-san, the Japanese accounting manager for the subsidiary, who has been here for nearly five years, wears elegant Paris fashions and James Joyce-style, wire-rimmed glasses. He tells me of the struggle over his first two years here to increase his fluency in French and so gain the respect of his local colleagues. (Those French managers who have been here throughout his stay acknowledge his efforts and successes with the language, as they implicitly criticize other Japanese managers for their poor French. Meanwhile, though the other Japanese managers are pleased that they can converse with me in Japanese, my conversations with Satō-san chart a trajectory based on time of day: we start out in French but as fatigue sets in we move into the mutually more comfortable Japanese.) Both of Satō-san's children were born in France and his family has enjoyed a spacious house and relaxed home life. He and his wife are bemoaning their imminent return to Tokyo.

Satō-san recounts to me the history of the start-up of this subsidiary over a decade ago. At the time he was still a student at Keiō, an elite, private university in Tokyo. The stories are complete with embellishments typical of multiple retellings: larger-than-life individuals and circumstances. The practical details revolve around a local French politician's seduction, via fine food and drink, of one of the company's high-level Japanese executives who visited the area several times over a two-year period. Satō-san tells me, with undisguised irony, 'The executive chose this site, several hundred kilometers from the most practical port, and is now well into his retirement.' Almost angrily he states that French government officials have been made aware that the company would never consider another 'green-field' investment in France, involving building a factory from scratch, until the tax rates on foreign operations, which are 'out of sync' with the rest of Europe, are reduced. However, Satō-san has clearly been seduced by France himself, and draws me several maps over the next few weeks of the nearest city's best, if least affordable, French restaurants.

The young wife of a Japanese engineer tells me about her and her husband's journey last weekend to the nearest Japanese restaurant, which just opened in a city 150 kilometers to the south. She says that even though the chef was Japanese the ingredients and the flavor were poor. Although in the first year here rice made up a good deal of their luggage on return trips from Japan, they have found a store in Paris that sells very good rice from Spain which she says is grown on a Japanese-managed farm. Along with two of the other wives of the seven Japanese managers, she has been teaching Japanese two hours a week to twenty-five interested employees at the factory. Although she is studying French, she says that after a year and a half she has only made one French friend, Gonzalez-san, one of her students of Japanese.

Mrs. Gonzalez' mother is Spanish, as are her husband's parents. Her main job is to maintain the computer program that tracks all of the 615 salaries in the firm. She has been very friendly and helpful in explaining the salary, flexi-time, and extremely complex benefit programs. She has been especially helpful in clarifying the thinking behind programs that are unique to the firm and were designed in-house, and the national programs which are subject to regular inspection by the French authorities. She says that her (French) boss's current headache is how to cope with a warning from the Bureau of Employment: by law employees may only work 40 hours a week with a maximum of 92 hours of overtime per year. Her boss suspects that someone in the firm has reported to the Bureau that several French production managers have been regularly spending 45–50 hours a week at work. She says that everyone knows about the fierce temper of the chief Japanese engineer, Katai-san, who has shaken up the production division since his arrival about three years ago. Human Resources staff now have a betting pool based on guesses about Katai-san's next day off; whoever chooses the closest date is taken to lunch by the other six. It is now a standing joke between them that they no longer know each other: of 75 potential lunches they have only had 16.

Coping with complexity on a large scale

I have offered these diverse vignettes to illustrate the point that large multinational corporations, especially manufacturers, are the Japanese organizations experiencing the most intense level of global interaction. These 'slices of organizational life' hint at the implications of these global operations for a few members of a subsidiary of a Japanese firm in France. When we think of keywords relating to 'Japan and the world' – for example, financial flows, government and private foreign relations, the media, the movement of ideas (including technology transfers), labor, law, families abroad, careers, education, etc. – it is difficult to find an arena that is not touched by Japan's multinational corporations. And this is the case for Japan more than any other nation. In the language of political science it would be written this way: Japan's contemporary global interactions are dominated by the spread of Japanese capital in a mercantilist form driven by business-state coalitions. In other words, Japanese corporations are the central filter through which 'Japan' interacts with the world, collectively surpassing the Japanese state as an actor in international affairs.[1]

Having established their significance, how is one to treat these challenging subjects? As a consequence of their scale and enormous complexity, large organizations, and especially multinational corporations, are indeed unwieldy subjects for anthropology, which favors far more discrete units of analysis. We might choose to derive analytical comfort, then, by treating each of the vignettes above as a window onto specific day-to-day concerns unfolding at various levels in a complex social field. As such we could generate insights into, say, individual or group strategies for coping with organizational life; such as localizing or scaling down information, potentially generated from a vast range of sources, to a more familiar and manageable level.

The argument in this chapter, however, moves in quite a different analytical direction. It focuses on the meanings and implications of globalising processes in Japanese multinational corporations which, in a very short period of time, have resulted in greatly increased organizational complexity.[2] The specific subject matter is the ideas, the experiences, and the conflicts surrounding globalization for Japanese managers in Japanese subsidiaries abroad. The goal is to stimulate thinking about 'globalization' as a complex process in general, and one with which our analytical experience remains relatively limited.

Anthropology has, I think, acknowledged that 'our' contemporary 'villages' are substantively influenced by global phenomena. As is typical of an early stage of interest, however, we are caught up in identifying the effects of globalization in the communities we study; we are naming rather than analyzing. The so-called 'macro-anthropology,' which takes on board global phenomena, has been less proficient, so far, in dealing with the by-now typical social arenas 'where diversity ... gets organized' (Hannerz 1989: 211), and which are increasingly the sites of field research.[3] This chapter is an attempt from within a particular social field to explore how 'globalization' is used, both by lay persons and academics, to explain such complexities.

The political economy of Japan's 'globalization'

The proliferation in time, space, and quantity of Japanese 'economic' exchanges has led to an expansion in Japan of use of the notions of 'globalization' and 'internationalization' in domestic economic, political, and social arenas.[4] By the late 1980s, with its global economic activities already in full blossom, Japan needed to tell the world – and, more importantly, itself – the story of its newly-achieved worldwide influence. With significant cash reserves in hand, especially following the 1985 revaluation of the yen, the Japanese government became the world's biggest donor of ODA (official development assistance). Japan spread 'butter rather than guns' to the developing world via its own bureaucracy and through highly visible (and arguably disproportionate) economic support for multilateral institutions, especially the IMF, the World Bank, and the Asian Development Bank (which always has a Japanese president). These moves coincided with a relative decline in U.S. government commitment to development, so that, in filling a gap, Japan could position itself as a major player in the 'development game' among its North American and Western European peers in the Group of Seven (G-7) nations.

At the corporate level, Japan's relative wealth was most explicitly exhibited by its trade surplus, not only with most of the G-7 nations, but also with the rest of the world (apart from the OPEC oil-producing states). By the early 1980s Japanese manufacturers, fearful of trade barriers to G-7 markets, moved into production abroad, especially in motor vehicles and electronics. The revaluation of the yen in 1985 generated international political pressures for more investment in countries with a trade deficit. Here we began to see highly visible investments by Japanese private capital in real estate or Hollywood, as well as in faltering industrial enterprises such as Rover in the U.K. and steel firms in the U.S. Meanwhile the Japanese government assisted the U.S. economy by buying a large volume of U.S. treasury bills. Elsewhere, with government development aid behind them, Japanese corporations positioned themselves to benefit from huge profit-making opportunities in rapidly expanding markets, especially in Southeast Asia and China. Thus, by providing investment, employment and/or development aid, Japanese organizations became in a very short period of time important economic, political, and social players in a large number of foreign countries.

The form taken by the globalization of business depends, of course, on the business sector under discussion. In Japan's business media, for example, 'internationalization' was for a long while the main subject attracting the attention of pundits; it sold newspapers, magazines, and talk shows, and drove publishers to place more reporters abroad.[5] For its part, manufacturing has the particular characteristic of direct, high-density, and wide-ranging interactions with local environments. In the foreign context this has meant that compared to other types of Japanese enterprises, such as banks or trading houses, Japanese manufacturers have caught up large numbers of foreigners and local institutions in their globalizing processes. The vignettes that opened this chapter are an attempt to make real this sense of things on the ground at a Japanese subsidiary in France.

It is in this context that in the late 1980s a proliferation of terms such as 'internationalization' and 'globalization' appeared in the slogans of Japanese corporations, as well as in the ministerial directives of the government and quasi-governmental organizations affiliated with them. As in government circles, these terms filtered down into Japanese manufacturers as overarching policies, reflecting as 'goals' what had in fact already occurred.

The 'globalizations' of Japanese managers: from the macro to the micro

Japanese managers posted to subsidiaries abroad experience 'globalization' at many levels, both through coverage by the mass media, and as an element of corporate ideology in internal company documents, such as synopses of the president's thinking on the corporate future, articles on the corporation's extensive projects abroad, and speeches delivered by top managers from Japan at corporate ceremonies.[6] These are examples of macro-globalization as rhetoric in two separate but complementary arenas: public and corporate.

Meanwhile, the 'work' that engages the day-to-day consciousness of the Japanese manager at a subsidiary abroad, is thoroughly involved in the cross-systemic/cross-cultural interchanges that are meant to supply the social content – the actual social processes, if you like – of the rhetorical vessels called 'globalization' and 'internationalization.' These activities are seldom explored in macro (or official) texts. For example, he might be analyzing why an assembly line is working inefficiently. He must communicate his findings in a mélange of English, French, and Japanese, through drawings on available sheets of paper, and by the physical handling of machines – the varied media in which communication in such environments precariously and creatively floats. As another example, he is at first surprised to find the office empty of French colleagues for an hour and a half at midday when he finishes his own lunch in fifteen minutes, but over several months he learns to appreciate the slow midday meal he takes once a week. And when he can pull himself together after a 70-hour workweek, he studies French at 8:30 a.m. on Saturdays.

Let me make explicit the subtexts in these descriptions of the effects of globalization at this intimate, micro-level. On the one hand I am describing efforts made toward cross-cultural communication. In spite of hierarchical and other relations of power, compromises are made by all involved in the work of generating understandings across cross-cultural boundaries. Anthropologists are professionally, and perhaps as a matter of temperament, style, and experience, familiar with these processes. Japanese managers, however, would suggest that their long hours and their authority over analysis and actions to be taken on, say, the assembly line enable communication across cultural boundaries. Although in the organizational chart of the overseas subsidiary Japanese managers are likely to appear as marginal 'advisers,' they see their authority as real. By this I mean not merely legal 49 percent, 51 percent or 100 percent Japanese ownership of the firm; I mean *de facto* power over the means of production in the broadest sense.

On the ground in subsidiaries abroad, the medium of this 'ownership' is in part the functional reach of technical know-how and financial resources, but it is, in addition, a series of dense explanations that link Japanese managers' techniques and their products with themselves. A range of icons focuses their attention. These include ideas as broad as 'their' firm's 'Japanese-ness,' or even their firm as the 'most internationalized among Japanese firms,' and as specific as personal identification with (and the fetishizing of) the particular objects upon which they have labored in the course of their careers. They are likely to be involved in the development of specific work practices surrounding the manufacture or distribution of these products. Remuneration enhances commitment, but the motivations of Japanese managers are deeply rooted in the particular visions they hold of their activities within the corporation. Their 'corporate culture' holds organizational value – it generates activity at their organization – because it is made personal. They are incorporated into the organization.

While they are abroad, the central task of Japanese managers and engineers is to maintain the 'product quality' upon which the very survival of the corporation is claimed to depend. This is carried forward through their attempts to pack the variations of foreign environments into a co-production, or equation, of 'men and machines.' While men and machines are, of course, not literally equivalent, they are linked together as equally important variables in the equations of industrial technique. Functionally, this symbolic manipulation lays down a grid to cope with different persons, contexts, and machines, and it results in achievement of the goal of standardized output. The means may be explicitly articulated manufacturing and accounting techniques – usually named and acronymed specifically by each corporation – in addition to an enormous range of unconscious configurations of a Japanese management model that is deployed as a 'natural' consequence of Japanese managers' postings abroad as a part of Japanese investment in foreign manufacturing.[7]

Although the above paragraph may seem to suggest otherwise, in subsidiaries abroad Japanese managers cannot and do not reproduce Japan, nor the 'Japanese corporation' as it exists in Japan. In practice, overseas production depends on the boundaries of the subsidiary being broadly permeable to its foreign host environment, with which it must sustain a complex range of technical, financial, and social interactions that underpin the physical production of goods. The contents of these interactions are as various and divergent as the many different global settings within which Japanese multinational subsidiaries are found. Thus, while the final product is largely the same throughout the world, it is produced differently within the particular social frames of each factory setting.

Thus I take day-to-day, formal and informal practices at the heart of the foreign workplace to constitute an ongoing 'negotiation' between the Japanese and their, say, French colleagues. Separated by language, knowledge, and hierarchical power, the French and the Japanese variously accommodate and resist each other's understanding of 'appropriate' organizational activity. As we would expect theoretically they generate a corporation that, after Bakhtin (1981), is an 'intentional hybrid.' Perhaps like all formal organizations, various notions of the 'corporation' are activated for each member of the overseas subsidiary according to the particular context. However, the differences between 'hybrid' organizations and 'domestic' organizations are important. By its French/Japanese constitution it can be neither Japanese nor French. From the perspective of each of its members, the overseas subsidiary can only be partially 'domesticated' as it will remain de-linked from other, more 'local' sources of personal identification and political discourse. Thus, work at a hybrid, cross-cultural organization is quite unlike what work has meant previously, either in, say, a French state bureaucracy or a Toyota automobile factory in Japan, especially for French and Japanese managers who interact closely with each other.

Our analyses of 'hybridized' and 'locally de-linked' cross-cultural organizations must rely on scrutiny of the ways in which their members deal with them on the personal and psychological level on the one hand, and at the organizational and operationalized level on the other. Variations experienced while working abroad are treated psychologically by Japanese managers as a 'sojourn' away from the purer set of corporate practices in which they are embedded in Japan.[8] And I choose this word 'sojourn' with precision to convey the experiential quality of an overseas posting as temporary and peripheral to essentially conservative corporate practices which have been experienced over long duration and with great intensity. The Japanese manager reproduces himself as he participates in his corporate practices in a powerful cycle of activity. This process allows him to reproduce the symbolic grid, described above, within which environmental and social variations abroad are controlled in order to meet the goal of standardized products. This experience differs substantively from that of expatriates at non-Japanese multinational corporations in foreign settings.[9] Meanwhile, at headquarters and at factories in Japan, information about variations at 'hybrid' overseas subsidiaries is played down as being 'particular' or 'unique,' and therefore of little significance to the larger organization. From the perspective of the Japanese manager, the large Japanese corporation emerges as a total institution – in Goffman's sense of an asylum, or a prison, but without the locked gates.[10]

On a daily basis in the subsidiary abroad, Japanese managers cope with discontinuities from – and, therefore challenges to – familiar patterns of social behavior, as they cope with markets that are structured differently. They build cross-cultural understandings out of frustrations, they get assembly lines to work 'almost as well as in Japan,' they do business, and they make friends. The tensions generated in these technical and cross-cultural forms of work reflect inconsistencies between the rhetorics and facts of 'globalization' and other rhetorics and facts of the firm, such as its 'corporate culture.' These are stresses characteristic of Japanese corporations' participation in global economic processes, which are perhaps captured in the logical acrobatics of another of corporate Japan's favorite contemporary slogans: 'global localization.' Is this slogan, which is targeted for consumption by both members of the firm and the public at large, meant to convey the idea of global homogenization or global heterogeneity, or is it to arouse, both in Japanese managers and ourselves, a sense of ambiguity, mystery, the exotic, or even irony, in relation to the processes of globalization?

For Japanese managers abroad, 'globalization' is complicated. It plays both within the tangible experience of day-to-day international corporate life and within the abstract metaphors of corporate rhetoric. 'Globalization' competes, furthermore, with other experiences and metaphors, both within the corporation itself and within the worldview of the Japanese manager, in a constellation that is paradigmatic of complexity both in large organizations and, indeed, throughout contemporary, modern life.

Positioning 'globalization'

Because of its presence in a wide range of discourses, I have focused in this chapter on 'globalization' as illustrative of the labeling produced to account for some of our experiences of complexity in our times. I doubt that I have fully exhausted the various 'positions,' or the reach of globalization as experienced by Japanese managers, by making explicit its rhetorical usage by the media, government, and the corporation, as a phenomenon connoting action as a matter of corporate policy, and as a 'thing' which occurs in complex and multi-dimensional ways in the day-to-day individual and organizational life of the subsidiary abroad. It is precisely my point that we generate terms like 'globalization' with meanings as varied, diffuse, multiple, and vague as the phenomenon itself. Eventually, definitions of 'globalization' will be made coherent by usage and habit. (Possibly this term will come to occupy a special status as representative of the current epoch.) So domesticated, 'globalization' will be superseded by other terms meant to account for blurry observation of a new contemporary reality.

Purposefully allowing definitional free-play to 'globalization' in this way is a difficult analytical position to sustain and one which I have attempted through a highly personal and nuanced description of the Japanese manager's experience abroad. I have taken the risk made explicit by Hannerz (1986: 365) that 'actor-centeredness...can become another means of avoiding the intellectual confrontation with problems of scale and complexity.' I push this approach because more fully abstracted alternatives to a focus on the processes occurring within and generated by actors seem only to provide boxes into which descriptions of global phenomena are categorized; they are lists of what globalization 'is.' Anthropology's most widely circulated example here is Appadurai's five 'scapes' of 'global cultural flow': 'ideo-scapes,' 'ethno-scapes,' 'finance-scapes,' 'media-scapes,' and 'techno-scapes' (Appadurai 1990). Such exercises are helpful at the start for defining the boundaries of an analytical field, but their feel is detached and externalized; they seem flat. We gain no sense of how these 'scapes' intersect with each other, as they obviously do, how persons move within and between them, nor a sense of what difference it might make to engage such categories at macro- or micro-levels of analysis. I have implicitly argued that such an engagement requires an analysis of the meanings and usages attached to 'globalization' by its users, not a listing of what globalization is or is not. Phenomena at this scale and at this level of complexity are best examined *through* actors' own engagements with the organisational contexts that produce their understandings of the 'global.'

Methodologically this may – and many would argue should – lead to a personalized investigation of some kind, that is a method that positions, or at least acknowledges, the investigator as structurally (and therefore analytically) entangled with his object of study. However while we have been informed – through the literary criticism movement, structuration theory, and in-depth debate in anthropology concerning the vicissitudes of fieldwork – that avoiding these entanglements is problematic intellectually, and perhaps morally dishonest, nonetheless many risks lurk behind these new analytic opportunities. In particular these exercises require great care to avoid overindulgence, disguised as self-awareness, where the reader wonders if the analyst ever left, metaphorically, his own campfire. (In this chapter I have partially deflected these complications through the rhetorical strategy of generating viewpoints on 'globalization' from the perspective of another; the Japanese manager.) In making analysis in some form personal, we would seem obliged to explore seriously, and to make explicit at the very least to ourselves, the motivations behind the analyses we generate. Personally, I am still waiting to be introduced to someone who is not affected by the complexities generated by processes of globalization. This person would provide a great deal of comparative insight into an analytical problem that I feel is important. However, at best I can only expect to design a project that allows analysis of the conditions under which other persons experience 'globalization' differently from myself.

Japanese managers working in corporate subsidiaries abroad are actors who – like ourselves – may deploy terms like 'globalization,' 'internationalization,' 'cosmopolitan,' or 'borderless' to describe the world around them and to explain their lives to themselves. They inject these words with multiple meanings that both overlap with and diverge from our academic usages of such terminologies as abstract categories. The practices of globalization are now inscribed on us to a far more intimate degree than at other times in history. We are all observers and participants now.

Conclusion

This paper has focused on the meanings implicated by increased structural complexities found in Japanese multinational corporations as a result of their expanding global interactions. I have argued that the term 'globalization' is likely to be used by Japanese managers during a posting at a subsidiary abroad to describe experiences which are both macro-level (i.e. public and pan-corporate), and micro-level (i.e. day-to-day life at work and at home). For these managers, the globalization of the firm competes, meanwhile, with other metaphors, rhetorics, and observed 'facts' of corporate life, such as the firm's corporate culture. As a result, the personal and organizational stresses that I claim as characteristic of participation in global political/economic processes are generated.

The mobilization of the perspective of the actor, in this case the Japanese manager, has been proposed as a valuable means for anthropologists to come to analytical grips with the implications of global processes. The emphasis on the actor has been proposed as an alternative to current anthropological perspectives, which have for the most part merely provided evidence of 'global' phenomena without accounting analytically for their implications and meanings. In addition I propose that we use reflections on our own global engagements as a resource for exploring the meaning of the 'global' to our subjects of study.

4 Trends in Value Change in Contemporary Japan

Ulrich Möhwald

The major goal of this paper is the assessment of recent trends in value change in Japan. In contrast to most of the other contributions in this volume, the approach that I adopt is not based on qualitative analysis or a case study but on a quantitative analysis of opinion survey data. It may therefore be necessary to start with some explanation of the concepts of 'values' and 'value change' used in this paper, together with the material, the goals, and the limits of the framework of analysis.

The concepts of 'values' and 'value change'

The concept of 'values' used in this paper is basically derived from Kluckhohn's definition (1962: 395), but since I am dealing with a reanalysis of survey data, I follow Klages and adopt a more general view of values as 'general orientations toward life concerning the selection of behavior or attitudes, to which one "should" or "should not" adhere' (Klages 1984: 9–10, 177). Much effort has been made elsewhere to distinguish values from other concepts in the social sciences, especially attitudes (Friedrichs 1968: 76–93; Kmieciak 1976: 151–202; Rokeach 1973: 17–25). This is a difficult task, but common to all these attempts in definition and distinction is the perception of values as orientations toward life in general, while attitudes are perceived as orientations toward specific objects. Nevertheless, as Manabe (1997) and Meyer and Rüegg (1979: 52–53) have pointed out, in the case of opinion surveys a clear distinction between values and attitudes is almost impossible.

For practical purposes in this paper, values and attitudes are distinguished by the degree of abstractness or concreteness of the survey questions. Questions that are directed toward life in general are treated as targeting values, and questions that are directed toward specific objects are treated as targeting attitudes.[1]

The concept of 'value change' adopted in this paper is not that of an intergenerational substitution of new for old values, like the one used for instance by Inglehart (1977, 1990). Following Herbert and Hippler (1991: ix–xi), I rather see value change as a multi-dimensional process, in the course of which the relative importance of values changes, new combinations of values emerge, and pluralization and differentiation of value patterns and mental conditions occur. Furthermore, while I admit that an important part of contemporary value change is intergenerational in nature, survey data from Japan and other societies strongly suggest that intra-generational change is also important. In the course of the change in the general mental climate we can observe a continuous diffusion of new ideas from the younger to the older generations at the aggregate level.

Therefore my perspective on the development of personal value systems also differs to a certain degree from much that is prevalent in contemporary value research. The standard approach asserts that personal value systems are formed during early socialization and become fixed by the end of adolescence, without much change happening thereafter. I agree with the standard approach insofar as I also think that early adolescence is especially important for the formation of the basic tenets of personal value systems, but I contest the idea that they are completely resistant to change thereafter, because this underestimates the impact of learning processes which occur in the various stages of socialization throughout one's life. Actually, longitudinal data both from Germany and Japan strongly suggest that changes in personal value systems frequently occur after the end of adolescence. In particular, what the German researcher Helmut Klages has called 'value synthesis,' i.e. the combination of conflicting values, and the ability to actualize different values according to different circumstances, is strongly related in my opinion to learning processes in adult life. In this case, value synthesis means that new values are added to the basic tenets of the personal value system, and previous values are to a certain degree relativized.[2]

The framework of analysis: goals and limits

Since the end of World War II, all highly industrialized capitalist societies – including Japan – have experienced continuous waves of societal change and accelerated modernization. Processes such as the advent of mass consumer society and the welfare state; the population shifts from primary into secondary and tertiary industries, and from the countryside into the big cities, with an accompanying weakening of traditional social bonds; the introduction and rapid diffusion of new media; and the expansion of higher education – all these have brought about fundamental changes in people's lifestyles and mental states. Due to these processes of change, continuing erosion has occurred of the customary social bonds that structure people's lives, whether of status group, class, or local society. Belonging to a reference group and adhering to its lifestyle and its way of thinking is less and less a matter of birth, and more and more a matter of personal, individual choice.[3] In fact, new patterns of consciousness are continuously evolving, and, despite some links with socio-structural groups, they increasingly cut across socio-demographic structures and have become typical of what marketing research calls 'lifestyle groups.'

The framework for analysis which is used in this paper proceeds from the assumption that no uniform set of basic or fundamental values exists in contemporary, highly industrialized, and continuously modernizing societies like Japan, but that social consciousness is fragmented and diversified between the various groups in a pluralized society.[4] As already stated, value change does not consist of a complete substitution of new for old values. What can be observed on the aggregate level is the appearance of new values that are incorporated into the value universe, and shifts in the relative importance of existing values. But what on the aggregate level appears to be merely a change in the relative importance of several groups of values hides more important changes at a lower level of aggregation.[5] This means that, in the course of value change, new combinations and mixtures of values appear and become typical of particular population subgroups. In this paper I call these kinds of typical combinations of values, *value patterns*, and the population subgroups that are representative of such value patterns, *value types*. These value patterns and value types are not constructed deductively but strictly empirically, based on the results of statistical analysis. Value patterns and value types have a strong influence on the selection of attitudes and behavior. But here too, I have to say that this influence is by no means absolute. Different value patterns or types not only imply different future and lifestyle orientations: they also imply different ways of perceiving and coping with problems. Hence, on the collective level, value patterns and value types display clearly different profiles in relation to attitudes and socio-demographic features.

This paper will focus on some aspects of the development, differentiation, and pluralization of such value types and value patterns. It will describe the characteristics of the population subgroups that adhere to these value patterns or constitute these value types, and will try to assess some of the short- and middle-range influences of this differentiation and pluralization on the development of Japanese society.

Several limitations of quantitative analysis must also be pointed out. First, we cannot gain information on the deep structure of people's consciousness through survey research and quantitative analysis. What we can get with these research methods are mappings of the surface structures and types of consciousness at the aggregate level, but these surface structures are strongly connected to the deep structures of the individual consciousness. Second, the results of quantitative analysis reflect tendencies at the level of collectivities and not of individuals. Hence we can say, for instance, that belonging to a certain collectivity increases the probability that an individual will hold a certain opinion, but we cannot say that s/he will certainly hold that opinion. Actually, the results of any statistical analysis are limited to indications that certain properties have higher or lower probabilities of being displayed by certain population subgroups relative to the whole population, or relative to other specified population subgroups.

Finally, a note of caution concerning the naming of value dimensions, value patterns, and value types. In opinion survey analysis, the naming of interconnected groups of variables is conventionally used to enhance the readability of reports. But it should always be kept in mind that this kind of naming is generally the result of interpretation of the content of a property, which is based on a small number of variables. It does not allude to all the possible connotations that a certain notion might have in natural language.

Aspects of the pluralization of value patterns in Japan

Since World War II, major changes have occurred in Japanese society, especially in the fields of economy, lifestyle, education, and the media. These changes have also been accompanied by changes in values, or, more generally, in Japanese social consciousness. This can easily be inferred from the data from surveys on the Japanese national character, like those presented in Figure 4.1. Indeed, this long-term trend in changes in Japanese social consciousness had already started in the Taishō period, but it was interrupted during the late 1930s and early 1940s.

Figure 4.1 Libertarian, authoritarian, and acquisitive values in Japan 1930–1993

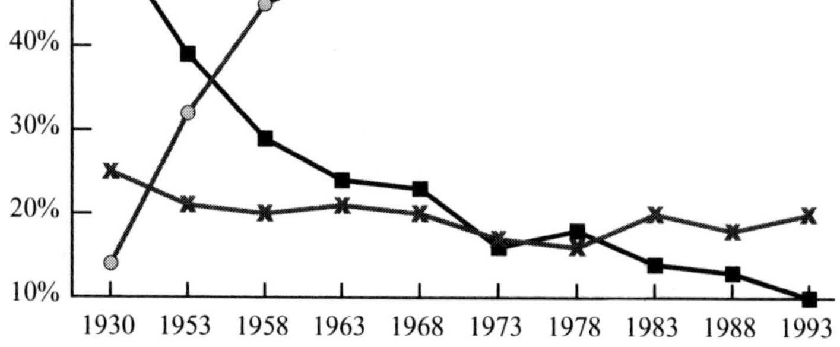

	1930	1953	1958	1963	1968	1973	1978	1983	1988	1993
authoritarian	53	39	29	24	23	16	18	14	13	10
acquisitive	25	21	20	21	20	17	16	20	18	20
libertarian	14	32	45	49	52	62	61	61	64	66

authoritarian — acquisitive — libertarian

Source: Tōkei Sūri Kenkyūjo

I am mainly concerned here with recent developments observable since the mid-1980s rather than longer-term trends. Nevertheless, Figure 1 allows us a glimpse of the background to more recent changes. The first volume in a series of studies of the Japanese national character, covering the results of the first two surveys from 1953 and 1958, was published by the Institute of Statistical Mathematics in 1961 (Tōkei Sūri Kenkyūjo Kokuminsei Chōsa I'inkai ed. 1961). It sparked a lively discussion of value change among Japanese intellectuals. By and large, this discussion was dominated by the question of to what degree Japanese social consciousness was moving away from 'traditional' or 'feudalistic' authoritarianism toward 'modern' individualistic values. As a matter of fact, the design of the surveys of Japanese national character and that of many other surveys on Japanese social consciousness up to the 1990 research project on value change by the German Institute of Japanese Studies was dominated by this kind of question. I do not want to enter into the 'tradition' versus 'modernity' debate now. It is sufficient to say that, to me at least, the dichotomies involved in this debate do not seem to provide a particularly sound approach to social change in Japan.

If we look at Figure 4.1, we can perceive a clear trend away from authoritarian and toward libertarian values, from the early 1950s to the early 1970s, with at least two periods of accelerated change, from 1953–58 and from 1968–73. After 1973 the increase in libertarian values largely came to a standstill, which lasted until about the mid-1980s, but since 1988 we can again observe an increase in these values, albeit on a much smaller scale than before 1973. Judging from the perspective of 'traditional' vs. 'modern' values, value change in Japan appears to have run its course, with only minor changes since 1973. In his penetrating analysis of long-term trends in the national character surveys, Hayashi (1988: 44–45) has pointed out that a major shift occurred in Japanese social consciousness between 1977 and 1983. Throughout the whole postwar era it had been dominated by the logic of a cleavage between 'modern' and 'traditional' value orientations. In this period, however, people started to dissociate themselves from this logic and to combine values that had hitherto been thought to be mutually contradictory. In a similar way, Watanuki (1986: 51–52) has pointed to the fact that, from the early 1950s, differences in political attitudes and voting behavior were dominated by a cleavage between 'traditional authoritarian' and 'modern' values. But in the early 1980s this cleavage started to weaken and to lose predictive power due to an increase in the number of value dimensions. Comparing the results of the 1991 survey by the German Institute of Japanese Studies with the results of the three surveys on Japanese life valucs by the Japan Institute of Life Insurers shows a similar trend. The point is not that changes in values have stopped, but rather that the change which has occurred since the mid-1980s no longer follows the logic of 'traditional' vs. 'modern' values. What has happened is a considerable change in the structure of Japanese values below the aggregate level of the relative importance of single values, which can best be described as an ongoing differentiation and pluralization of value patterns.

This process of pluralization of value patterns becomes apparent if we look at Figures 2 to 4, which are based on the results of the three Japanese life value surveys. In these surveys the central

Figure 4.2 Value patterns in Japan 1976/77

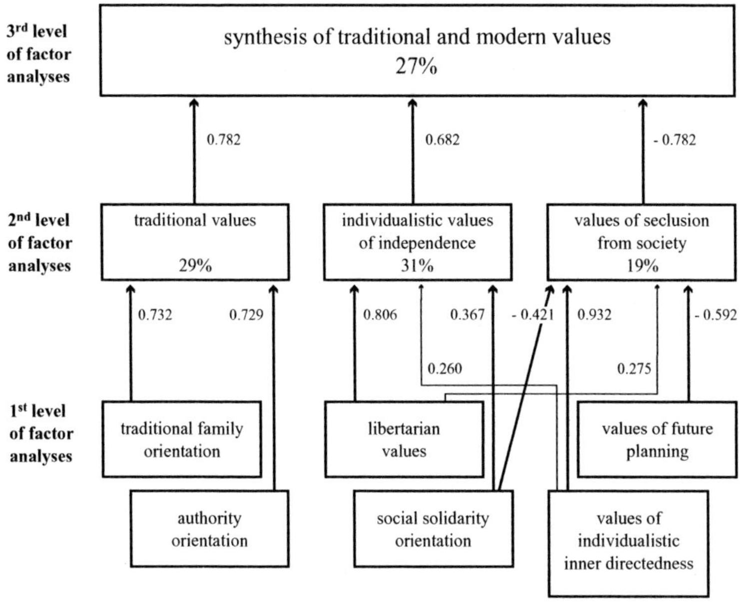

Source: Seimei Hoken Bunka Sentaa. Percentages refer to high scorers.

approach to data analysis was a method which quantitative sociologists call 'data reduction.' If the data fulfil certain prerequisites,[6] we can use factor analyses in order to explore whether a small number of latent dimensions is hidden behind a large number of questions. If we have a very large number of questions, as in the case of the hundred or so used in these surveys, these factor analyses can result in quite a large number of latent dimensions which then can be submitted to secondary factor analysis. This kind of analysis can be continued until the resulting factors are no longer correlated with each other. In the case of the Japanese life value surveys, three-step hierarchical factor analyses have been used in order to condense the value orientations.[7] If we look at the Figures, all three levels of factor analysis have been included only for the 1976/77 data, because at that time the first level factor analysis resulted in only six factors, whereas in 1985 and 1991 it resulted in twenty-two. This fact by itself already points to a shift from a relatively uniform structuration of the Japanese value universe toward an increasing fragmentation and differentiation, which is also apparent at the second and third levels of the factor analysis.

A closer look at the 1976/77 results reveals a differentiation at the second level between 'traditional' authoritarian and 'modern' individualistic values as the main cleavage that structured the value universe. But at the third level we can see a synthesis of values from both sides of this cleavage, forming something like a basic common pool of values that were shared more or less strongly by the majority of the Japanese.[8] This pattern can be called the 'mainstream' in the development of Japanese social consciousness between the 1950s and the 1970s. Nevertheless, as the negative correlation between one of the sets of second level value patterns ('values of seclusion from society') and the third level value synthesis indicates, a certain disengagement from this mainstream already existed in 1976/77.

In 1985, the Japanese value universe was more differentiated and fragmented than in 1976/77 and at the third level, the disengagement from the mainstream of Japanese social consciousness had developed into a pattern which competed with the synthesis of 'traditional' and 'modern' values, that of 'hedonistic and materialistic values of ego-centeredness.' This represented the

Figure 4.3 Value patterns in Japan 1985

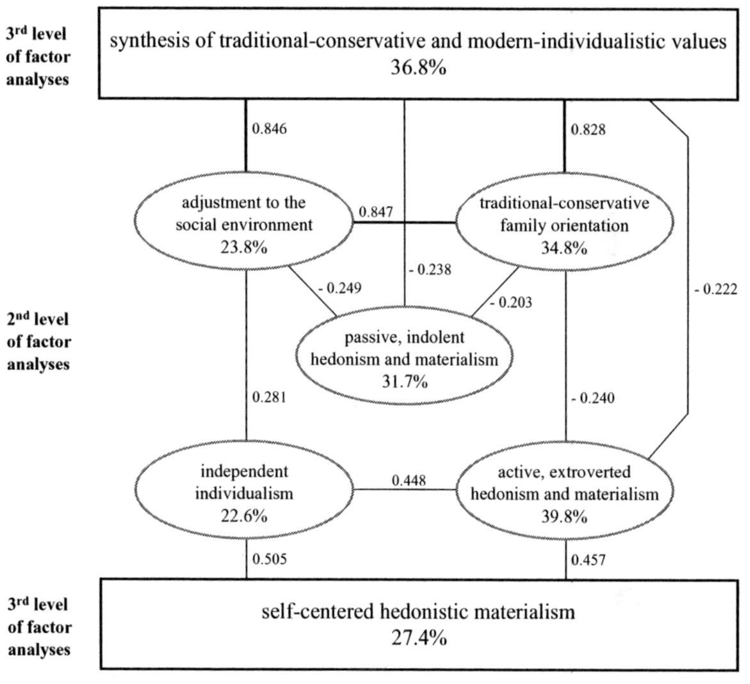

Source: Seimei Hoken Bunka Sentaa. Percentages refer to high scorers.

emergence of a new and much stronger kind of value cleavage. Now, not only a new second-level pattern (that of 'active, extroverted hedonism and materialism'), but also important elements of a previously observed second-level pattern ('independent individualism') were linked to this new third-level pattern. But a certain dissociation of another second-level pattern (that of 'passive, indolent hedonism and materialism') from this new cleavage could still be seen.

Between 1985 and 1991, the development of Japanese values became increasingly fluid, and in 1991 new combinations of values and a certain restructuring of the relations of the value patterns could be observed. Individualistic values had moved closer to the former mainstream synthesis, while both types of hedonistic and materialistic values had become connected and formed the basis of the opposing third-level synthesis of 'ego-

Figure 4.4 Value patterns in Japan 1991

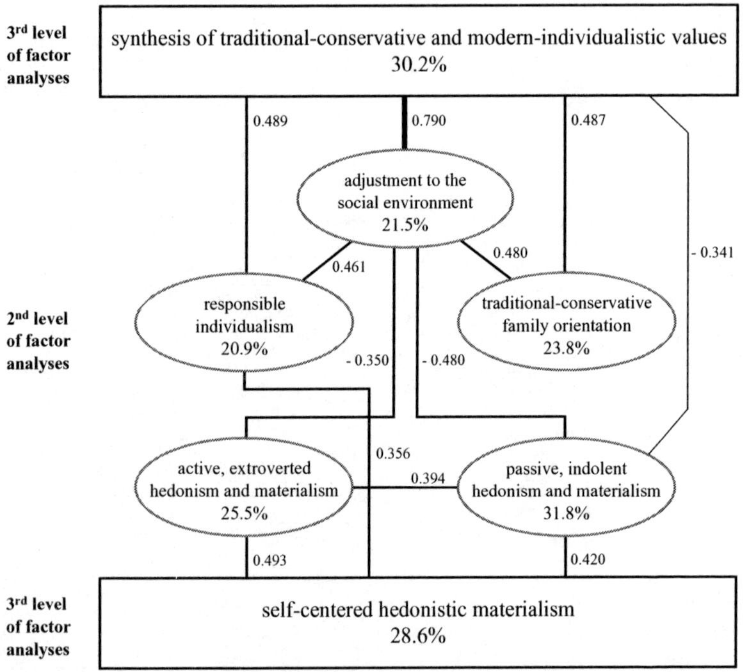

Source: Seimei Hoken Bunka Sentaa. Percentages refer to high scorers.

centered hedonism and materialism.' Hence a new cleavage in the value universe has emerged, which goes beyond the division of 'traditional' and 'modern' values. At the same time, among the old traditional values, hierarchical and authoritarian orientations have lost much of their strength, while modern individualistic values display a connection with the 'old' type of value synthesis, as well as with the 'new' type of synthesis based on hedonistic and materialistic values.

The same kind of disengagement from the mainstream of Japanese social consciousness and from the cleavage between 'traditional' and 'modern' values can also be seen in the results of the 1991 survey of Japanese values by the German Institute for Japanese Studies. This survey did not aim at a complete analysis of the value space, and the basic value dimensions explored were limited to the two dimensions of individualistic and conformist values. In this case four value types were constructed by classifying the respondents according to their proximity to these two value dimensions. This approach has also been replicated in two non-representative surveys in 1996 and 1997. What is interesting in the results of these surveys is that a considerable proportion of the Japanese – close to 20 percent – appears to have dissociated itself from the 'traditional-modern' values cleavage and attached itself to new groups of values. These new processes of value change and pluralization can no longer be meaningfully analyzed if we limit ourselves to the 'tradition' vs. 'modernity' framework. Similar developments can be observed not only in Japan, but also in most Western European societies.

In order to interpret these developments, an important point is the increasing affluence of Japanese society during the 1980s, which culminated in the bubble economy of the late 1980s. During these years, permissiveness in Japanese society increased considerably, and pluralized lifestyles and patterns of consumption became the major vehicle for self-expression and self-definition.[9] Nevertheless, when compared with Western societies of the same period, a relatively high degree of social control still persisted, especially in the lives of Japanese young people, which caused a number of contradictions and frictions. A new element in the fluidity of Japanese values was introduced by the bursting of the economic bubble,[10] which produced new insecurities, together with new groups of losers in the modernization processes. Since about 1990 we can also observe an increasing relaxation of control over the lives of Japanese young people, combined with a further general increase in permissiveness in Japanese society.[11] If we explore the vast amount of survey data that is produced every year in Japan, we can see a clear relativization and weakening of values in every area of life since the mid-1980s, especially in relation to the family, marriage, work, and everyday behavior: areas which had hitherto formed the core of the consensus between 'modern' and 'traditional' values. This, in my opinion, also affects the stability of value orientations at the individual as well as the collective levels.

This kind of change especially affects young people, among whom support for the ego-centered hedonistic and materialistic value patterns lay almost twenty percentiles above the average in the 1985 and 1991 surveys of Japanese life values. Similarly, in our own surveys, we also found that disengagement from the 'traditional-modern' values divide was strongly over-represented in the youngest age groups. But it should also be noted that support for the individualistic and idealistic value pattern was also clearly above average among the younger generation. Therefore it is fair to assume that the younger age groups have by and large moved away from traditional values.

What is the content of these new value patterns and value types that have emerged since the mid-1980s? In order to gain some insight into this problem, it might be useful to look at the common features of the value patterns and value types that imply dissociation from the mainstream of Japanese social consciousness.[12] They are distinguished not only from those of average respondents, but also from the individualistic and rather idealistic value patterns and types among young people.

In socio-demographic terms, these traits of dissociation are strongly associated with males, young people under thirty, lower educational levels, and employment in production and clerical jobs. In terms of human relations, they are associated with avoidance of relationships that imply strong obligations, and with selectivity in their establishment. But they are also associated with weak bonding with groups and with small social support networks. While a group of more active, extrovert people sharing these value patterns tends toward self-assertion and showmanship, and demands to be at the center of attention, a more passive, introverted group is strongly inclined toward social seclusion. In general, they strongly reject hierarchical social relations and structures, conformity, and respect for customs. Their orientation toward social engagement and solidarity with the socially disadvantaged is very weak. They tend toward avoidance of foreigners, and display strong anxiety and insecurity in relation to them. They show very little interest and no practical engagement concerning politics.[13]

Their general value orientations are marked by a strong sense of self-interest and a tendency toward individualistic values that border on egoism. They show disregard for duties toward the family and tend to push for their own rights without regard for others. They display a strong orientation toward the hedonistic values of pleasure, amusement, and consumption, and a relatively strong orientation toward acquisitive materialism and social advancement. They also tend toward instant gratification.

On a more psychological level, they show a low degree of satisfaction with life. They harbor considerable insecurity, unhappiness, and anxiety and show a low degree of self-esteem and self-reliance. They display a certain tendency toward *anomie*, mistrust, and jealousy. They are rather uneasy with contemporary society, and, it has to be said, are not well adapted to the changes now taking place. Concerning employment, they are characterized by the avoidance of responsibility and strenuous work. They show a weak loyalty toward the firm and a propensity to change jobs easily, and they display weak solidarity and bonding with colleagues. They place importance on free time and high wages, but if they have to choose between them, they tend to opt for free time. They regard work primarily as a means to earn money, and tend to accord precedence to other areas of life over work and the firm.

One of the big questions is to what degree the adherents of these new value patterns will take on more traditional values during their future socialization, especially after they enter the labor market, and thus move in the direction of value synthesis and the customary mainstream of Japanese social consciousness. Here, value synthesis means that new values are added to the basic tenets of the personal value system, and previously held values are to a certain degree relativized during the life course. These processes can be demonstrated in the cases of purely 'traditional-authoritarian' or 'modern-individualistic' value patterns. What remains unclear, however, is how the new value patterns of disengagement from the 'traditional-modern' divide will be affected by future socialization processes.

Let me now make a few comments on how the value patterns or value types that imply disengagement from the customary mainstream of Japanese social consciousness affect attitudes toward work, gender equality, and foreigners.

A Work

In the 1976/77 survey on Japanese life values, the basic value synthesis comprised a number of values which stressed the importance of diligence, hard work, and work as an end in itself. In 1985 and 1991 this was no longer the case. Work is still of great importance to the majority of the Japanese, but there no longer exists a consensus concerning the moral superiority of work, diligence, and endeavor regarded as basic virtues and ends in themselves. Thus, these values have detached themselves from the basic value synthesis. Generally, Japanese time series data on values and attitudes show that important elements of Japanese attitudes in relation to work have been subject to change since the mid-1970s.

As may be seen from the outline of these new value patterns and value types above, they have very little in common with the stereotype of the 'workaholic Japanese' as depicted in much Western social science writing on Japanese work attitudes. In 1990, the Labor Ministry's Employment Security Bureau conducted a survey on work-related attitudes among youths who consulted the Tokyo and Osaka regional offices. They found that the majority of the respondents belonged to a type which they called *shinjinrui-gata*, characterized by very low loyalty to the firm, dislike of hard work, a preference for leisure over work (opting generally for free time rather than extra income where the two conflicted), attachment of high value to short working hours and high salary, no interest in the content of work, rejection of socializing with colleagues after hours, and frequent change of job. As one can easily see, this description fits very well with the new value patterns concerning work described above (cf. Rōdōshō Shokugyō Antei-kyoku 1991: 113).

The value type covering young and idealistic individualists in our surveys does not fit very well with the workaholic image of the Japanese either, but in this case we can say that they have a very strong latent work motivation which can be activated by the right incentives, even at the expense of their private lives. These incentives include interesting work, responsibility, and respect for the opinions and interests of fellow employees, but level of remuneration is less important. Motivation can also be frustrated or deactivated by the wrong treatment. Fostering motivation requires major changes in Japanese personnel management practices, something that is very difficult in itself. But if this kind of adaptation does not occur, the idealistic individualist is most likely to react with frustration, declining work motivation, withdrawal from additional tasks, and a search for self-actualization elsewhere. The data indicate that this is already happening in the case of younger, better-educated, and more highly qualified female individualists. These talented women no longer have much hope that Japanese companies will change their attitude toward women, given that the impact of the Equal Opportunity Law vanished along with the demise of the bubble economy, as described by Bishop in Chapter 6.

In the case of value patterns and types that imply disengagement from the 'traditional-modern' values cleavage, this kind of latent work motivation is lacking, and research in Germany suggests that it is impossible to generate it through incentives of any kind. The Japanese data gives a similar impression. Those who share these kinds of value patterns and value types are neither interested in the content of work nor in responsibility. They aspire to high salaries and positions of power, but the utility of these aspirations as incentives is clearly limited, since at the same time they strongly reject hard work and long working hours.

What is important here is that it will no longer be possible for Japanese companies to conduct personnel management on the assumption of the existence of relatively uniform attitudes toward work and leisure among their workforce, or on the assumption that it will be relatively easy to re-socialize new entrants into the labor force to company values and rules. They will have to take into account the necessity of dealing with diverging desires, motives, and needs, and trying to find a way of balancing them. This is true not only of work motivation, but also of the way in which companies deal with women, as will be clear from the next sub-section.

B Gender equality

Time series data from Japanese opinion polls since the 1970s clearly show that attitudes toward women's roles and gender equality have been changing rapidly. This development is especially pronounced among women, the younger generation, and people with higher levels of education, but it is by no means limited to them. Again, what is hidden behind the obvious changes at the level of aggregate data is a considerable pluralization and differentiation of attitudes. Based on the 1991 and 1996 surveys by the German Institute of Japanese Studies, we can isolate the following three relatively independent variables in attitudes toward women's roles and gender equality: (1) customary gender role attribution to women, (2) discrimination against women in the work place, and (3) the degree of conjugal partnership. A non-hierarchical cluster analysis of these three dimensions generates six combinations of high and low scores on these dimensional variables. The distribution of the six patterns is strongly influenced by value types, gender, age, educational level, and, especially in the case of women, stage in the life course.[14]

Women show a clear trend toward a high evaluation of conjugal partnership, combined with a rejection of the customary gender roles attributed to them, especially among the younger generation. This is not very surprising, because it fits well with the general trend of change in attitudes toward gender role division that can be seen in time series data since the mid-1970s. The younger women in particular increasingly express dissatisfaction with a role attribution that largely leaves them alone in charge of household work and childrearing. A majority of people unconditionally endorsing the customary role division between men and women could only be found in the over-sixty age group.

What was more astonishing was the strong rejection of discrimination against women in the work place. This was extremely pronounced in the younger age groups, but extended far beyond them into older groups, up to fifty-five years of age. Of course, I am not talking here about changes of behavior or company practices, which until now have not been very much affected by changes in consciousness. What we can see, rather, is a rapid decline in the degree to which discriminatory practices against women in their working lives are regarded as legitimate. As a matter of fact, open discrimination and sexual harassment are not only despised by women, but also increasingly by young men.

But in the latter case we also have to take into account the effect of value types. Among the younger age groups especially, the idealistic young 'individualists' endorse a new family ideal based on conjugal partnership, combined with a rejection of both customary role divisions and discrimination against women in work. The young 'non-committed' are again a special case, insofar as they display a very ambivalent attitude toward gender equality. At a general level they are characterized by indifference toward gender equality; a reaction occurs only when their own life situations are affected or when it suits their interests. Young working 'non-committed' females strongly reject discrimination against women in work. But young working 'non-committed' males tend to favor ascriptive criteria for promotion and remuneration, including gender, age, and seniority, because these give them an edge over more qualified competitors, including women. They also tend to endorse discrimination against women in the work place.

C Attitudes toward foreigners

In our 1996 survey we also included a number of items on attitudes toward foreigners, since we wanted to explore the relation between values and prejudices. What we found was a clear association between value types and attitudes toward foreigners, though these are very preliminary results. A far more thorough survey of relations between values and prejudice among young Japanese is now in preparation. Nevertheless, I will report some of the results, since they indicate a potentially dangerous trend.

To start with, I have to refer to some results of German research on the problem of youth violence. A survey carried out by a research group at Bielefeld University found that, in particular, males with value patterns that imply a disengagement from the customary 'traditional-modern' value cleavage show an increased inclination toward violence in general, and toward foreigners and the socially weak in particular. This inclination toward violence is further increased by the experience of personal problems, social *anomie*, unhappiness, and insecurity (cf. Heitmeyer et al. 1995).

In Japan up to now we have not seen such a strong trend toward youth violence and hatred against foreigners as in the U.K. or in Germany for instance. But youth violence has recently become an increasing problem in Japan, and in the Nagoya area at least three incidents of xenophobic violence by gangs of youths have occurred in the last few years: harassment and attacks on female students of a Korean school in Kasugai in early 1997; an attack on young Okinawan high school students in the amusement area around Sakae in Autumn 1997, resulting in the death of one of them; and an attack on young Nikkei from Brazil in Komaki in the winter of 1998, which also resulted in the death of one of them.

In our 1996 survey we found that the idealistic young 'individualists' displayed a marked openness toward foreigners. But the 'non-committed' young, especially males, showed a strong inclination toward anxiety and avoidance in relation to foreigners, bordering on hostility. This inclination was mitigated if the respondents had had contacts with foreigners, but it increased strongly if they were dissatisfied or unhappy with life.

In our 1996 questionnaire we did not include items targeting social *anomie* or the inclination to violence, and indeed, only a minority of the 'non-committed' might actually be inclined to violent behavior. But to an alarming extent these 'non-committed' display personality factors that are associated with an increased disposition to justify, or even use, violent behavior in order to achieve their goals or to act out their frustrations, especially if we take into account the results of the 1997 survey.

The 'non-committed' in general display a strong inclination toward egoism and the instrumentalization of human relations, both personality traits that easily lead to the justification of violent behavior. They display a rather strong orientation toward acquisitive materialism (the acquisition of material benefits and a powerful social position), but they also have a strong tendency to have lower levels of education and to hold low-level positions in small firms, so that they are in a rather bad position to realize their aspirations. Accordingly, they show a strong trend toward dissatisfaction with life in general and particularly with work or school. Insecurity, jealousy, and worries about the future are common among them. They have low self-confidence but at the same time they are marked by a strong tendency to reject criticism directed at themselves, combined with strong egoism and a desire to be the focus of attention. They have problems in integrating with groups, and tend to form loose cliques. They show a strong tendency to develop a cluster of personality factors of this kind.

Conclusion

In this paper I have stressed trends that can be observed among younger Japanese in particular, and pointed to some of the problems that might arise from them.

But value change is by no means limited to the young generations. Even if the main agents of value change are the younger generation, general value change in a society creates a climate in which new values diffuse from the younger to the older generations, and this results in the adaptation of personal value systems to new ideas. What is important in this respect is that value change does not mean the substitution of new values for old ones, as some researchers think, but a change in the relative weight or importance of various values, and a pluralization and differentiation of value patterns. Therefore, quite complex structures and considerable variation may actually lie hidden behind what appear to be only minor changes or trends at the level of aggregate data.

This kind of pluralization and differentiation of patterns has occurred in Japan, especially since the mid-1980s. This has led to an increasing fragmentation of the Japanese value universe and to the emergence of new cleavages, which go beyond the customary divide between 'traditional' and 'modern' values. New value patterns and value types have emerged which are especially appealing to the younger generation, and this has strongly affected Japanese attitudes toward work and gender equality.

It cannot be said that work has lost its importance among the Japanese in general, but different value types show differences in work motivation and stress different aspects of work. They also react to different kinds of incentives in improving their work motivation and performance. Japanese firms will have to take this into account if they want to cope with changes in work-related attitudes. But adaptation to this state of pluralized value patterns is far from easy, since it does not allow for uniform personnel policies.

As with work-related attitudes, those related to gender equality have also fragmented into various patterns. Nevertheless, a common denominator, especially among the younger generation, is a strong rejection of gender discrimination in the work place; and this is another point that Japanese firms will have to take into account in the treatment of their work force.

Finally, the pluralization of value patterns also shows the emergence of problematic traits among those who share the new value types and value patterns which imply disengagement from the customary divide between 'traditional' and 'modern' values. A relatively high proportion of these people show a multi-faceted accumulation of negative traits: *anomie*, personal problems, dissatisfaction with society, anxiety, and unhappiness, combined with weak integration with their social environment. This could lead to an increased disposition toward violence, some of it linked to xenophobia or discrimination.

Observation of the future development of Japanese social consciousness is therefore necessary in my opinion. This observation will have to make use of more sophisticated approaches to survey research, as well as international comparisons and qualitative in-depth analysis of the personality dispositions of the various value patterns and value types.

Note on the Material

The materials for this paper are data from nationwide representative sample surveys. These include especially the three *Nihonjin no seikatsu kachikan chōsa* ('Survey of the life values of the Japanese') by the Seimei Hoken Bunka Sentaa (Japan Institute of Life Insurers), dating from 1976/77, 1985 and 1991. The main objective of these surveys can be said to be the mapping of the structure of Japanese social consciousness on the aggregate level by making use of very large measuring instruments covering about 100 items. For this paper I relied on the published reports (Seimei Hoken Bunka Sentaa and Nomura Sōgō Kenkyūjo eds 1980; Seimei Hoken Bunka Sentaa ed. 1987, 1988, 1992, 1993). Also central to the argument of this paper is the 1991 *Nihonjin no kachi ishiki chōsa* ('Survey of the Value Consciousness of the Japanese') by the German Institute of Japanese Studies. The objective of this survey was not a complete mapping of the Japanese value universe, but was limited to the problems of individualism and equality in the areas of family and work. I was able to use the raw data from the survey. In addition to the results of the 1991 survey, I was also able to make use of data from two non-representative surveys by the German Institute of Japanese Studies from 1996 and 1997. These surveys replicated parts of the 1991 survey, but also aimed at an enlargement of the value dimensions covered and added new areas of attitude and person-ality inventories. Additional information has been drawn in particular from the *Nihonjin no kokuminsei chōsa* ('Survey of Japanese national character') by the Tōkei Sūri Kenkyūjo (Institute of Statistical Mathematics), which has been carried out every five years since 1953 (Tōkei Sūri Kenkyūjo Kokuminsei Chōsa I'inkai 1961, 1970, 1975, 1982, 1992, 1994), and the *Nihonjin no ishiki chōsa* ('Surveys of Japanese consciousness') by the NHK Hōsō Bunka Kenkyūjo (NHK Institute of Broadcasting and Culture) (Nihon Hōsō Kyōkai Hōsō Yoron Chōsasho 1975, 1980; NHK Yoron Chōsa-bu 1991, 1998; Hayashi, Nishihira, and Suzuki 1965; Hayashi 1988; Hashimoto and Takahashi 1994).

5 Education Reform in Japan: Fixing Education or Fostering Economic Nation-Statism?

Brian McVeigh

Repairing education or reproducing the status quo?

'Educational reform' has a positive, progressivist ring which appeals to a large number of observers of Japan and members of the Japanese public. But whatever hopes one places in reform, it is worth noting that the Japanese education system has witnessed fundamental change only twice, during the 1870s after the Meiji Restoration, and during the Occupation at the end of the Pacific War, both times of extreme crisis. It is also worth remembering that the sweeping reforms of both periods 'were followed by a more conservative reaction that served to temper the earlier changes' (Beauchamp 1994: 3), evidence that deep ideological substructures lie buried under the edifices of foreign-imposed policies, expedient alignments, and partisan promises. In a certain sense, then, 'educational reforms' are nothing new, and the Japanese elite has, since the Meiji Restoration, always been searching for ways to 'improve' schooling for its own purposes, while taking into account (if only ostensibly) the concerns, complaints, and criticisms of teachers, parents, students, and international neighbors. Different socioeconomic groups have had very different opinions on what constitutes 'reform,' and the distinction between actual reform and improving status quo arrangements (i.e. superficially changing procedures, slightly adjusting methods, and reworking current operations) is often difficult to make. The media hype that usually surrounds reforms seems to blur the lines between the official announcement and initiation of reform discussions, lengthy deliberations, and the actual effects of the implementation of any decisions, so that the education system always seems to be heading toward some type of positive change.

In this chapter I contend that 'reform' means change, but a special type of change as understood within the context of Japanese education. 'Reforms' are attempts, orchestrated by statist and capitalist interests, to maintain a certain status quo implicated in elitist definitions of Japanese identity and nation-state power. When discussing reform in Japanese education, a distinction should be made between fundamental change and modification; the latter is periodic, while the former has happened only twice so far. Simply stated, then, though the educational bureaucracy has displayed institutional innovation and flexibility since the Meiji period, Japan's leaders have never deviated from safeguarding the continuity of ideologies of identity. They have ensured that schools have instilled the knowledge that underpins Japan's capitalist developmental state into Japan's pre-war and wartime imperial subjects, and into its post-war citizens. These forms of knowledge, especially literacy, numeracy, and science, are designed to produce workers who are rational, diligent, and aware of the significance of 'being Japanese.'

Educational nationalism and 'Japaneseness'

'Being Japanese' requires some analysis because merely to call it a form of 'nationalism' obscures the powerful semantics and dynamics of identity. 'Just to call nationalism an identity...explains little in itself' (Billig 1995: 7). Moreover, discussion of the meaning of 'nationalism' is admittedly fraught with conceptual difficulties, though this is not the place to attempt to sort out this terminological confusion. However, a few explanatory words are in order. 'Nationalism' is used in a variety of ways, and any set of ideas or institutions can be 'nationalized' and intimately bound up with national identity. In the case of Japan, we can speak of state nationalism, racial nationalism, agrarian nationalism (Havens 1974), economic nationalism (Levi-Faur 1997), cultural nationalism (Yoshino 1992), gendered nationalism (Tamanoi 1998), linguistic nationalism (Miller 1982), techno-nationalism (Samuels 1994), and religious nationalism. Nationalism may also mean (1) heightened ethnocultural awareness; or (2) the belief that a people/

nation deserves to recover, obtain, or establish a unified political structure (state). These two meanings need to be distinguished for many reasons, such as the fact that some nationalisms target their own states ('anti-state' nationalism), creating circumstances in which the second definition ('every people a polity') may conflict with the first.

For the sake of conceptual clarity and for the purposes of my present argument, my use of 'nationalism' subsumes three types of identity: (1) *ethnocultural* (conventionally referred to simply as 'nationalism'), ranging from pride in one's cultural heritage to xenophobic ethnocentrism; (2) *statist*, involving political structures, membership as a citizen, and control structures ranging from general regulatory legal functions to highly centralized and totalistic bureaucratic control; and (3) *racial*, ranging from classifying individuals based on perceived physical differences or innate traits (e.g. 'blood') to pseudo-scientific theories about the inferiority/superiority of different 'races.' These three ideologies of identity (as in some other societies besides Japan) intersect, interrelate, interact, and legitimize each other, weaving complex tapestries of identity. However, the key point I want to stress is that, because these three different ideologies have become so fused, they should be understood as having been forged into a hard alloy, resulting in a folk theory of 'Japaneseness' at the popular level. 'Japaneseness,' linked to the projects of Japan's capitalist developmental state, produces what we can call an overarching ideology of economic nation-statism. This latter ideology (really an array of merged ideologies) is sustained and reproduced by education. At this point, Gellner's (1983) thinking is pertinent. He argues that modern nationalism came into being because states were able to successfully instill in their populations the basic levels of education (literacy, numeracy, etc.) required by industrialism. 'At the base of the modern social order stands not the executioner but the professor...The monopoly of legitimate education is now more important, more central than is the monopoly of legitimate violence' (Gellner 1983: 34). We can speak, then, of 'educational nationalism,' driven by statist sovereignty, ethnocultural affiliation, and the promise of economic power.

In order to effectuate, actualize, and articulate economic nation-statism and, more specifically, educational nationalism, Japan's policy elites have designed a system of 'strategic schooling.'[1] Institutionally, this system of highly organized schooling can be understood as comprising a three-tiered organization with the Ministry of Education (Monbushō), the education-socializing arm of the state, at the apex. The three tiers are: (1) *strategic*: executive bodies that design comprehensive plans (state officials, government circles, business associations, advisory councils, the Education Minister's Secretariat); (2) *intermediate*: mediating levels of implementation, composed of ministerial bureaus, their divisions, prefectural and municipal education commissions, and education-related associations and legal entities (*hōjin*) authorized by the state, linking the strategic and tactical levels; and (3) *tactical*: schools and other sites administered and monitored by the Monbushō.[2]

The meaning of 'educational reform,' then, becomes more understandable if one views it a series of policy maneuvers that were begun in the Meiji period – and which continue to this day – whose aim is to tune up and lubricate the bureaucratic machinery that runs the ideological and institutional gears of Japan's economic nation-statism. In order to appreciate these policies, some history is necessary.

Post-war Japanese education

Discussions of how to improve education can be traced all the way back to the Meiji period, within and outside official circles, and the state has used officially appointed and staffed councils to investigate and recommend reform (e.g. the 1935 Education Renovation Council, *Kyōgaku Sasshin Hyōgikai*, which was comprised of ultra-conservative scholars, and which was replaced by the 1937 Education Advisory Council, *Kyōiku Shingikai*). But the most famous push for reform, of course, occurred immediately after the Second World War. Even before the Occupation forces had settled in, the Monbushō initiated a series of 'voluntary reforms' through orders and notifications that anticipated the American reforms.

There are two ways to interpret the Monbushō's 180-degree ideological about-face. The first is cynical: in order to please the conquerors, the educational authorities simply said what they assumed the occupying forces wanted to hear. Moreover, bureaucratic elites, out of sheer practicality born out of a threat to their own survival, realized they had little choice but to reverse their policies. But most importantly, the educational authorities cannily danced to the tune of the times while keeping their own policy agenda intact for future deployment once the occupiers had left. The second interpretation accepts at face value the idealism and enthusiasm for reforms based on equality, democracy, and internationalism. It must be remembered that the sudden change in the Monbushō's policies was certainly welcomed by segments of the general population. The wartime Monbushō and its bureaucratic allies were never completely successful in their socializing projects and, in any case, not all Japanese agreed with these projects.

Both of these interpretations have some merit, and the choice between them depends on which circle of individuals one chooses to investigate. But as we shall see, the first is perhaps more convincing. This is not to deny the courage, sincerity, and achievements of those who dismantled the militaristic aspects of pre-war education. However, to overemphasize the second interpretation is to ignore the deep ideological structures that inform both pre- and post-war education in Japan: the structures of economic nation-statism. Furthermore, in spite of any anti-elitist feelings that the average Japanese may have had immediately after the war, very few would have opposed the fundamental imperative of the elite agenda: that of rebuilding Japan as quickly as possible. How this reconstruction was to take place was heatedly debated and, at times, violently contested. However, the basic goals of the contending groups – whether they were Monbushō officials, workers, managers, teachers, or students – were not essentially different: a strong and prosperous Japan, secure in its time-honored identity. This broad support for revitalizing Japan involved state projects affirmed in a moralistic tone that seemed to merge the interests of the elite and the masses. Ultranationalism, then, was swept away by traumatic defeat, the Occupation, and an injection of foreign-ordered reforms. But the deeply-rooted ideologies of economic nation-statism and Japaneseness, though forced to present themselves in a more 'internationalist' light, were left intact.

The Occupation authorities were primarily concerned with defanging the virulent nationalist elements of Japanese education (e.g. State Shintō, highly prescriptive moral education, mythical depictions of history), resocializing Japanese educators, and decentralizing and democratizing the educational administrative system. Some key features of the new framework included the unification and standardization of schooling, resulting in the '6–3–3–4' system;[3] the abolition of state-sanctioned sexual discrimination; the offering of some financial aid; provisions for part-time and correspondence courses; integrating special schools into the regular school system; and extending compulsory education to nine years, something that had been discussed in Japan long before the Occupation.

American assistance in the institutional continuity of the Monbushō

The agendas of state and corporate interests, the ideological substructures supporting economic nation-statism, institutional inertia, and the so-called 'reverse course,' in which the Occupation abandoned its more progressive policies to turn Japan into a bulwark against Communism at the onset of the Cold War, can all help explain trans-war continuity in Monbushō projects and policies. But the failure of the Occupation authorities to understand the role of the ministries in Japan was also partly responsible. Of all the groups criticized and held accountable for Japan's disastrous defeat and impoverishment – the military, politicians, *zaibatsu* (industrial combines), the imperial household, and ministerial officials – it was the last two that were the least weakened by Occupation reforms. The imperial institution suffered a loss in mystique and prestige, though it still spoke to many at a deep ideological level, even those who considered themselves internationalist and pacifist, about the importance of 'being Japanese.' The state structures, which had been greatly strengthened by the war experience, were basically left intact by the Americans.

The Americans assisted the augmentation of the Monbushō's power in two ways. First, SCAP (Supreme Command Allied Powers) believed it could implement its mission through the centralized bureaucracy; and second, because SCAP did not establish adequate mechanisms at the local level to finance local education, the central authorities were able to continue their role overseeing education by controlling taxes, grants, and subsidies.

Thus, 'Although central control over the educational system might have been seen originally as a temporary accommodation to the requisites of carrying out revolutionary change, nevertheless SCAP in effect sowed the seeds of the resurgence of the Education Ministry in Tokyo' (Marshall 1994: 150). Though the American authorities would have the final say in policy direction, SCAP hoped that the Japanese themselves would take the lead in revising their educational system. Thus, American-initiated reforms were carried out indirectly, through Japanese state agencies. Indeed, the American misunderstanding of the pre-war and wartime function of the Monbushō offers a powerful lesson in the dangers of assuming that institutions perform the same functions everywhere:

> 'It seems that most of the Americans who participated in the reforms in Japan considered the Ministry of Education as a low power, non-independent organization because in the United States the Education Section of the Office of Health, Education and Welfare has a more advisory function. But traditionally in Japan the Ministry of Education had a much stronger role in determining educational policy than that of the United States Office of Education' (Kayashima 1993: 53).

Signs of ideological and institutional continuity

The practices, policy tools, and traditions that the state elite utilized in the early and mid-1950s did not suddenly appear from thin air, but were the direct descendants of pre-war and wartime state operations. Though there was much resistance from various quarters against the strengthening of the statist and capitalist elite, the state's colonization of society and the building of social substructures during the pre-war and wartime periods ensured that changes deemed too radical would not be allowed. Many state officials saw little need for some of the changes espoused by more liberal groups: 'They were willing to reject the militarism of the late pre-war period, but they did not want to lose the "traditional Japanese morality" of the Imperial Rescript [on which see below]. Neither did they want to see the efficiency of the pre-war system sacrificed in the name of "western" egalitarianism' (Schoppa 1991:

31). The elements of 'traditional morality' (e.g. hierarchy, loyalty, obedience, and diligence) that comprised the deep ideological meanings of Japaneseness were not to be swept away by military defeat. Some Japanese officials expressed doubt as to whether the American reforms were suitable to their 'culture': in his address to the United States Education Mission to Japan, Monbushō Minister Abe Yoshishige stated that 'I fear that we shall never be able to have a true Japanese education which is firmly rooted in our soil and which can work on the innermost soul of the Japanese people. If so, it will also be impossible to have a true development of Japanese culture' (Abe 1994: 84).

As one example of trans-war continuity, consider the debate about the fate of the Imperial Rescript on Education during the immediate post-war period, a symbol that deserves comment because it was so charged with nation-statist meanings. This serves as an excellent example of the 'problem of rupture and continuity' between the pre- and post-war periods.

According to Horio (1988: 132–7), there were basically four responses to the problem of how to deal with the Rescript. The first was 'open advocacy of the Imperial Rescript's continued validity.' Even Monbushō ministers who criticized wartime excesses, and who in other respects seemed liberal, supported this view. For example, Maeda Tamon (minister from 18 August 1945–13 January 1946) linked the Rescript to the *kokutai*, the mystical 'national essence'; Abe Yoshishige (13 January 1946–22 May 1946) linked it to 'daily morality'; Tanaka Kōtarō (22 May 1946–31 January 1947), a practicing Christian, believed the values embodied in the Rescript were based on 'natural law'; and Amano Teiyū (6 May 1950–12 August 1952) called the Rescript 'the standard of Japanese morality.' The second response advocated a revised Rescript that would be more fitting for the new era. This was the view of the Committee for Japanese Educators, formed to cooperate with the United States Education Mission. Ashida Hitoshi, who in 1948 became the fifth post-war prime minister, doubted whether the Japanese people could understand the new Constitution. Therefore a new Rescript was necessary, since it would come from the most popular figure in Japan, the Emperor himself, and would help make the people understand the Constitution. Yoshida Shigeru, who became prime minister in 1949, wanted to replace the Rescript with an 'educational statement' (*kyōiku sengen*) on morality. On 6 May, 1950, Monbushō Minister Amano publicized his views on morality, and in November 1951, a newspaper published 'An Outline of Practice for the Japanese People' (*Kokumin Jissen Yōryō*) and stated that Amano was its author. It espoused pre-war values, such as 'love and respect for the Emperor,' and carried a heavy statist moral tone, declaring that 'The State is the parent body of the individual; without the State there can be no individuals.' Amano was severely criticized in many circles, and his ideas were called 'Amano's Imperial Rescript.'[4] The third response contended that a new Rescript was needed that would declare the 1890 version invalid. This was advocated by Morito Tatsuo (minister from 1 June 1947–15 October 1948). These three responses indicate that, even though they may have been committed to democratizing Japan, some post-war leaders 'were themselves not free from the mystique of Imperial Rescripts' (Horio 1988: 135).

The final response, forcefully argued by the historian Hani Gorō, stated that the Rescript should be repealed (Hani 1979). Though it was this response that would finally be officially adopted, Horio points out that even after the new Constitution had been in effect for a year and imperial sovereignty had been replaced by popular sovereignty, a special Diet measure was needed to annul the Rescript and other Imperial documents officially. The Fundamental Law on Education was intended to replace the Rescript, which was eventually removed from schools. 'Here we find striking evidence both of the persistent reluctance of Japan's leaders to renounce the Imperial Rescript and of the difficulties the Japanese people had to overcome to establish a genuine democracy' (Horio 1988: 138).

The 'reverse course': the re-assertion of state and capitalist interests

Other examples of trans-war continuity are visible in the maneuvers of the Occupation authorities and Japanese elites in their response to the increasingly chilly atmosphere between the United States and the Soviet Union during the late 1940s and early 1950s. These maneuvers, collectively known as the 'reverse course,' demonstrated the staying power of the state and the capitalist elite, as well as the American concern for containing communism. The

Occupation authorities, worried about the spread of labor unrest, lost their initial interest in pro-labor legislation. General MacArthur banned a general strike planned for February 1, 1947, and the 'Red Purge' of 1949–50 resulted in the firing of 22,000 people in both the public and private sectors. Cold War tensions exploded into heated battle when the North Korean army invaded South Korea on Junc 25 1950. Meanwhile, under a liberal interpretation of the new Constitution's war-renouncing Article 9, Japan's rearmament began with a paramilitary National Police Reserve of 75,000 personnel. In 1952, this was renamed the National Security Force, and air and naval forces were eventually added.[5] Around this time a campaign was launched by some politicians and bureaucrats who formed the 'Committee for the Investigation of Revising Governmental Decrees' (*Seirei Kaisei Shimon I'inkai*), to 'correct the excesses of post-war democratization.'

The effects of the reverse course can be seen in how the Monbushō's top positions changed. Immediately after the war, scholars such as Maeda (Minister), Tanaka (School Education Bureau Director-General), and Yamazaki Tasuku (Science Education Bureau Director-General), were brought into the Monbushō from outside. Called the 'rostrum clique' (*kōdan-ha*) by the media, these individuals were expected to 'democratize' the educational bureaucracy (Yamamoto 1992: 32). Even the socialist Morito became a Monbushō minister. But in the later stages of the Occupation, Monbushō ministers were conservative politicians, businessmen, or individuals with pre-war associations such as the controversial Ōdachi Shigeo (minister from 21 May 1953 to 10 December 1954) who had been a pre-war Ministry of Home Affairs official, and who had been purged as a war criminal before his appointment, and Amano (minister from 6 May 1950 to 12 August 1952), who advocated the idea that 'the center of ethics is the Emperor.'

In 1955, legislation was proposed to alter – or in the opposition's opinion, weaken – parts of the Fundamental Law on Education. Of the three pieces of legislation, only the 1956 Law Concerning the Organization and Operation of Local Educational Administration was eventually passed, and then only with special riot police brought in to maintain order in the Diet. Between 1957 and 1959, the Monbushō maneuvered on four fronts in order to implement its projects: education board/commission reform, textbook screening, teacher evaluations, and student achievement testing. The Monbushō made substantial advances on the first two fronts, but had only partial success on the latter two.

LDP views of education

Circles within the Liberal Democratic Party (LDP) have consistently expressed profound reservations about the schooling system installed during the Occupation, arguing that a 'multi-track' and 'diversified' educational system similar to the pre-war system would better suit Japan. They have specifically targeted the symbols of foreign imposition: the Fundamental Law on Education and, by implication, the post-war Constitution and its 'peace clause.' Their nationalistic agenda has included strengthening moral education (which more recent state campaigns have termed 'education of the heart') (McVeigh 1998a), revising textbooks, teaching Japanese 'traditional' values, instilling respect for the Emperor, and using the Hinomaru and Kimigayo (the national flag and anthem) in school ceremonies. Some LDP politicians have openly voiced their wish to weaken the Japan Teachers' Union.

The controversy over the use of the Hinomaru and Kimigayo in school ceremonies still simmers. The Monbushō, under pressure from certain politicians, decided that though these were not 'official' emblems of Japan (they were not made official until the legislation of 1999), they were 'customary' symbols to which all Japanese should pay homage. But resistance to, and resentment of, official directives runs deeper than the appearance of daily life in Japan might at first suggest. Some schools, under pressure from parents or students, simply refused to raise the Hinomaru or sing the anthem. There are stories of schools complying with Monbushō directives by raising the Hinomaru for one minute behind the school among trees where it was not visible, or playing a tape of the Kimigayo while students listened.

The LDP has received strong support from the *zaikai* (business world), which has often requested that the educational system produce more disciplined and obedient workers instilled with the proper attitude toward labor, especially during the period of high-speed economic growth of the 1960s. The 'GNP-first' period appeared to be an extension of the wartime economy and the ethos was the same: 'During the war the Japanese were made to work selflessly in the attempt to win. After the war similar sacrifices were evidently expected in the interest of GNP growth' (Taira 1993: 171). Leading business organizations have regularly published reports about what kind of worker the educational system should be producing. These reports, along with the general public discourse about reform, employ terms that sound high-minded, but also evoke a strong sense of *déjà-vu* since they have been recycled through the post-war decades. The calls for more 'creativity,' 'individuality,' 'liberalization,' 'diversification,' 'flexibility,' and 'internationalization' are in large measure demands from business and industry for workers who are more innovative, efficient, open-minded, and skilled in the latest technology needed for Japan's economic nation-statism.

Consider the meaning of 'liberalization,' which does not mean creating a 'spiritually freer form of schooling,' at least from the *zaikai* perspective, but rather deregulation in order to continue the current education system into the future (Horio 1988: 367–8). For some, the liberalization or privatization of schooling means the introduction of market forces, which, it is believed, would force the education system to improve. But the privatization of education does not mean limiting state involvement in the system, but rather shifting the costs to the people themselves.

Another key word in the discourse on reform is 'diversification,' used to describe a schooling system in which multi-tracking is used to segregate students into various academic streams (rather than the current single-track system in which students study the same curriculum). Critics of diversification claim that multi-tracking will only increase elite/mass distinctions.

Reforms of the 1970s

During the mid- and late 1960s, various concerns – such as how to respond to Japan's rapidly changing economic needs and to the over-standardization of education, combined with student unrest at universities – led Monbushō Minister Kennoki Toshihiro (3 December 1966–25 November 1967) to issue a 'request for advice' (*shimon*), asking the Central Council for Education to deliberate on problems in Japanese education. In June 1971, the Council submitted its suggestions for reform. Many of these were not put into effect, but some were implemented: (1) aid to private universities, (2) aid to private schools, (3) expansion of kindergartens, (4) expansion of education for the handicapped, (5) salary raises for teachers, (6) formal recognition of assistant principals, and (7) the establishment of graduate teacher-training universities. Reforms that were partially implemented included the establishment of the *shunin* (administrative teachers) system and diversification of high schools (Schoppa 1991: 207).

Reforms of the 1980s and 1990s

In the early 1980s, school violence and bullying, excessive competition in university entrance examinations, and overly standardized and inflexible structures and methods of education compelled further reform measures. Conservative corporate interests argued that 'the economy of the 1980s (and even more, the economy of the future) required creative scientists, fluent foreign-language speakers, specialists in extremely complex technology and workers who could express their views rather than just follow orders' (Schoppa 1991: 50). By 1984, the stage was set for further adjustments in Japan's educational system, when the Nakasone Cabinet established the Ad Hoc Council on Education (*Rinji Kyōiku Shingikai* or *Rinkyōshin*), which would deliberate for three years and submit four reports.

The Council identified eight areas for deliberation and possible reform: (1) major challenges toward the twenty-first century; (2) promotion of 'lifelong learning' and the easing of emphasis on the educational backgrounds of individuals; (3) improvement of higher education and the development of the individual characteristics of each institution; (4) further improvement and diversification of elementary and secondary schooling; (5) improvement of the quality of teachers; (6) a strategy to cope with internationalization; (7) a strategy for the advent of the information age; and (8) a review of educational administration and financing.

Nakasone was particularly intent on strengthening state control over teachers, changing the post-war 6–3–3–4 system, and emphasizing 'traditional Japanese morality' in order to stop school violence and bullying. But it is worth pointing out Nagano's contention that conservative voices used the 'dilapidation of education' as a pretext to strengthen the state-guided selection, training, and evaluation of teachers (1992: 208), and Horio writes that the Ad Hoc Council on Education was an attempt to 'settle the score' on the post-war reforms (1988: 362). Schoppa echoes Horio when he writes that Nakasone's desire to stress 'Japaneseness' and alter the 6–3–3–4 system 'can be seen as a reflection of his desire simply to erase a symbol of Japan's defeat' (1991: 56). The Monbushō did not agree with many of Nakasone's ideas, and only some of his reforms were implemented: (1) expansion and reinforcement of moral education; (2) a more flexible curriculum; (3) school expansion programs; and (4) a probationary teacher-training year.

Conclusion: Japanese education and 'stealth ideology'

Since the Meiji period, the state, along with corporate interests, has so successfully instilled an orthodoxy about capitalism and Japanese identity that it is very hard for many to conceive of alternatives. Thus, the implementation of fundamental change becomes exceedingly difficult.

A significant aspect of post-war educational reform, notwithstanding any input from the Japan Teachers' Union and other relatively progressive groups, is its conservative and elite-defined nature. Indeed, if education has been so distorted, provoking loud and incessant complaints, why have genuine educational reforms been so lacking? According to Refsing, perhaps 'a substantial number of Japanese in influential positions are actually – secretly – quite satisfied with the way things are' (1992: 127). Moreover, and perhaps just as significantly, state projects have colonized so much of daily life and become such a large part of the aspirations of the masses that there is little need for state structures (and corporations) to convince people to participate actively in the education system and to pursue academic credentials diligently. Consequently, rather than the state/capital nexus existing for the sake of the citizens and society, the citizens and society are working hard to benefit state and capital.

As an example of how deeply state and capitalist agendas have penetrated society, consider the case of the Monbushō's campaign to reduce school hours. In the early and mid-1990s some schools abolished Saturday morning classes twice a month in order to give more free time to students and relieve the pressures of studying (previously all schools had held classes on all Saturday mornings). Current reform plans aim at abolishing all Saturday classes by 2003. However, as evidence of how difficult it is to disengage state agendas that have permeated society, it was reported that 'under half of all elementary and middle schools have actually cut down on academic hours' and 'over 75 percent of schools at all three levels said the academic workload of students does not seem to have changed substantially' ('Five-day week doesn't mean less studying,' *Japan Times*, September 4, 1997: 2). The problem is not just with the schools; it is with society. Indeed, according to a survey, 'the number of parents who object to the planned five-day school week is larger than those who accept it' ('More parents oppose 5-day school week,' *Daily Yomiuri*, August 21, 1997: 2). Some parents complain that they do not know what to do with their children on Saturdays and worry that their children will lose out in the educational race.

An examination of the history of Japanese education reveals that, contrary to the view that Japanese are merely motivated by a 'non-ideological' reductionistic economism, there is an ideology in Japan, one that rests upon 'being Japanese,' and this has shaped in no small way Japan's educational plans, policies, and priorities. But because ideologies of identity have not been fully appreciated, Japaneseness has become what may be termed a sort of 'stealth ideology,' whose movements, tactics, and targets are not always clear. There are basically two reasons for this.

First, as noted above, Japaneseness is better understood as being formed from the intersection of three types of identity: (1) ethnocultural, (2) statist, and (3) racial. Japaneseness is built by essentializing and confusing one's political affiliation (statism), nation (ethonocultural heritage), and 'race' (biological traits that are assumed to be common to a group). The merging of these concepts forms a logic of tautological equivalencies: 'one looks Japanese because one is ethnically Japanese because one possesses Japanese citizenship.' Though the average individual can readily disentangle citizenship, ethnicity, and physical appearance if asked to, the point is that, quite often, the habitual and unconscious sentiments forged by socializing patterns weave them into a tight web of mutually defining concepts: 'Racial, ethnic and national [i.e. statist] categories almost completely overlap in the Japanese perception of themselves' (Yoshino 1992: 25). This is why the term *tan'itsu minzoku*, meaning 'homogenous nation,' 'is used as a convenient phrase to indicate the homogeneity of Japanese people without specifying whether one is referring to their racial or cultural features' (Yoshino 1992: 25–26). Note how ex-prime minister Nakasone conflates physical traits with nationality and uses a mysticism cloaked with science to link Japanese with their past:

> 'Starting with DNA, scientists have clarified the mysteries of life in the whole universe. We were born in Japan not because we desired to be born in this country. We have been given this nationality by providence within the context of the great law of the universe...Our lives have been given by DNA, which goes back to the immemorial past through generations of our ancestors' (Nakasone 1997).

But if the average person conflates different types of identity, then so do some researchers who, rather than appreciating how the three aforementioned ideologies coalesce into a potent racialized nation-statism, use 'nationalism' as a vague catchall term that conceals more than it reveals. The result is that some fail to see how one type of ideology of inclusion and exclusion can combine with and be articulated through other ideologies.

The second reason for confusion has to do with how 'being Japanese' has become so deeply wrapped up with the nation-state system, consumerist capitalism, the acquisition of educational credentials, and labor. We often fail to recognize how the norms of political economics – which appear so 'commonsensical' and universalistic to some – reinforce and legitimate national identity and state projects. From the point of view of the average Japanese, receiving compulsory education, as required by the state, has become indistinguishable from being a 'good Japanese' – even if it does involve discipline instead of learning, cramming instead of studying, and training instead of education, in order to participate obediently in the labor force, as required by corporate culture. It is almost as if one is condemned to suffer in 'exam hell' because one is born Japanese.

My impression is that many foreign observers who are interested in political economic studies do not give enough attention to the power, subtlety, and – most importantly – the motivating force of ideologies of identity. Moreover, they fail to notice the dynamics of 'banal nationalism' (Billig 1995): 'Only the waved or saluted flag tends to be noticed. If sociological categories are nets for catching slices of social life, then the net, which sociologists have marked "nationalism", is a remarkably small one: and it seems to be used primarily for catching exotic, rare and often violent specimens' (Billig 1995: 43). As in other societies, Japanese nationalism is successful largely because the education system instills forms of knowledge designed to reproduce the nation-state and its economic machinery. In the modern world, identity – whether ultranationalist, nationalist, or merely banal – cannot be disentangled from economics or, more significantly, from education. This may seem like a truism, but it is one whose significance requires exploration, not presupposition, especially if one is interested in questions related to 'educational reform' in Japan.

6 The Diversification of Employment and Women's Work in Contemporary Japan

Beverley Bishop

Introduction

Most attempts to explain the relatively low level of industrial strife and remarkable productivity of Japanese industry during the post war period have focused on the organization of work for male employees of large corporations (see Abegglen and Stalk 1985; Dore 1973, 1986). However, the 'classical Japanese model' of the firm as a community marked by worker commitment and flexibility in exchange for employment security, the seniority-plus-merit (*nenkō*) principle in pay and promotion, and enterprise unionism (Kato and Steven 1993) only ever pertained to a minority of workers. Large corporations have been able to afford these benefits for their workers by externalizing risk. Generally they have made use of *keiretsu* – intricate vertical relationships with small and medium sized subcontractors, which are almost entirely dependent on the larger company, provide flexible pricing and production, and even absorb surplus employees of the larger company in times of economic difficulty.

The precarious position of smaller companies has been evident in the current recession. Of those employees laid off through bankruptcy or restructuring between 1997 and 1999, 47 percent worked at companies with fewer than thirty members of staff, while only 14 percent worked at firms with 500 or more staff members.[1] Employees of small and medium-sized enterprises also tend to receive lower wage rises in times of economic hardship than their counterparts in larger companies. In 1999 the average wage rise of workers in the former sector was only 1.67 percent compared to 2.21 percent in the latter (Labor Relations Bureau 2000).

A higher proportion of women than men are employed within these small and medium-sized companies. Women are also more likely to work as members of other groups excluded from the full benefits of the Japanese employment system, such as contract workers, temporary, casual or day laborers, family workers, part-timers, agro-industrial workers, and home-workers.

As well as being more likely to be found in peripheral sections of the labor market, women have also had a peripheral position within the core. Even within large companies, supposedly permanent women workers would usually retire upon marriage or the birth of their first child. In fact without women's short tenure and confinement to lower level positions, it would not have been possible for men to rise upwards through the company and take on more responsibility as the *nenkō* system required.

Post-war state policies encouraged the marginalization of women's paid labor. The tax system penalized men whose wives earned a full-time salary. The 1948 Labor Standards Law institutionalized several provisions for the 'protection of motherhood,' including six weeks maternity leave both before and after childbirth, the right to request leave for child care, paid menstruation leave, restrictions on overtime, and a ban on night work. Carney and O'Kelly (1990) argue that this institutionalized the contingent and marginal character of women's work, noting that thousands of women workers in railway transportation and similar occupations immediately lost their jobs when the Labor Standards Law came into effect. In effect the rights were difficult to exercise: until 1966, the Ministry of Labor took the view that terminating a woman's employment upon marriage did not violate the Labor Standards Law, and the courts upheld a firm's right to refuse a bonus – which could be worth several months' salary – to employees who took menstrual leave. Even so, most women's groups have continued to support this motherhood protection and have argued that overtime restrictions should be extended to men.

In white-collar jobs, women's work was often, in effect, that of an assistant or 'office wife' to men: it was common practice for male employees to expect female workers to serve tea, clean the offices, and even polish their shoes. As they were expected to retire on marriage, they did not receive the same high quality of on-the-job training as their male co-workers. Lo (1990) gives the example of the Brother Corporation's recruitment literature, which presents the ideal career of an OL (office lady): she enters the company at 18, acquires ladylike skills through company classes in tea ceremony and flower arranging, then leaves in her early twenties, when she marries a co-worker and uses her savings to set up home. That is not to say that all women followed this path. Roberts (1994) describes the longer working careers of some blue-collar working women who worked to pay for household necessities, but makes it clear that their determination to continue working flew in the face of the company president's expectations.

Cook and Hayashi (1980) carried out interviews with managers, who justified the differential treatment accorded to women in terms of women's lesser mental and physical powers, lack of commitment to work, and lack of time to devote to paid work because of domestic labor (in the case of married women). Women's short working lives did not justify investment in training, and women did not deserve the same wages as men because they had not acquired the same skills. Of course this contains a certain amount of circular reasoning: being confined to routine work at low wages did little to encourage women to remain in the workforce, and women could not be expected to acquire the same skills as men without the same training. Furthermore, married women were almost solely responsible for housework and childrearing (Lebra 1984), because of the long hours worked by male workers. In fact companies implicitly recognized the dependence of their male employees on the reproductive labor of their wives, as they provided family allowances, housing allowances, and company housing.

Also of course, Japan's spectacular economic growth permitted a family to survive on the wages of one earner alone. Iwao (1993) argues that this placed women in a more favorable position than men, in that they had the time to pursue a range of cultural activities and did not have to be obedient to company demands in the same way as men. In 1960, only 8.8 percent of married women worked outside the home.

Although a series of court judgments from 1966 onwards formally outlawed the practice of companies requiring women to retire at marriage, social expectations and the culture of the workplace continued to lead to most women leaving work upon marriage or pregnancy. A trading company employee told me of the practice of one large firm that would only take on women who lived with their parents. This, she assumed, was to ensure that they were *ojōsan* – respectable young ladies. Parents were expected to attend the firm's welcome ceremony for new employees and were told that it was their responsibility to ensure that their daughters retired at marriage. Ms. Shirafuji, whose lawsuit against her employer, Sumitomo Electric, has been continuing since 1995, described how at every year-end party her boss would ask the women what their plans were for the next year, implying that there was no expectation that they would stay with the firm. Another employee of the Sumitomo group claimed that, on returning to work after giving birth, she was segregated from other office workers, placed at a desk by the window sitting alone behind her boss, and given no work to do for six years.

Women workers' short tenure enabled firms to adjust the size of their workforce during economic slowdowns, without threatening the jobs of male core workers. Rohlen (1988) shows how the number of women employed in manufacturing fell rapidly in the first two years following the 1973 oil crisis, due to 'natural' wastage, i.e. freezing the hiring of female workers, while women continued to retire at childbirth or marriage. Other strategies employed by companies in the 1970s included laying off part-time workers (predominantly female), and suggesting that because of the special economic circumstances, women should give up work even before they reached these conventional departure points. Approximately 700,000–800,000 women left the labor force between 1974–1975 (Fox 1999: 2). It should be noted though that in the more recent recession of the 1990s, women have been increasingly drawn into the workforce, albeit into relatively disadvantaged positions within it.

Economic, social, and demographic factors have been gradually altering women's positions in the Japanese workforce. Women now participate in the workforce in numbers comparable to other modern industrialized societies, accounting for 38.3 percent of workers in 1994 (Japan Institute of Labor 1999: 22). Among married women, 60 percent work *(Japan Insight* 1999a). The average age of female employees increased from 23.8 to 36.1 between 1949 and 1994, with average years of service increasing from 3.2 to 7.6 (*Japan Insight* 1999b: Data 18.1). This can be partially attributed to increased longevity, a declining fertility rate (the number of births per woman has fallen from 4.54 in 1947 to 1.4 today), an increase in housing and education costs, the return of 'baby boom' wives to the labor market, and changing social attitudes concerning women's place in society (Whittaker 1990, see also Chapter 4 by Möhwald). Furthermore, the Equal Employment Opportunities Law (EEOL), which came into effect in 1986 and was revised in April 1999, was enacted with the ostensible aim of giving women equal opportunities in the workplace.

However, other legal and industrial changes mean that, even though women are increasingly likely to work outside the home, the work they do is becoming even more segregated from that carried out by men. Instead of using women's early withdrawal from the labor market as a way to achieve numerical flexibility, firms are using women's employment in insecure, irregular jobs to achieve the same ends.

This chapter will examine the characteristics of women's work in an increasingly diverse Japanese labor force, and the reactions of women toward the work roles that they are expected, or permitted, to play.[2]

The diversification and casualization of the workforce

One of the main explanations given by business and political elites for the diversification and casualization of the Japanese workforce is the increasingly fierce competition to which Japanese goods and services have become subject in a globalized economy. Keidanren (the Japan Federation of Economic Organizations) has also used the rhetoric of survival in a globalized economy to argue for 'workforce reduction' and an end to lifetime employment (see for example, Keidanren 1995). The 1996 Global Competitiveness Report of the World Economic Forum caused shock waves in Japan when it ranked Japan as the world's thirteenth most competitive economy: the previous ten years had seen it ranked first. Globalization is not only leading to more competition from outside Japan, but also to the Japanese market becoming increasingly subject to penetration by foreign capital. Japan's dependence on the U.S., both for security and as a vitally important export market, has made it particularly susceptible to U.S. pressure for deregulation (Carlile and Tilton 1998).

Government and business elites are currently trying to counter the negative effects of globalization on the Japanese economy through deregulation and restructuring of the Japanese model of employment. In 1995, Nikkeiren (the Japanese Employers' Federation) published an 'Employment portfolio,' recommending a shift toward a 'new Japanese style of management.' They argued that the workforce should be divided into three types of labor power: the core workforce, which would receive all the benefits of security of tenure and seniority wages as at present, but which would be much reduced in size; specialists, who would be hired on short term contracts and paid according to merit rather than seniority; and a third group which should be used for numerical flexibility. As men and women have traditionally had very different positions in the classical Japanese model of employment, the reshaping of that model is affecting men and women in different ways.

The case of the airline industry provides one of the clearest examples of how globalization has led to the restructuring of the workforce. The airline industry has been progressively deregulated since 1986. Reforms have included permitting Japanese airlines to compete against each other, allowing All Nippon Airways (ANA) to enter international markets, permitting code-sharing with U.S. airlines, and allowing discount tickets to be bought through legitimate channels. This shift from nationally protected businesses to international alliances competing with other alliances both globally and locally has led to a substantial worsening of conditions for the overwhelmingly female flight attendants in Japan.

In 1994 Japan Air Lines (JAL) announced a reorganization of per-sonnel. All regular workers would be assigned to international flights, while temporary workers on short-term contracts, earning approximately half the wages of regular workers, would work on domestic flights. Consequently many female regular workers who had domestic or childcare responsibilities left work rather than accepting reassignment to international flights (Nakura 1997; JAL Cabin Attendants' Union 1995). Meanwhile, the annual working hours of regular workers increased from 840 to 900. Uchida Taeko, a flight attendant and activist in the aviation industry labor union, claimed that, as contract employees are paid by the hour, they tend to report to work even when unwell (Uchida 1998: 7). She also claimed that JAL was taking on a higher proportion of attendants from Singapore, Hong Kong, Germany, and Britain, as women from these countries could be hired for up to 75 percent less than their Japanese counterparts. Unlike most private companies, where there is a clear division between full-time workers and others, contract workers can be upgraded to the status of full-timers, but this depends partly on the evaluations of their full-time colleagues, with obvious implications for workforce solidarity.

It is however somewhat disingenuous to attribute restructuring solely to the exigencies of globalization. These goals were not necessarily new: Nikkeiren has always opposed the protective legislation of the Labor Standards Law and has been arguing for more 'flexible' working practices since 1948, but the increasingly hegemonic nature of the *laissez-faire* Anglo-American model of capitalism has, in recent years, made the government more susceptible to its requests.

Furthermore, the prospect of economic slowdown and the subsequent desire to restrain public spending has led both government and industry to treat women both as poorly-rewarded part-time workers and unpaid care givers. The goal of the Ministry of Health and Welfare's 1994 Angel Prelude Plan was to encourage women to 'raise healthy children as well as supporting efforts to make childrearing and employment compatible' (Gottfried and Hayashi-Kato 1998: 39). The 1995 New Gold Plan stressed the increasing role of family members, particularly women, in providing care to elderly relatives, while the 1995 Child Care and Family Leave Care Law permits workers leave for a period of up to three months to care for infirm family members.

Table 6.1 (below) shows the growth in the proportion of the workforce that is irregular, while Table 6.2 shows how women are disproportionately represented within the irregular workforce.

It is important to explain that regular and irregular work are not necessarily distinguished by a difference in job content or hours worked, but rather in the rewards that accrue to the workers.[3] The term 'regular workers' applies to those workers who have

Table 6.1 Regular and Irregular Workers in the Japanese Labor Force, 1986–97

	Regular workers	Irregular workers			
Year		Total	Part-time	Temporary	Other
1986	83.4	16.6	9.4	3.5	3.7
1997	76.8	23.2	12.9	6.2	4.2

All figures are percentages.
Source: MITI, White Paper on International Trade 1998

employment security, age and tenure related pay rises, bonuses, and other fringe benefits. As the bonuses alone of full-time employees are usually equivalent to several months' salary, this is a very significant difference.

Contract workers are employed directly by companies for a temporary period specified in a contract which is often renewable, while 'dispatched workers' (or *haken*) are those employees who are dispatched by personnel agencies to companies on a contract basis. By 1996 around half of all women workers were engaged as 'part-time,' temporary or dispatched workers (Nakano 1996: 4).

Non-regular workers

One of the main responses of employers to the unstable international economic climate has been the increased use of part-time workers.

Table 6.2 Male and Female Regular and Irregular Workers in the Japanese Labor Force, 1994

	Regular workers	Irregular workers				
		Total	Dispatched	Contract	Part-time	Other
Total	77.2	22.8	0.7	13.7	4.4	4.1
Female	61.4	38.6	1.2	28.6	5.1	3.7
Male	86.9	13.1	0.4	4.4	3.9	4.3

All figures are percentages.
Source: General Survey on Diversified Types of Employment, Ministry of Labor, 1994

In 1999, 10.1 million out of 27 million women workers were working part-time, compared to 6.6 million out of 23 million in 1983 (Annual Report on the Labor Force Survey, 1999).

Part-time work is often presented as a way for women to 'harmonize' family life and work, providing care for children and Japan's rapidly swelling elderly population, as well as meeting the 'growing need for flexible and highly-skilled labor'(Kurokawa 1995: 72). This is far from being the case for all part-timers. Sakai (1999) reports that part-timers are often not allowed to take childcare leave. According to a survey of 2,319 working women (excluding dispatched workers), 34.5 percent of irregular workers in private companies and 56.4 percent of irregular workers in the public sector said they were doing irregular work 'involuntarily' (Part-Time Work Research Group to Consider Women's Working Life 1999).

In many cases, part-timers have trouble 'harmonizing' family care and work, because they are actually working full-time hours. Furthermore the wage difference between female regular and part-time workers has increased. A female part-time worker was earning 80.7 percent of a female full-timer's wage in 1977, but only 68.0 percent in 1997 (Sakai 1999), even before bonuses and pensions were taken into account.

As well as part-time work, there has been an increase in other types of non-regular employment, such as agency and contract work. As the revised Equal Employment Opportunities Law only refers to jobs where men and women do the same tasks, non-regular jobs in which no men are employed do not fall within its scope. According to records kept by the Tokyo Josei Union (personal communication, December 1999) the majority of callers to their Working Women's Helpline were experiencing problems stemming from a change in their status from regular to irregular employees.

The 1947 Employment Security Law prohibited worker-dispatching activities to ensure the employment security of workers. The limited legalization of temporary agencies in 1986 was therefore controversial, although an illicit worker dispatch industry had flourished since the late 1970s, mainly supplying white-collar female workers. The Worker Dispatch Law originally limited worker dispatching to a very limited range of specialist activities and a Cabinet Order designated sixteen forms of such work. However the law has been liberalized in stages and by the end of 1999 agencies were allowed to supply workers for virtually all types of jobs. The result has been a boom in the temping business, with the number of dispatched workers nearly doubling from 1,140,000 in 1992 to 2,040,000 in 1997 (Rengo White Paper 1999: 77). While some women are undoubtedly attracted by the chance to experience different workplaces and to take extended leave, 22 percent of temporary workers claim that they became temporary workers because they could not find regular work (Japan NGO Report Preparatory Committee 1999: 53).

Some banks, securities companies, and trading and manufacturing companies have set up their own agencies. Female regular employees are often invited to register with the firm's subsidiary agency when they leave upon childbirth or marriage (Nakura, personal communication, March 2000). The workers, who are by definition skilled and experienced, are no longer covered by the seniority system, and employers can replace female regular workers with non-regulars. Shiga (1990, cited in Nakura 1997) suggested that the number of agency workers in banking was already equivalent to the number of regular female staff by the late 1980s.

Temporary workers may face hidden costs: they are themselves responsible for keeping their skills updated. One temporary worker told me of the practice of agencies requiring workers to take courses run by the agency before they were offered assignments. At the same time the job of a dispatched worker is become less well rewarded. A survey conducted by the Dispatching Network found that the 1,706-yen average hourly wage in 1994 had decreased to 1,660 yen in 1998 (Sakai 1999).

Temporary workers may also find themselves isolated in offices where regular workers feel threatened by their presence.

> 'What I didn't like was that...although there were several dispatched workers, everyone in the group was [called] *Haken-san* (Ms Temp)...I mean, we didn't say '*Seisha'in-san*' (Ms Regular Worker)...It wasn't discrimination but...for example...sometimes in Japanese companies there are sweets. A customer comes and brings sweets as a present. In the office they would hand them round, but when they got to a *haken-san*, they would skip you. It's

> unbelievable isn't it?...That's really dreadful, isn't it?' (34-year-old former dispatched worker)

Sakai (1999) also claims that dispatching companies often exhibit a preference for young and attractive women. One company ranked their employees' appearance in three categories. When the information later appeared on the Internet, a lawsuit was brought against the company.

In some cases, a position as a dispatched worker can lead to more secure employment. Three quarters of workers placed by the Girl Friday agency with foreign firms became permanent, suggesting that these firms are using agencies as a way of 'checking out' workers, rather than risking taking on the responsibilities associated with employing full-timers in Japan immediately. However, only 1 percent of the employees of Tempstaff, whose customers are predominantly Japanese, are retained in this way (Hulme 1996).

November 1999 did see the establishment of some legal rights for dispatched workers, when the Nagano District Court judged that temporary workers doing the same work as regular workers were entitled to 80 percent of the pay of regular workers, and to the same standards of bonus and pensions. It remains to be seen to what extent this judgment will be used as a precedent for dealing with the treatment of other irregular workers.

Regular workers

The United Nations Decade of Women and International Women's Year (1975) stimulated much popular and media debate in Japan, and had an impact upon public opinion (National Institute of Employment and Vocational Research 1988). In 1980 Japan agreed to ratify the UN Convention on the Elimination of all forms of Discrimination against Women (CEDAW). However, as a signatory, the Japanese government had to pass laws forbidding discrimination against women in wages, recruitment, training, and promotion. Thus in May 1985 the Equal Employment Opportunities Law was passed, to take effect from April 1986. Following a number of high-profile court cases and protests about the shortcomings of the EEOL from feminist groups, the law was revised in 1999. Neither the 1986 nor the 1999 version of the law offers much protection to non-regular workers, as they often have no male co-workers with whom their situations can be compared, but among regular workers it has certainly been influential.

The passing of the EEOL initially served to exacerbate women's marginal position in the workforce. The law only asked companies to make voluntary 'endeavors' to treat women equally in recruitment, hiring, assignment, and promotions, and no sanctions were attached to violating directives on vocational training, fringe benefits, retirement age, and dismissals.

Many larger firms reacted to the law by introducing a formal tracking system for employees: new employees could enter either the *sōgōshoku* (career/management) track or the *ippanshoku* (general) track (Shire 2000). As the law only forbade the 'exclusion' of women from positions, it was perfectly legal to recruit, for example 90 men and 10 women for the *sōgōshoku* track and to ask for higher or different credentials for female applicants. The law had no provision to cover the exclusion of men from positions. This made it difficult for women working in sexually segregated workplaces to use the law. When women working at Sumitomo Mutual Life Assurance applied to the Osaka Women's and Young Workers' Office for mediation in a case where, they claimed, married women on the clerical track were being passed over for promotion, they were told that mediation could not be started as there were no men on the general clerical track with whom the women could be compared.

One interviewee with a 'career' type position won it through an entrance examination where the pass mark for men was lower than that for women. It seems that entry to the *sōgōshoku* track for men is more or less automatic, while women are expected to show exceptional commitment. A bank worker took an MBA through an American company at her own expense to enter the *sōgōshoku* track, which was, she said, 97 percent male, compared to the general track which was 94 percent female. She also spoke of working from 7.30 in the morning until 9.00 or 10.00 at night. At the same time that the EEOL was passed the Labor Standards Law was also revised and the provisions restricting night work and overtime were declared not to apply to women in management or specialist jobs – in other words, women doing 'men's' jobs would be expected to work the same hours as male core workers. This sort of schedule was obviously unworkable for someone with childcare responsibilities. In April 1999 the law was again revised and overtime and night-work restrictions were abolished for all women. This still ignores problems with company practices such as compulsory transfer of employees: in a ruling on 28 January 2000, the Supreme Court upheld a lower court case ruling that a company had the right to dismiss a woman who rejected a transfer due to the care needs of her 3-year old child.[4]

Opinions were mixed among respondents about the benefits to women of abolishing overtime and night-work restrictions. Tokyo Josei Union's help-line records show that the number of female callers requesting advice about their heavy workload increased after April 1999. The records cite the case of a woman who became ill after the revision because of having to work until 11 or 12 p.m. as well as on holidays. In contrast, another respondent claimed that women often worked illegally long overtime hours that went unrecorded, and was glad that women workers could finally gain recognition for the extra work they did.

Unsurprisingly the low rate of retention of women on the *sōgōshoku* track has become a topic of concern in recent years. This does not however mean that women who have left the *sōgōshoku* track have necessarily given up their career ambitions. Renshaw cites many case histories of women who started work as company employees, then left and began their own businesses as the 'glass ceiling' became all too visible. In fact 23 percent of Japanese businesses are owned by women (Renshaw 1999: 158) and 87 percent of women entrepreneurs worked for a company before starting their own business (Renshaw 1999: 166).

The entry of foreign firms into the Japanese market may provide slightly more attractive opportunities for high-achieving women who intend to continue working. Certainly this is a common impression held by Japanese female students seeking employment. Higuchi (1993: 176) noted that the rate of retention of female university graduates for between 5 and 10 years was 75.7 percent in foreign-affiliated companies, compared to only 57.9 percent in Japanese companies. The foreign enterprises are no angels, however. Company documents provided to me by the union at Showa Shell, a subsidiary of Royal Dutch Shell, demonstrate that, while women's tenure in the company is far longer than the average for Japanese companies, women are nonetheless greatly over-represented in the lower employment grades. As the following anecdote shows, some Western employers may also be inclined to exploit stereotypes of Japanese women as passive and undemanding workers, in order to save on their wages bill.

> 'Actually I had one interview with an American person and...he offered me 150,000 yen a month for doing secretarial work. And it wasn't...well I think it was full-time, and I asked him if I could get a little bit more, because it was...the time was I think noon till ten or five to ten at night or something like that. The hours were really bad. So I asked him if I could get more, and he said, "Well, women in Japan are not supposed to ask for money...Actually the average pay the women are getting is 110,000 yen in Japan, so I'm really surprised that you asked for more although you're a Japanese woman." So I guess I gave him a bad impression.' (Part-time worker, early 20s, describing her search for full-time work)

Despite its shortcomings, Gelb (1998) feels that the original EEOL has had an impact on the aspirations of young women. She notes the prevalence in the popular press of articles on working women, and cites a 1993 study by Knapp in which 70 percent of young women interviewed indicated that they would like to apply for the *sōgōshoku*. There is also some evidence that the discussions and publicity around the Law may have had a consciousness-raising effect on the general population. Surveys suggest that the proportion of people believing it was acceptable for a woman to continue working after giving birth rose from 16.1 percent in 1987 to 32.5 percent in 1995 (Araki 1998).

Few women felt that the law was sufficient. In fact an opinion poll commissioned by the *Economist* and published on October 9, 1999 found that 0 percent (*sic*) of Japanese women believed that they had the same rights as men. But the law has proved to be a focal point for feminist campaigners. Since Japan's endorsement of the CEDAW convention, Japanese women's groups have increasingly been networking and campaigning on a global stage.[5]

If women are still vastly underrepresented in the *sōgōshoku*, they are slightly over-represented in the cadre of specialists. Of women in their 30s, 62 percent answered that they felt the most desirable way to work was to become an expert in a certain field, compared to 12.1 percent who thought the most desirable way to work was to work for the same company for a long time and obtain a managerial position. Shinotsuka (1994) notes that a greater proportion of women (13.8 percent) than men (11.3 percent) work as specialists. My respondents gave the impression that women were aware of job discrimination, and felt that this was one way to ensure career success – albeit that the requisite training is usually at the worker's own expense, rather than at the company's expense as in the traditional employment system. In a focus group session, a university lecturer noted,

> 'My female students are very eager to get licenses and so they go to another vocational school as they study at university, because they think that girls are disadvantaged[6] ...Girls have to have some weapon, so they take some course, such as bookkeeping, or they become specialists in real estate.'

Another woman commented to me,

> 'I know a young woman...and on her name card there are a lot of qualifications (*katagaki*). She said, "With these certificates, I'm just...I'm on the starting line with the boys."'

Specialist work too is being de-regulated. From 1 April 2000, employers have been permitted to draw up written agreements with thirteen different types of specialists, including certified public accountants, researchers, and designers, stipulating that payment is to be made for a certain length of time, regardless of how long a job actually takes. An advertising copywriter that I interviewed complained that the price for her work was the same (one day's worth), whether the job took her one hour or three days.

Company workers outside the *sōgōshoku*, who do not have specialist vocations, continue to work in stereotypically feminine jobs. In fact, often women referred to workers doing 'professional jobs' simply as 'the men,' e.g. in complaining that only 'the men' could take English language lessons.

A woman who was employed on the *jimushoku* (office track) after being told that women could not apply for the *sōgōshoku* unless they had first worked for a year complained

> 'I had to make a lot of tea. At my company, we were scheduled to make tea three times a day, at fixed times. Also we were required to serve tea every time a male employee came back to the office. Even when I was busy, I still had to make a cup of tea for male workers. I did not like it...One time a client complained about how I was handling a phone call. Since my voice wasn't high-pitched, the client scolded me for that. I did not like it. According to the client, I had to be cheerful because I am a woman...I guess if I were a man, I would not have to be cheerful. I did not think it was fair for the client to complain about that.'

Another respondent complained that women on the general track were not given name cards, the exchange of which is practically essential to establish any kind of business relationship with someone outside the firm.

Ogasawara (1998) writes that the exclusion of women can in some ways liberate them from office authority. She writes about how OLs (office ladies) use gossip, withholding of gift-giving, and even total non-cooperation with the requests of male co-workers in order to manipulate the behavior of these men. Ironically, this behavior reinforces management stereotypes of women as emotional, irrational, and lacking in commitment to work, and provides a further excuse not to promote women or give them responsibility.

Conclusion

Women in the traditional Japanese employment system had a very limited role. They were usually confined to routine jobs with little or no training and expected to leave upon marriage or childbirth. Societal and demographic change, educational advance, and increased acceptance of the ideology of equal labor rights have encouraged a gradual increase in Japanese women's determination to continue working.

However, as economic globalization has made the Japanese economy more vulnerable to foreign competition and cyclical flows, Japanese policymakers have attempted to remain competitive in the international market by reducing labor costs through the segmentation and flexibilization of the Japanese workforce. It has also been made clear through government documents that if middle-aged women work in part-time jobs, this will enable women to provide low-cost care for elderly people. Within this new model of Japanese employment, women are filling a more diverse range of jobs. A disproportionate number of these are less stable and less well-rewarded than those performed by men, though a few very determined and well-qualified women are beginning to break through into managerial and professional jobs, aided by legal changes.

While most of the legal changes that have occurred have removed legal protection from workers, some, like the EEOL, have at least provided a focus around which groups can campaign for global standards on a global stage.

7 Blurring the Boundaries of the Buraku(min)

John H. Davis, Jr.

An emerging trend within scholarship on Japan is research focusing on groups that have been marginalized within Japanese society. Recent works in the West on Koreans, Ainu, and Nikkeijin (ethnic Japanese who have come to Japan decades after their parents or grandparents departed) among others collectively point to a multi-cultural dimension of Japanese society which poses a serious challenge to the image of Japan as a racial and cultural monolith.[1] Burakumin, members of a formerly outcaste group still subject to social discrimination, are frequently included in the group of diverse communities adduced as evidence to belie the notion of Japan as a homogeneous people (*tan'itsu minzoku*),[2] a notion which has been labeled a 'myth' and 'illusion' by various scholars (e.g. Coates ed. 1995; Weiner ed. 1997). Ironically, this idea of Japan as a racially and culturally homogeneous nation that is under attack in the West has played a critical role in efforts to combat discrimination against Burakumin.

This chapter will argue that the ambiguity inherent in the category 'Burakumin' can provide pointers to ways of developing conceptual frameworks which are no longer based on boundaries demarcating a racially and/or culturally pure Japanese majority (whether real or imagined) from an equally homogenized 'Other.' Although well-intentioned attempts to 'prove' that diversity exists within Japan proceed by documenting the existence of diverse communities within the country, they can sometimes undermine their own purpose, that of helping the disadvantaged, by reinforcing the *uchi/soto* distinction (i.e. between insiders and outsiders) – which then becomes the basis for continued exclusion.[3] If we acknowledge instead the arbitrary and constructed nature of social categories, it becomes possible to question the boundaries separating groups from one another, and to identify those social forces which produce and manipulate particular modes of categorizing people in order to control them. Here I hope to identify the racial ideology at work in various efforts to deal with the *buraku* issue in contemporary Japan. I will argue that one theme common to efforts made by the government, the Buraku Liberation League, and educators is the attempt to combat discrimination against Burakumin by challenging the idea that Burakumin are not the same sort of Japanese – which in effect preserves the national fiction of the *tan'itsu minzoku*. Another aim of this essay is to show how the conceptual boundary between non-Burakumin Japanese and Burakumin is becoming blurred. By discussing the contingent nature of being (or being identified as) 'Burakumin,' I want to urge scholars not only to focus on diversity within Japan, but also to reflect on how to construct discourses that open up space *within* the national community for those who threaten the popular myth of racial and cultural purity.

A case of mistaken identity

In 1998 news broke of a scandal involving Japanese companies engaged in discriminatory hiring practices.[4] Because hard evidence had been obtained documenting the illegal *mimoto chōsa* (background checks) of an investigating company whose services had been contracted by more than 1,400 businesses, some of which were affiliated with the local government, many regarded this as one of the most significant discoveries since the *Buraku Chimei Sōkan Jiken* (Buraku Lists Incident; see below) in 1975.[5] Citizenship, political and religious affiliation, and location of residence were among the types of information collected by investigators and used to weed out 'undesirable' applicants.

According to information faxed anonymously to the office of the Buraku Liberation League, the following notations were scribbled on the resume of one applicant: 'D,' '4 *shusshin*' and 'Buraku Liberation League smack in the middle.' All three of these remarks identify the applicant as Burakumin. The letter D is taken from the word *dōwa*,[6] which is a euphemism for Burakumin used most commonly in official documents and in discussions of this topic by the public. The number '4' together with the word *shusshin* (birthplace) refers to the derogatory term *yottsu* ('four'), which debases Burakumin by suggesting that they are four-legged animals and not human (Ninomiya 1933; Price 1967: 11). The final notation points to the location of a branch office of the BLL in the heart of the community in which the applicant resides. The presence of the office is taken as proof that the community in question is of *buraku* origin. The nature of this investigation indicates that employment discrimination continues to be a problem in contemporary Japan for Burakumin and other groups deemed to be undesirable.

However, in this essay I want to focus on something less obvious but nevertheless critically important: the fact that in this particular case the investigator simply got it wrong. The applicant was not Burakumin, nor did s/he reside in a *dōwa* community. Because there was no suitable location to build the BLL office within the *dōwa* community it represents, it was necessary to construct it in an alternative location outside the *buraku*. Thus the community identified as a *buraku* by the investigator was actually an ordinary community. How could a professional investigator make such a critical mistake?

An error of this sort is easier to make than one might imagine. Several factors have worked collectively to blur the geographic boundaries and overall recognizability of the *buraku*, and to obscure the very category of 'Burakumin': the decline of exclusively Burakumin occupations, the implementation of government programs aimed at rebuilding *dōwa* communities, the combined effect of formal and informal *dōwa* education activities aimed at rooting out prejudicial attitudes which foster discrimination toward residents of *dōwa* areas, and the flow of people into and out of *dōwa* districts. Below I will discuss each of these factors in some detail to document the extent to which the *dōwa* phenomenon has changed in recent years. But before doing so, I will briefly outline the historical development of Japan's *dōwa* communities.

Historical roots of the *dōwa* issue

The *dōwa* issue is typically traced back to the Tokugawa Era (1603–1867).[7] Although there are *buraku* areas which existed prior to this period, the status system of *shi-nō-kō-shō* (warrior-farmer-artisan-merchant) was created to help the Tokugawa family maintain control of the land. Two additional status groups fell outside this four-tier ranking order, *Hinin* (literally 'non-human') and *Eta* ('filth-abundant'). [8] As their names suggest, these two groups occupied the lowest rungs of the social order and various types of measures were enacted to accentuate their visibility and control their interaction with the rest of society. Occupation was the primary basis upon which the status of Hinin and Eta was determined. Both groups engaged in occupations considered polluting according to religious proscriptions.[9] Killing and death were frowned upon by Buddhist doctrines which taught reverence for all living things, and these two groups engaged routinely in work involving dead animals such as leather-making and butchering. In the case of Hinin, the pollution was not absolutely permanent; in rare cases Hinin status could be shed (Ninomiya 1933: 100–101, Price 1967: 6). Eta, however, were considered to be hereditary outcastes whose polluted state was regarded as permanent and transferable to offspring.

The Meiji Era (1868–1912) ushered in various changes, one of which was the abolition of the status system. As part of a push toward modernization, the Meiji government issued the Emancipation Edict in 1871. Legally, the distinction between the former outcastes and the rest of society was ended because the Emancipation Edict declared the former outcastes to be *heimin* or commoners. However, the status of the former outcastes was recorded in the *koseki* (family register) as '*shin-heimin*' (*new* commoners) or '*kyū-Eta*,' 'former Eta.' This made the former outcastes easily identifiable by the rest of the population, which was not eager to see themselves put on a par with a group which had formerly been beneath them. Despite the legal change, outcaste status proved to be difficult to elude. Even without the force of law to support it, social sanctions continued to restrict the mobility and participation of outcastes in Japanese society. The former outcastes continued to be subjected to social discrimination, particularly in marriage and employment.[10] Even after death former outcastes were given *kaimyō* or posthumous names which sometimes identified them as Eta (Ooms 1996: 283–84, Osaka Jinken Rekishi Shiryōkan, 1994: 23).

In addition to the dogged persistence of discriminatory attitudes and practices, the living standards of many former outcaste communities deteriorated severely due to the loss of outcaste monopolies and rapidly changing economic times. The stigma that previously provided a protective barrier of sorts for outcaste occupations weakened. The new competition often proved to be too stiff for people living in *buraku* areas because they still tended to be small-scale family operations (Watanabe 1999: 42–46). At a time when they were losing their economic niche, it was difficult for former outcastes to find other types of employment. So many left rural areas and headed to large cities such as Osaka, where temporary employment could be found in the ship construction industry or other types of transient labor. Because most of the work to be found in large cities was of a temporary nature, it provided little more than a tenuous economic base for many families.

To help resolve the problems of social discrimination and poverty, Burakumin organized politically and demanded better treatment from society and from the government. The roots of the BLL can be traced to the Levelers' Association (*Suiheisha*), which was founded on 3 March 1922.[11] Suiheisha members challenged the collective conscience of their peers and the public through a strategy known as *tetteiteki kyūdan* ('thorough denunciation'), whereby the organization would openly protest against discriminatory treatment and demand a public apology from those accused of committing discriminatory acts against Burakumin. This marks a significant turning point in the liberation politics of Burakumin. Unlike many previous attempts to mitigate social prejudice by focusing on self-improvement (*yūwa* movements), this confrontational strategy clearly located the problem within society and not within the *buraku*. This point of view also conditioned the manner in which the Suiheisha and its successors dealt with the government.

According to the logic of those supporting the Suiheisha movement, if society was responsible for the prejudices and problems afflicting those residing in *buraku* areas, then it stood to reason that the government should bear the brunt of responsibility for improving the situation. Some members of the organization began to make appeals to the government to implement programs aimed specifically at *buraku* residents. This led to some tension within the organization, however, because many supported socialism and believed that the *buraku* problem was essentially part and parcel of the class struggle characteristic of capitalist societies. Some felt that seeking special programs to deal specifically with the *buraku* issue would undermine the solidarity of the class struggle.[12] This tension eventually led to the breakup of the organization.

Several of those who had been active within the Suiheisha movement met after the war to form the Buraku Kaihō Zenkoku I'inkai (National Committee for Buraku Liberation). This organization changed its name in 1955 during its tenth convention to Buraku Kaihō Dōmei, (the Buraku Liberation League). To this day the BLL continues to be the largest, and arguably the most powerful, organization representing Burakumin. The BLL continued to pressure the government to implement measures to deal with the *buraku* issue. After the 1965 report of the Dōwa Policy Council recommended that the government take an active role in resolving the *dōwa* issue,[13] support grew for some kind of legislation.

In 1969 the Special Measures Law (SML) was implemented. This law helped rebuild thousands of *dōwa* areas, some literally from the ground up, with the money for such projects coming from national, prefectural and local governments.[14] Between 1969 and 1993 ¥13,880 billion was allocated to *dōwa* projects (Sōmuchō 1995: 184–196). In addition to the money that was spent rebuilding communities, funds were used to subsidize housing, provide scholarships for Burakumin youth, and underwrite other programs to reduce the financial burden on Burakumin families. Another attempt by the government to end discrimination against Burakumin entailed revision of article 10 of the *koseki* law in 1976 to restrict access to family registers (Neary 1997: 65). This made it much more difficult to investigate people's backgrounds.

The Buraku(min) today

Many buraku communities (and the lives of substantial numbers of the people residing in them) have changed significantly as a result of the SML. If you travel to one of the officially designated *dōwa* areas, you are unlikely to find any semblance of the impoverished communities described in early studies of the Buraku issue (e.g. Brameld 1968; DeVos and Wagatsuma 1967; Shimahara 1971). In fact, you are more likely to find a community that boasts *more* services and facilities than the average Japanese neighborhood.[15] Let me describe one community in Osaka to illustrate how much things have improved. Residents of Saiwai Chiku[16] no longer reside in dilapidated housing but in high-rise apartment buildings. The community affords its residents a level of convenience and access to services that few places can match. A health clinic, a community center with an auditorium, a grocery store, a youth center, a senior citizens' center, a swimming pool to combat the summer heat, and a nursery are all located within the community. Many joke that they don't have to leave the community for anything. When it is necessary to travel outside the community, residents have ready access to a railway line that practically carries them to and from their doorstep.

Just as impressive as the physical improvements is the economic stability that many have attained. Prior to the SML stable employment was hard to come by. For this reason many community residents were engaged in seasonal occupations such as shipbuilding or peddling vegetables in nearby towns. Poverty is a recurrent theme in the recollections of many of the older generation. Many identify poverty as the central barrier to their obtaining an education. In the words of a resident of Saiwai Chiku, 'There were many days I could not go [to school] because I was expected to work and supplement the family income. Even when I was able to go, I would often skip classes because I was always embarrassed during lunchtime. The teacher routinely punished me for forgetting my lunch money. Of course, I did not forget. We were poor and I did not have any lunch money. Rather than being punished by the teacher, many of us would get together and play instead.' This is an illustration of the *akujunkan* (vicious cycle) of which many informants spoke. Poverty impeded educational attainment, and without an education it was impossible to secure well-paid jobs.

The employment situation has now improved for many families in Saiwai Chiku. The number of government employees, for example, has risen sharply. Approximately one-third of the people in Saiwai Chiku hold jobs as *kōmuin* (government employees). This percentage tops the national average for *dōwa* communities (10.6 percent for men, 11.2 percent for women) (Buraku Kaihō Kenkyūjo 1997: 71) and dwarfs the corresponding figure for Japanese living outside *dōwa* districts (4.2 percent for men, 1.5 percent for women) (Saiwai-chō Kyōgikai 1993). Access to well-paid jobs has sparked an increase in household income for many families, particularly households where both men and women have secured well-paid positions. Within *dōwa* areas there has been a gradual increase in the number of families earning enough to be taxed at the standard tax rate. In 1971 43.7 percent fell within this earning bracket (Buraku Kaihō Kenkyūjo 1997: 60–61). By 1975 this number had climbed to 53.9 percent, peaking at 58.2 percent in 1993. In 1992 80 percent of Japanese families were paying tax at this rate, so that despite the entry into this tax bracket of a further 15 percent of Burakumin families between 1971 and 1993, their earnings still lagged behind the rest of the population.

While there has been a substantial increase in the earning power of a number of families residing in *dōwa* areas, there also has been an increase in families whose income level is low enough to exempt them from paying taxes. In 1971 20.4 percent of families in *dōwa* areas qualified for tax-exempt status (Buraku Kaihō Kenkyūjo 1997: 60–61). This number remained virtually unchanged in 1975 (20.5 percent), and rose to 21.8 percent in 1985. It climbed an additional 4 percent by 1993 to peak at 25.8 percent. The national figure for families with tax-exempt status is 15.9 percent. Meanwhile there seems to have been only a modest decline in families receiving social welfare. Thus there has been an increasing bifurcation among *dōwa* area residents.

The majority of those whose economic outlook has not changed considerably are *kōreisha* (senior citizens) and *shōgaisha* (people with various disabilities), two populations who remain at the core of the *buraku* community as the BLL continues to lobby for social welfare measures to help them.[17] It seems that the community has always provided a safety net of sorts for those who have needed one. There have been many cases of individuals who have left the community to pursue either jobs or marriage. When tragedy struck (sudden illness, divorce, etc) and left them without a job or a place to stay, many returned to Saiwai Chiku.

Those who do leave temporarily often find new faces when they return. The SML has resulted in increased mobility for many Burakumin families. As the upwardly mobile move out, those seeking less expensive housing move in to take their place. One statistic indicative of the rapid flow across the borders of the *buraku* is the declining percentage of Burakumin families residing in *dōwa* areas. The majority of families residing in *dōwa* communities today are not related to the outcaste groups of feudal Japan by family or by occupation. Statistics show that between 1971 and 1975 the percentage of Burakumin residing in *dōwa* districts dropped from 71.9 percent to 60.8 percent. By 1993 the figure had slipped to 41.4 percent (Sōmuchō 1995: 28–29).

Dōwa education: rooting out discrimination

In addition to the abovementioned efforts to improve the living environment and economic circumstances of *dōwa* area residents, education has also played a major role in attempts to solve the problem of discrimination against Burakumin. Extra resources were allocated to schools whose student populations included residents from *buraku* communities. The money was used for various purposes, ranging from hiring extra teachers to improving the diet of children (see Clear 1991; Hirasawa 1989), but the overall goal was the same – improving the educational attainment of *buraku* youth.

There has indeed been significant improvement, particularly in the percentage of Burakumin youth advancing to high school, which at 92 percent has closed to within approximately 4 percent of the national average (96.5 percent) (Sōmuchō 1995: 62–63). This marks a drastic reduction from the 36.5 percent gap in 1963, when the average for Burakumin students stood at 30.3 percent compared to a national average of 66.8 percent. The number of high school students advancing to college, however, continues to be a concern in many communities. On average, only 24.3 percent of high school students from *dōwa* areas continued on to higher education in 1994, compared to an average of 36 percent for the public at large. This gap in the college advancement rate actually closed to within about 11 points in 1986 (19.1 percent compared with 30.3 percent), but the national average then climbed at a faster pace than the average for Burakumin youth, thereby widening the gap once more (Buraku Kaihō Kenkyūjo 1997: 109). Contemporary Japan is often described as a *gakureki shakai*, a society based on educational qualifications. Many parents in Saiwai Chiku worry that without a college education young people will have difficulty securing well-paid jobs. This, they note, could potentially trigger another vicious circle of poverty and low educational attainment.

Dōwa education has also targeted discrimination by non-Burakumin Japanese. The Dōwa Policy Committee identified 'psychological discrimination' (Buraku Kaihō Kenkyūjo 1981:255) as the root of discriminatory behavior directed at *dōwa* area residents. *Dōwa* education has also served as a means of educating the general population about the history of the *buraku* issue. *Dōwa* education courses are offered in most schools located near *dōwa* communities and in some colleges and universities. The atmosphere in many courses is rather tense, due to a general uncertainty about what kind of statements are acceptable. At worst, an inappropriate statement by a teacher or student can ultimately result in a confrontation with the BLL.[18] The main thrust of *dōwa* education programs is to teach about the development of the *buraku* problem within the context of Japan's status system. Another goal is to destroy the myth that Burakumin are different from other Japanese. The importance of this step in terms of combating prejudice against Burakumin was recognized by the Council in 1965 when it wrote: '...in order to do away with the prejudice of the general public, it must be clearly stated that the residents of the *Dōwa* districts are neither a different race nor a different people, but are without any doubt Japanese, both by race and nationality' (Buraku Kaihō Kenkyūjo 1981: 252). History is frequently used to underline the 'Japanese-ness' of Burakumin by pointing out that outcaste communities in feudal Japan engaged in many occupations that played a critical role in developing some of the traditional arts that have come to define Japanese culture.[19]

Efforts to combat discrimination through *dōwa* education have not been limited to schools. Several companies have *dōwa* education programs in place to promote awareness of the *Buraku* issue and other social issues among employees. Such efforts were stepped up after the Buraku Community List Incident (*Buraku Chimei Sōkan Jiken*) of 1975, when several major Japanese companies were found to possess lists containing the names and locations of *dōwa* districts.[20] The lists were used during recruitment and hiring to identify and weed out Burakumin applicants. The incident led the Ministry of Labor to administer 'guidance' to the companies involved, instructing them to commit some of their personnel to full-time research on the *Dōwa* issue and the promotion of understanding of the issue within the company. The Ministry's guidance was not mandatory; nevertheless many companies have in fact established *dōwa* education programs.

In society in general, a multitude of activities have taken place to battle discrimination by raising public consciousness. Local governments in various parts of the country have worked with local political organizations to establish human rights museums, produce television programs, and distribute booklets, posters, and other material designed to promote awareness of human rights. With respect to the *dōwa* issue these often underscore the message that the Burakumin are not a different racial or ethnic group, but are Japanese.

The BLL has also been active in confronting discrimination through the tactic of 'thoroughgoing denunciation' (*tetteiteki kyūdan*) mentioned above. This continues to be one of the most distinctive and controversial features of the BLL. It was legally challenged after the Yōka Incident (Rohlen 1976), but the courts upheld the right of Burakumin to engage in such protests because of the lack of any other effective remedy to compensate for the discrimination to which they were subjected.[21] Many within the BLL argue that, done correctly, this tactic is consistent with the goals of *dōwa* education because it is a means of helping the accused to realize the error of their ways.[22] Representatives from the local government are routinely present to witness the proceedings. Any information confirming foul play or a general attitude of prejudice toward Burakumin gives the BLL leverage to press the government (and the institution with whom the person denounced is affiliated) to devote more resources to *dōwa* education. Consistent with their other efforts to educate the public, the BLL also uses denunciation sessions as an opportunity to challenge the notion that Burakumin are somehow different from other Japanese.

It is worth underscoring here that most people in Japan agree that the *dōwa* issue bears little resemblance to the problems caused by ethnic and cultural diversity in the West. Perhaps for this reason the key to solving the problem may seem counterintuitive from the perspective of countries that imagine themselves as multicultural entities. Embracing diversity seems to be at the heart of multiculturalism, whereas the emphasis placed on the same-ness of Burakumin often seems to perpetuate false notions of Japan as a homogeneous society. Perhaps more troubling is the fact that it is often suggested that discrimination against Burakumin is wrong *because* they are the same, suggesting that discrimination against other groups of foreign origin is of a different order. This idea is evident in a human rights poster in Osaka featuring a close-up of an owl, which rhetorically asks the reader, 'This kind of discrimination exists?'[23] before urging the reader to work toward ending *buraku* discrimination. The poster is indecipherable unless one recognizes the implicit contrast being drawn between the same-ness of Burakumin and the other-ness of other groups perceived as fundamentally different from the Japanese. This has led to some friction between the BLL and other human rights groups. According to a human rights activist for *Zainichi* Koreans, 'Even a racist can be convinced that discrimination against Burakumin is wrong.' Some have criticized *dōwa* education for re-introducing racial categories that often lead to discrimination against minority groups.

Conclusion

This chapter has surveyed some of the recent changes in officially designated *dōwa* districts in Japan. One aim has been to document the extent to which the description of the Burakumin as a group with distinct boundaries ignores many of the complexities in their position. It also reduces the potential of the Burakumin issue for exposing some of the limitations of theories of race and ethnicity developed in the West. By showing the constructed nature and arbitrariness of the category 'Burakumin,' together with the historical, political, and material changes which have altered its meaning and public perception within Japanese society, I have tried to illustrate the flexible nature of group identity and identification.

With all of the changes that have taken place, the present seems like a good time to rethink our approach to the *dōwa* issue. Perhaps this issue will be useful in developing theoretical approaches that permit a critique of the 'homogeneous' image of Japan without drawing rigid boundaries between 'Japanese' and 'others.' An approach based on social categories and boundaries may provide us with a glimpse of a Japan hardly known to much of the world, but their use may also lead us to assume that the categories that often dictate the allocation of power and privilege are in some sense 'natural.' I have attempted here to move in the direction of 'denaturalizing' and deconstructing these categories, by illustrating the ambiguity of the boundaries believed to separate Burakumin from other Japanese by scholars both in Japan and in the West. Hopefully, additional research can shed more light on the processes by which other groups pushed to the periphery of the nation are also constructed as 'others' within Japanese society, and allow us to initiate academic as well as public debate which will create space for these 'other' groups within the body politic of Japan.

8 *Yoseba* and *Ninpudashi*: Changing Patterns of Employment on the Fringes of the Japanese Economy

Tom Gill

Introduction

The 'collapse of lifetime employment' has become one of the clichés of the Great Heisei Recession. Far from enjoying the security of a job for life, many Japanese face a struggle to stay in work from year to year or even from month to month. Low unemployment was one of the great achievements of the post-war Japanese economy, but unemployment edged up through most of the 1990s and rose to 4.8 percent for the year 1999, climbing above the U.S. level for the first time since just after World War II. Some economists argue that differences in statistical practice mean that in reality the rate has been higher still.

The 1990s were a decade of stagnant growth and faltering markets, played out in the shadow of an American economy that boomed on relentlessly. In the 1970s and 1980s there had been serious talk of Japan overtaking the United States as an economic superpower, and the 'Learn from Japan' movement gained a considerable following among pundits around the world. In the 1990s the tide was reversed completely. Intellectual trends followed the pattern of American economic dominance, and the U.S. economy became the sole model for Japan and other countries to emulate. This meant less regulation, more privatization, and remuneration systems increasingly governed by principles of merit rather than fairness. The special relationship of trust between employer and employee became an unaffordable luxury: henceforth workers would get pay rises if they were productive, the sack if they were not. For some observers, the ever-rising rate of unemployment was not so much a symptom of malaise as a positive sign that the strong medicine of monetarism was taking effect.

Yet of course, for some workers the old pre-1990s regime had never been the bed of roses depicted by some admirers of Japan. Norma Chalmers' book on the peripheral workforce (Chalmers 1989) was one of many works drawing attention to the pyramidal hierarchy in the Japanese labor force. One of the reasons why big Japanese corporations were able to maintain excellent standards of job security for their employees was because they maintained relatively small workforces. Compared with other capitalist countries, a much larger portion of production was out-sourced: entrusted to smaller companies that stood in a variety of relationships to the main company. Some were wholly- or partially-owned subsidiaries, some were nominally independent companies that were tied to the main company by ties of custom, obligation or personnel.

Collectively these chains of related companies were known as *keiretsu*, a Japanese term that has become part of the global economic vocabulary (see also Chapter 6 by Bishop). Some industries had horizontal *keiretsu*, as in the related banking, trading and manufacturing companies in major combines such as Sumitomo or Mitsubishi. But construction *keiretsu* were generally vertical: the smaller companies acted as a kind of safety valve for the main company. When times were hard, the main company could avoid laying off its own staff. Instead it would scale down orders to suppliers in the *keiretsu*, or enforce price-cuts that the suppliers were seldom able to resist because of their heavy dependence on a single client: the main company. The peripheral workforce of the supplying companies had a far lower level of income and job security than the elite workforce of the assembler.

The *keiretsu* system is chiefly associated with the manufacturing sector, as a structure linking small makers of parts to the giant companies assembling the finished product: cars, machinery, computers, consumer electronics etc. But as we shall see, much the same hierarchy of elite and peripheral workers may be observed in the construction industry. At the very bottom of this hierarchy are day laborers. They are unaffiliated men who are sometimes employed literally by the day to help out on building sites. In this chapter I propose to address the question of how these marginal workers live and what happens to them in a time of prolonged recession and climbing unemployment. My investigation will focus on two important institutions: the *yoseba*, or casual labor market, and the *ninpudashi*, or workers' boarding house. Let us start our inquiry, however, by visiting a building site.

A tunnel in Yokohama

They are building a tunnel in Yokohama. It is a water drainage tunnel, for use in the event of a major flood in Yokohama – the kind that occurs roughly once in ten years.

It is a massive tunnel, about ten meters high, and already several kilometers long. It will discharge floodwater into the sea somewhere near the port, and they are tunneling back inland from the sea end. The contract is worth ¥5 billion, and was originally won by a consortium led by a corporate behemoth, Kajima Construction. Kajima 'voluntarily' renounced the contract, as it had to with many others, after its leading role in a series of bribery and bid-rigging scandals emerged in the media. The contract was re-advertised and went to a new consortium led by Tōkyū Construction, a somewhat smaller but still substantial company.

Around the entrance to the tunnel stand various temporary buildings associated with the project. Just inside the main entrance are four flagpoles from which flutter the corporate logos of the prime contractors – Tōkyū Construction (the leading contractor or 'sponsor' in Japanese-English), Nissan Construction, Kyōwa Construction and Ishida Construction. The first three are large general contractors with nationwide operations; the fourth is a small local company. The client, which is the government of Kanagawa prefecture, specified that consortia tendering for the contract should include one business from within the prefecture, with a view to stimulating the local economy.

But all is not as it seems at this construction site. Ishida Construction, which gets 10 percent of the value of the contract, i.e. ¥500 million, or roughly $5 million, is in fact a front for a gang of *yakuza* (the Japanese mobsters described by Herbert in the following chapter). Mr. Watanabe, my on-site informant (not his real name), says he has never met a person from Ishida Construction at the worksite; their contribution to the project exists only on paper. The portions of the project allocated to Ishida in fact have to be shared out among the other three companies, which have to shrug their shoulders about the consequent reduction in profit margin.

They put up with this because they have to – meaning that certain politicians, policemen etc. want it that way. Either a portion of the money is passed on to them by the *yakuza*; or the *yakuza* have some relevant blackmail material. The other contractors can afford to shoulder this burden because the profit margin on tunneling is considerably bigger than on other kinds of construction work. This is because it is much harder to estimate the cost of a tunnel project accurately than it is for a road or a dam or a building, because one never knows, until one starts boring, what technical problems may arise. So the original estimate is made on the assumption that there will be no problems, and when these problems do arise, extra demands for payment are submitted to the customer in the name of *sekkei henkō* (changes to plan). At the end of the day, a substantial profit margin somehow emerges from this procedure.

None of the actual boring is done by the prime contractors themselves. That work is sub-contracted to a company based in Shizuoka prefecture that specializes in tunneling. This company in turn uses labor supplied by a pair of sub-sub-contractors, both based in Tokyo. And when the project is in an especially busy phase, they may look to midget construction firms in Yokohama for extra help. These firms may have no more than three or four regular employees. The rest they will pick up as required from the casual labor market at Kotobuki. Mr. Watanabe showed me around the site headquarters of the prime contractors, which was pretty well built and comfortable for a temporary building. It had air-conditioning. He also pointed out a smaller, humbler, prefabricated building, for the use of the sub-contractors. He says the sub-contractors do well over half of the actual physical labor on the project, yet their efforts go unacknowledged. Their flags do not fly alongside those of Tōkyū and the rest, while that of Ishida Construction, which does not actually do any work at all, but still collects 10 percent of the money, wafts proudly in the breeze.

'Isn't life unfair,' I said.

'It certainly is,' he said.[1]

Figure 8.1 A day laborer of Osaka, photographed in his tiny doya *room. The graffiti on the wall says "One-shot gamble" – a gambling reference.*

Credit: Nakajima Satoshi.

Day laborers at the *Yoseba*

Yoseba are open-air casual labor markets. Most major Japanese cities have a *yoseba*, and the biggest ones, in descending order of size, are Kamagasaki in Osaka, San'ya in Tokyo, Kotobuki in Yokohama, and Sasashima in Nagoya. Among minor *yoseba* are Takadanobaba in Tokyo, Chikkō in Fukuoka, Shinkaichi in Kobe, Uchihama in Kyoto, Don in Hiroshima, Tenmonkan in Kagoshima and Shūri in Naha, Okinawa. There is a massive Japanese-language literature on *yoseba* and an academic society devoted to their study.[2] There is also a fast-growing *yoseba* literature in English, including de Barry (1985) and Fowler (1996) on San'ya, and Ventura (1992) and Stevens (1997) on Kotobuki, while Matsuzawa (1988) provides a useful brief overview of the institution. The *yoseba* at Kotobuki is the main source of casual labor for the construction industry in Yokohama. It also supplies warehouse and longshoring labor to the docks at Yokohama and other ports, but containerization has greatly reduced this sector of the market for casual labor. Other once-significant employers, such as transportation and manufacturing, have all but disappeared.

Yoseba have a long and complex history, which I discuss elsewhere (Gill forthcoming 2001). The word literally means a 'gathering place,' and denotes an open-air labor market, where men gather early in the morning to negotiate employment for the day with street-corner labor recruiters known as *tehaishi* ('arrangers'). There are many kinds of *tehaishi*: some are independent small businessmen, while others are employees of the companies that use the labor, or have a special association with one or several of those companies. Some are themselves *yakuza*; those who are not will generally be paying off the *yakuza* in some form for the right to operate unmolested in the *yoseba*. These protection payoffs are called *shobadai*.[3] *Tehaishi* tend to have specialties: some will specialize in dock-work, others in construction. In Kotobuki, which has far more foreign workers than most other *yoseba*,[4] some *tehaishi* specialize in recruiting Korean, Chinese, or Filipino laborers. The day wage varies with degree of skill and the balance of supply and demand, but by the time the *tehaishi* has taken his cut, popularly estimated at 25 to 30 percent, the unskilled laborer will likely have roughly ¥10,000, or $90, in hand. Men who do skilled or dangerous work may get up to twice that amount.

Day laborers tend to be single men. Some are lifelong bachelors, others are divorced or separated. Many of them live in cheap lodging houses called *doya* – a slang reversal of the word *yado*, standard Japanese for an inn. *Doya* charge anything from ¥1,000 to ¥3,000 a night for rent of a tiny room just big enough to lie down in. This makes them very cheap compared with most other kinds of hotel, but surprisingly expensive compared with small apartments rented by the month. Their appeal to day laborers stems from the fact that unlike apartments, they do not require a major non-returnable down payment or letter of guarantee from a responsible citizen, or even proof of identity. In Kamagasaki, San'ya and Kotobuki, there are concentrations of a hundred or more *doya*: hence these places are sometimes referred to as *doya-gai* (lodging-house towns) as well as *yoseba*. These locations are associated with gambling and heavy drinking, and are sometimes compared with the American skid row (Caldarola 1968; Giamo 1994; Marr 1997).

Government attempts to regulate the day labor market date back to the mid-seventeenth century (Leupp 1992: 160–4), and still persist today, in the form of public casual labor exchanges that have been set up in each of the four main *yoseba*. Kamagasaki, San'ya, and Kotobuki actually have two casual labor exchanges each, one run by the Ministry of Labor and the other by the local authorities. The Ministry of Labor also runs a system of unemployment insurance tailor-made for day laborers. The worker carries a handbook, in which revenue stamps are affixed and franked by employers for each day worked. So long as a man has the stamps to demonstrate 26 days' work done in the previous two calendar months, he is entitled to a payment of ¥7,500 (roughly $65) per day of weekday unemployment in the following month. As well as the *tehaishi* and the labor exchanges, the modern day laborer can also seek work through personal connections or by responding to job advertisements carried in sports newspapers. A few of the most efficient men even have mobile telephones with which they can swiftly ascertain demand for labor at several different building sites on any given morning.

Although *yoseba* workers are often referred to as 'day laborers' (*hiyatoi rōdōsha*), they do not necessarily work only on one-day contracts. Some *tehaishi* come looking for men to work for periods ranging from a week to several months, often on large-scale rural construction projects. Among these men are some who have been exposed to radiation while being employed to do dangerous work at nuclear power stations. The topic of the 'nuclear gypsies' (*genpatsu jipushii*) is one where fact and street-myth mingle, but there certainly have been some cases of this. Tanaka (1988) has a valuable account of subcontracting and day laboring in the nuclear power industry. Another *yoseba* myth is of sick men being allowed to die by hospitals because they lack health insurance, or even being given lethal doses of medicine and then being sold as cadavers to medical schools or for illegal organ transplants. Once again it is impossible to guess how much truth there may be in these rumors, but enough cases have surfaced to suggest that the answer is not zero.

But besides these extreme cases, there are plenty of other everyday threats to the lives of the day laborers. *Bentō to kega wa jibun mochi* ('Your lunch-box and your injuries are your own affair') is a popular *yoseba* saying. It can be very difficult to make construction companies take responsibility for worksite accidents, especially where the end employer is separated from the worker by a chain of subcontractors such as I described above. A further serious issue is the safety of the on-site dormitories where men are housed during major construction projects. In eastern Japan these dormitories are referred to as *hanba*, a term which confusingly enough is used synonymously with *ninpudashi* in western Japan. They tend to be thrown up with scant regard for safety, and cases of fires at them are regular minor news items. Several occurred during my own *yoseba* fieldwork (1993–5). One was at a very dangerously designed worker's dormitory in Ebina, 20 miles from Yokohama, where eight men died in a nocturnal fire on July 6, 1994. Most of the 53 men staying there were migrant workers from Hokkaido and Tohoku. Press reports said the dormitory belonged to a small construction company called Komuro-gumi.[5] In fact it belonged to Tōkyū Construction, the same company that was in charge of the tunnel project described above. Tōkyū was using Komuro-gumi as a subcontractor. Komuro took the blame; Tōkyū may have had to make a quiet payoff to its subcontractor, but the firm escaped negative publicity. Life is indeed unfair.

Day laborers at the *ninpudashi*

In sharp contrast to the very extensive literature on *yoseba*, relatively little attention has been paid by academics and journalists to the *ninpudashi*.[6] Yet this is an institution which is arguably every bit as important as the *yoseba* in contemporary Japan, if not more so.

The word *ninpu* is a fairly coarse Japanese term for a navvy or manual laborer. *Dashi* derives from the verb *dasu*, to produce, give, or supply something. Hence *ninpudashi* are navvy-suppliers, businesses that specialize in supplying casual laborers. It is a crude term, considered downright insulting by the people who run these businesses. They prefer the term *rōdō geshuku*, or 'workers' boarding house,' or better still *jinzai hakengyō*, or 'personnel supply business.' I use the term '*ninpudashi*' here because it is the standard term used by the day laborers who patronize them.

I first came across the word in the summer of 1994, on a fieldtrip to northern Kyushu. In retrospect it is amazing, not to say shameful, that I had not become aware of the institution during over a year of fieldwork with day laborers before then. But in Fukuoka and Kitakyushu, even the most insensitive fieldworker cannot miss the *ninpudashi*, for they dominate the casual labor market in these two neighboring industrial cities on the north coast of Japan's southernmost main island. The *ninpudashi* combine the roles of the *yoseba* (casual labor introductions) and the *doya* (cheap, low-grade accommodation). The owner of the *ninpudashi* supplies the worker with a room, either a small *doya*-like individual room, or a larger room shared with several other workers. Meals will generally be provided, though probably at extra cost. He also supplies the worker with employment, activating a network of contacts to find casual work around the city or neighboring cities. Very often he will also supply transportation, having his own minibus, or even a fleet of minibuses, to get the men to the worksites.

The attractions for the worker are manifest: a roof over his head, two or three square meals a day, and no need to get out of bed at half past four to look for a *tehaishi* and negotiate a contract with him. But at the same time, the *ninpudashi* is potentially a powerful tool of exploitation. Wages are generally paid to the *ninpudashi*, not directly to the worker. At the end of the month, the *ninpudashi* will calculate how much the man has earned, then subtract the cost of room rent, meals, and sundries. Some will charge extra for TV-watching and showers, for example, or will supply alcohol and tobacco on credit at higher prices than in the shops. Nor will the wages necessarily be paid immediately at the end of the month. Payment may be delayed, typically until the 15th or 20th of the following month, sometimes even later. Since day laborers are often short of money, they may be unable to wait that long for payment – in which case the *ninpudashi* may lend him an advance against wages, often with high rates of interest attached. Combining the roles of landlord and recruiter gives the *ninpudashi* decisive advantages over both these *yoseba* figures. In the *yoseba*, the *doya* manager must always calculate how likely a man is to get enough work to pay the room rent, and how many days he should allow arrears to mount up before cutting his losses and throwing the man out. In contrast, the *ninpudashi* owner determines the man's level of employment himself and gets the money directly, passing it on only after he has taken off what he determines the man to owe him. And whereas the *tehaishi* must compete against other *tehaishi*, offering higher wages or better terms at times when labor is scarce, the *ninpudashi* owner can monopolize the labor of the men working for him through the hold he has over them as their landlord.

Perhaps most significantly, *ninpudashi* do not guarantee to find employment for their tenants every day. There may be 40 men staying at the boarding house, but only enough work available for 20. In that case men will be 'rested,' on average, every other day. But not all men will necessarily conform to the average. Trouble-makers who complain about conditions may find themselves 'resting' considerably more often than their more docile brothers. Hence the *ninpudashi* is in a strong position to erode solidarity between workers and stimulate mutual competition among them in its place. Rent is payable every day, whether a job is supplied or not. Hence it is all too possible that after a prolonged lean spell, some of the men may find that far from earning money for their own use, they are grappling with a steadily mounting debt owed to the *ninpudashi*. Many men voiced suspicions that *ninpudashi* would deliberately take on more men than they could find work for, because filling the rooms and keeping many of the men idle was more economically advantageous to the *ninpudashi* than having their men fully employed and some of their rooms empty. In the worst cases, day laborers can get so deeply into debt that they are effectively stripped of their human rights and reduced to the status of rather literal wage slaves. In such a situation the worker's one recourse may be to do a runner – or a *tonkō* as it is known. Unions of *ninpudashi* owners maintain blacklists designed to avoid employing men who have absconded from other *ninpudashi*, however, and in some cases the ultimate sanction against abscondence may be the threat of violence, by *yojinbō* – hired bully-boys.

Shortly after World War II, *ninpudashi* were made illegal under article 44 of the Employment Security Law, a piece of legislation inspired by the leaders of the allied Occupation. This article outlawed the practice of taking money for job introductions in any form, and hence criminalized the *tehaishi* at the *yoseba* as well as the *ninpudashi*, and indeed more conventional temporary employment agencies as well (as discussed by Bishop in Chapter 6). Kamata (1971) contends that illegality just made the boarding house business more brutal, while the police usually turned a blind eye. In 1986 the government of Nakasone Yasuhiro passed the Labor Dispatch Business Law (*Jinzai Hakengyō-hō*), which legalized the practice of agencies taking money from an employer and paying their own, lower wage to the worker. This, I believe, was a major factor favoring the renaissance of the *ninpudashi* business, which had been going through some lean times with the decline of the coal and steel industries that spawned it in northern Kyushu.

During the mid-1990s I gained the impression that there was a pattern to casual employment practices in Japan, with *yoseba* tending to predominate to the east of Osaka and *ninpudashi* to the west, especially in Kyushu. Osaka itself has Japan's biggest *yoseba*, in Kamagasaki, but also a concentration of boarding-houses at the nearby district of Taishō, estimated by day-laboring activists to be home to some 7,000 workers.

The dominance of *ninpudashi* in Kitakyushu was explained to me by local labor activists as being related to the district's traditional association with the iron and steel industry. Kitakyushu is an artificially constructed city, formed by the union of five formerly independent cities – Kokura, Tobata, Wakamatsu, Yahata, and Moji. Moji was a port city, while Yahata and Tobata were both dominated by a single employer – Nippon Steel, formerly known as Yahata Steel. The area was naturally suited to steel production, having a plentiful water supply and coal from the nearby Chikuhō coalfield. During the 1970s and 1980s, however, Japan's steel industry was steadily supplanted by rivals in South Korea and elsewhere. Today the once mighty plant at Yahata is long closed, and Nippon Steel has built an amusement park, Space World, on part of the disused site. The Tobata plant continues to operate at a reduced scale, while the closure of the Chikuhō coalmines in the 1970s left Chikuhō as one of the most economically depressed areas in all Japan (Allen 1994).

Nippon Steel used to employ something like the subcontracting system that I described above for the construction industry. Like construction, iron and steel is an industry highly sensitive to changing economic trends, and the advantages of a flexible workforce are obvious. So rather than relying entirely on its own directly-employed workforce, the company would delegate parts of the smelting operation to bosses (*oyakata*), who would be entrusted with supplying the required amount of labor on each day. The *oyakata* would run their own boarding houses, where they would provide board and lodging for men who were effectively their own private workforce. Their wages would be paid by the *oyakata* rather than by Nippon Steel, and hence the company had no responsibility to provide them with 'lifetime employment' or anything like it. Meanwhile, there was a constant struggle for control of the casual workforce among rival labor racketeers – a struggle that was bloody and sometimes murderous.[7]

The boarding houses peaked in 1960, when there were nearly 200 of them. When the steel industry went into decline, the owners of the boarding houses gradually shifted their attention to construction, and today they are the prime suppliers of casual labor to building sites in the Kitakyushu area. Meanwhile, the notorious pre-war *yoseba* at Harunomachi ('Spring-town'), a slum district in the lee of the Yahata steelworks, is long gone. The main post-war *yoseba* was at Senbō, just next to the Tobata steelworks. However, when I got to Senbō in the mid-1990s I found that the *yoseba* had virtually withered away, with no more than a couple of dozen men standing in the street. In the neighboring city of Fukuoka, there is a small *yoseba* located at Chikkō, very close to the Hakata docks, reflecting the fact that like Kotobuki in Yokohama, it used to supply labor principally to the longshoring industry. Even today some 40 percent of work is at the docks, the remainder in construction. In the mid-1990s there were only about 200 day laborers looking for work at Chikkō on the average morning, whereas a day laborer union activist estimated that there were some 10,000 day laborers in the city as a whole. The rest were mostly staying at *ninpudashi*, which for all their drawbacks still represented a surer way of keeping oneself housed and fed than the uncertain prospects of the daily hunt for work on the street corner. Several day laborers said that they would use the *yoseba* when employment prospects were good, retreating to a *ninpudashi* when they were bad. During the 1990s they were usually bad. The small *doya-gai* in Fukuoka was

*Figure 8.2 Volunteers check the blood pressure of day laborers at Kotobuki, Yokohama, during the annual summer festival. The portable shrine (*omikoshi*) can just be seen in the background.*

Credit: Kagoshima Masa'aki.

located some way from the *yoseba*, and the casual labor exchange was in yet a third part of the city. Hence there was no concentration of facilities for day laborers to compare to the *yoseba/doya-gai/*

labor exchange package at Kamagasaki, San'ya, and Kotobuki. Life is less convenient, and the potential for solidarity far lower, than in cities with major *yoseba*. As for the boarding houses, they varied greatly in style. Some were shabby little buildings resembling *doya*; others were smart new multi-story buildings, with covered forecourts where fleets of minibuses stood ready to take the men to work. In Fukuoka and Kitakyushu, the going rate for unskilled casual labor in the late 1990s was in the region of ¥8–9,000 a day, compared with ¥12–13,000 in the major *yoseba* cities of Osaka, Tokyo, and Yokohama. Regional variation in standard of living accounted for some of this differential, but the relative weakness of labor *vis-à-vis* capital was undoubtedly a factor too. All the big *yoseba* have day laborer unions; there are none active in *ninpudashi* districts.

The widow Kawamoto and a sad tale from Kyoto

One common factor which links the *yoseba* at Kotobuki, Yokohama, with the workers' boarding houses of northern Kyushu is that they are both largely owned by ethnic Koreans. Contrary to the stereotyped liberal view of Japanese society, which insists on seeing ethnic minorities as the brutalized victims of a racist, authoritarian state, the Korean ethnic minority in fact includes some very successful, wealthy businessmen. That does not mean that they are not subject to discrimination: they are. However, rather like Jews in medieval Europe, who responded to prejudice by finding a niche in the financial industries, they have carved out sectors of the economy spurned by the ethnic majority and made them their own. *Pachinko* (Japanese-style pinball, with a strong gambling element) and *yakiniku* restaurants (serving Korean-style grilled meat) are the most famous examples of this. However, in some parts of Japan ethnic Koreans have also carved out a niche in the management of casual labor – another sector of the economy low in status but potentially lucrative.

Virtually all the *doya* at Kotobuki are owned by Koreans, and the Yokohama branch of Chongryun, the General Association of Korean Residents in Japan, an organization sympathetic to North Korea (cf. Ryang 1997), is located in the *yoseba*. The *doya* owners are divided among those who support Chongryun, those who favor

Mindan, the equivalent organization loyal to South Korea, and independents. This lack of political unity, coupled with a drastic fall in land prices during the 1990s, has probably saved Kotobuki from being knocked down to make way for a 'Koreatown' modeled on the nearby Chinatown which is arguably Yokohama's premier tourist attraction. To the best of my knowledge, however, there is no significant Korean presence among the *doya*-owners of San'ya and Kamagasaki.

Down in Kitakyushu and Fukuoka, practically the entire boarding house industry appears to be in Korean hands. Both Chongryun and Mindan had branches in the *ninpudashi* district of Kitakyushu, and the former was a sumptuous new building. No one I asked could name a Japanese-run boarding house. The widow Kawamoto was a Korean lady using a Japanese name, and she ran a *ninpudashi* in Tobata called *Shin'ei Kōgyō* (Shin'ei Industries), a name which made it sound like a construction company.[8] One worker said it was embarrassing to admit to fellow workers that one was with a *ninpudashi*, and better to simply mention this respectable-sounding name. It was a sizeable operation: when I visited in 1994 it was dispatching 90 to 100 men to worksites in Kitakyushu and neighboring cities every weekday morning, in a fleet of 20 vehicles. It was semi-residential, with 30 men living on the premises and another 60-odd showing up for work. The company paid ¥8–10,000 a day, rising to ¥12,000 for more skilled work. It charged ¥900 a night for a three-mat room (including a ¥100 TV charge) and ¥300 for breakfast (optional). The final employers were billed monthly in arrears, and the widow said the company's margin was ¥1–2,000 per person-day.

When work was short, some men might be asked to 'rest' for a period. The widow said that residents of the boarding house would generally be given preference in job allocation, but if they were laid off for some time and ran short of cash, they would be allowed credit against their room-bill. She also said that she looked after ill workers and helped them to get compensation and social welfare in serious cases. She stressed that the business was run like one big family (*katei-teki*) and was providing shelter and gainful employment to men who would otherwise be sleeping in the street. Certainly I noticed only one possibly homeless person while in Tobata.

Wages were paid in cash, at the end of each day's work. I observed this happening. The widow said this was the usual practice in Tobata, but mentioned some larger, more impersonally run boarding houses in nearby Kokura where wages were withheld for a week or ten days. She had heard of many cases of abuse at these places, such as deliberately forgetting about overtime, or refusing to pay a worker's wages if he wanted to leave before payday.

She confirmed that Koreans ran the entire industry. Asked if there were also Koreans in the workforce, she said there were very few: the Koreans in Tobata could get better work. At the very least they could get steady employment at a cousin's *pachinko* parlor. She said the recession had damaged her business, but there seemed to be plenty of activity, and her father appeared to be driving a Bentley in British racing green.

Men working for this boarding house confirmed most of the above, and said it was one of the better places. One of them claimed, however, that the cozy, family-style relationship between employer and workers only lasted for as long as the latter was fit enough to generate income for the former. The boarding house would dump anyone who was reckoned to be past it. The widow did say that she never employed old people, and that the average age of her workers was about 45.

She repeatedly described her workers as 'diligent' (*majime*) and 'obedient' (*sunao*). She contrasted them with the workers in Senbō, who she said were sometimes very badly behaved.

Later that summer, I met a man in Kamagasaki who told me that he had recently finished a stint at a *ninpudashi* in Kyoto. He was so angry about the conditions at this *ninpudashi* that he borrowed my notebook and wrote them out in great detail. The following is a direct translation; note that he uses the term *hanba*, which in the Kansai region around Osaka and Kyoto is used in the same sense as '*ninpudashi*.' Only the dollar conversions are added by myself.

> Wages:¥12,500 [c. $115] a day. Payment to *hanba* (including room, meals, TV, electricity etc.): ¥3,300 [c. $30] a day. The payment to the *hanba* is payable even on days when one is made to rest because it suits the convenience of the owner, and on Sundays and public holidays.

From January 1994, my days worked and payments to the *hanba* were as follows:

Month	Days worked	Payments to *hanba*
January	9 days	¥3,300 × 31
February	8 days	¥3,300 × 29
March	9 days	¥3,300 × 31
April	2 days	¥3,300 × 30
May	0 days	¥3,300 × 31
June	2 days	¥3,300 × 30

Total income in 6 months:	30 × ¥12,500 =	¥375,000	[c. $3,500]
Total expenditure:	182 × ¥ 3,300 =	¥600,600	[c. $5,500]
Net loss:		¥225,600	[c. $2,000]

[Also employed through the *hanba* are] workers who live in their own places in Kyoto and come to work on bicycles, motorbikes, etc. When the prime contractor or leading sub-contractor which is the end employer only needs a few people (1 or 2), the labor supply business (*hanba*), because it does not use the workers who stay at the *hanba* (and whose wages are about ¥1,000 higher than for general workers) and does not supply a light van or minibus, gives priority to the above-mentioned workers who come to work on bicycles and motorbikes. Because of this the 22 people staying in the boarding house are all (by order) made to take the day off work.

He then bitterly complained that prostitutes were better off than day laborers in the *hanba* – at least they didn't have to pay rent on the rooms where they worked and slept. They also had their clothes and make-up paid for, etc. He and his fellows actually had to pay for the privilege of being exploited, he said. 'Both psychologically and economically we are below them,' he said.

The changing patterns

The bursting of the speculative bubble at the start of the 1990s sent the Japanese construction industry into a drastic decline. Real estate prices collapsed, housing starts plummeted and heavily indebted companies cut back on investment in new plant. The bloated construction industry, which a 1998 OECD report found to account for a portion of the economy roughly double the figure for most industrialized countries, was forced into a contraction which saw layoffs even at the big general contractors, while thousands of smaller companies were forced into bankruptcy.

Naturally, the first workers to feel the pinch were day laborers. Employment at all the big *yoseba* collapsed. For example, the number of person-days transacted at the Kotobuki Labor Center, which accounts for over 90 percent of formal labor contracts transacted in Kotobuki, fell from 154,574 in 1986 to 38,348 in 1999. This was a crippling 75 percent fall, which had all but killed off the system of state-mediated casual labor by the end of the century. The *tehaishi* do not supply statistics for the informal labor market, but by the end of the 1990s a lot of familiar faces had disappeared from the morning streets of Kotobuki, as many *tehaishi* simply withdrew from the market. With the market so weak, freelance manual work out of a *yoseba* ceased to be an option for the young working-class men that had once formed a large part of the population. Consequently the *yoseba* population aged dramatically – far faster than the rate for the general population. The mean age of workers using the Kotobuki Labor Center rose from 39 in 1975 to 45 in 1985 and then to 52 in 1997.

Growing numbers of day laborers were forced into homelessness, and throughout the later 1990s Yokohama City Hall (located a ten-minute walk from Kotobuki) was surrounded by over a hundred cardboard boxes in which homeless people would spend the night. Shanty towns and tent cities spread out in every major city – at the west exit of Shinjuku station and along the left bank of the Arakawa river, to name but two famous Tokyo locations, and around Tennōji Park in Osaka [9] and in Wakamiya Park in Nagoya, among many others. The great majority of these homeless people were unaffiliated men of middle age and above – the kind of people who used to be able to make a living as day laborers. The fast-rising numbers of homeless bore testimony to the important role that the day-laboring system had played as the employer of last resort in the Japanese economy, and the degree to which the system was being eroded.

The inescapable fact of rising homelessness, coupled with vigorous campaigning by day laborer unions and homeless support groups, has led to a gradual softening of attitudes toward *yoseba* on the part of city governments. For many years it was virtually impossible for men based in the *yoseba* to acquire welfare payments, largely because of an unwritten rule made up by bureaucrats, to the effect that one had to have a fixed address to apply for welfare, and that a *doya* room did not constitute a fixed address. In Yokohama that rule has been relaxed to the point where some 80 percent of the region's 6,500 *doya* rooms are now occupied by welfare recipients, a figure that has doubled in the last five years or so. Kotobuki is now well on its way to completing the transition from 'workers' town' to 'welfare town' discussed by Stevens (1997), and it has in fact become very difficult for the traditional wandering day laborer to get a room in Kotobuki. Other city governments have been slower to move, and consequently there are far more empty *doya* rooms in San'ya and Kamagasaki than in Kotobuki, and far more homeless men in Tokyo and Osaka than in Yokohama.[10]

Right at the end of the 1990s, the Tokyo government finally started to show signs of relaxing its hard line on welfare for *doya* occupants, and started to approve a number of applications. Some *doya* owners responded by making slight cuts in room rents to meet the ¥2,300 maximum that the metropolitan government had set for nightly accommodation expenses for welfare recipients. Even so, the *doya* population of San'ya is a fraction of what it used to be, and the place has something of the atmosphere of a ghost town. Rising numbers of homeless and of welfare recipients, and a high mortality rate, account for some of the disappearances, but not all of them.

According to activists with a day-laborer union called the San'ya Dispute League (*San'ya Sōgidan*), quite a large part of the day-laboring population of San'ya has disappeared into *ninpudashi*. The word has been much less common in the Kanto region around Tokyo and Yokohama, and has tended to be used in a different sense to that understood in the Kansai: as a straightforward job introduction agency, without the residential component. However, *Sōgidan* activists say they have clear and mounting evidence of a new wave of residential *ninpudashi* cropping up in Tokyo's four main satellite prefectures: Kanagawa, Saitama, Chiba, and Ibaragi. Rather than looking for workers in the *yoseba* – which are invariably located in fairly central urban places – employers keep them in boarding houses in quiet, out-of-the-way places, where land is cheap and few prying government officials or journalists are likely to show their faces. They are bussed into construction sites in the Tokyo-Yokohama region and bussed out again at the end of the day.

It would appear, then, that a sea change is coming over the unobserved outer margins of the Japanese economy. The old way of life associated with day laboring out of the *yoseba* is crumbling away, and the *yoseba* working population is draining away in three directions: toward welfare, toward homelessness and early death, and toward the *ninpudashi*. *Ninpudashi* are far more resilient than *yoseba* to changing economic forces, because of the system described above, of rotating under-employed workers while deducting their board and lodging from their pay packet at source. They have remained viable at levels of economic activity so low that the *yoseba* have steadily lost their function as labor markets, metamorphosing into slum districts for single men like the U.S. skid row, or in Kotobuki's case, into a vast economy-class welfare institution.

One reason why *ninpudashi* have attracted far less attention than *yoseba* from academics and journalists is because they are far less noticeable, and also far harder to study. A *yoseba*, by definition, is a gathering place: a concentration of largely unattached men with little to lose in terms of possessions or social status. As such they have always had a certain rebellious potential. While the *yoseba* have never fulfilled the quixotic hopes of utopian Japanese Marxists, that they might be catalysts for the revolution, they do have a history of street-rioting[11] and far higher rates of alcoholism and crime than other urban districts. They can be studied by anyone who chooses to walk into them. By contrast, *ninpudashi* are closed environments that are very difficult for researchers to penetrate, especially foreign researchers. They are also strictly controlled environments, in which much smaller groups of men are concentrated, and where the balance of power is far more decisively on the side of the recruiter/landlord. The gradual shift from *yoseba* to *ninpudashi* represents a small, barely noticed, yet decisive defeat for labor in its never-ending struggle with capital on the fringes of the Japanese economy.

9 The *Yakuza* and the Law

Wolfgang Herbert

> 'Social control activities may unintentionally generate functional alternatives. The relationship between controllers and controlled may often be characterized as a movable equilibrium. As in sports or any competitive endeavor, new strategies, techniques and resources may give one side a temporary advantage, but the other side tends to find ways to neutralize, avoid or counter them. The action may become more sophisticated, practitioners more skilled, and the nature of the game may be altered – but the game does not stop. A saying among Hong Kong drug dealers in response to periodic clampdowns captures this nicely: "Shooting the singer is no way to stop the opera"' (Marx 1993: 13).

Introduction

In this paper I want to outline the interplay between the law, as represented by the police, and Japan's underworld gangsters known as *yakuza*.[1] I will concentrate on the Yamaguchi-gumi, Japan's biggest *yakuza* syndicate. My basic thesis is that the state and organized crime have developed a form of interaction that can be described as a 'supergame.' The players in this game are the public, politicians, the law, the police, the mass media, business leaders, and the *yakuza*. The latter have to be seen as an enterprise purveying legal, semi-legal, and illegal goods and services. Changes in attitudes or formal rules (laws) lead to a shift in the balance of social power between the actors. But it will not lead to the 'eradication' of the *yakuza*, an outcome the police repeatedly predict with a somewhat heroic optimism.[2] *Yakuza* may renounce certain activities, but at the same time they occupy new economic niches.[3] After some time a new informal social contract will come into existence. If it is blatantly broken, or if one of the players feels particularly endangered or that they are losing the game, legal or other steps are taken. I want to demonstrate this with reference to the legislation against *yakuza* that came into effect on March 1, 1992. However, this was not the first time that law enforcement agencies had tried to curb the activities of the *yakuza*, so I shall also give a concise outline of post-World War II developments, again focusing on the interplay between police action and *yakuza* re-action.

In the immediate post-war period the existence of a huge black market and the lack of state control was an ideal breeding ground for organized crime and racketeering. It was then that the 'traditional' *yakuza* groups of gamblers (*bakuto*) and peddlers (*tekiya* or *yashi*) moved into areas of business previously foreign to them, e.g. prostitution, extortion, and drug dealing (mainly in amphetamines). They competed with aggressive groups of young delinquents 'without tradition,' called *gurentai*. The lines between these groups began to blur, alignments and mergers occurred, and all of them were forced to diversify their businesses – a process which continues up to the present. They also fought against gangs of so-called *sangokujin* (Koreans, Chinese, and Taiwanese resident in Japan as a legacy of the colonial period) for control of the black market. The *yakuza* finally broke up these other gangs or absorbed them. The economic resurgence during and after the Korean War led to a construction boom in Japan. *Yakuza* profited widely from their growing involvement in the construction business – a link that still continues, as Gill's chapter in this volume shows. In 1959 the *Yomiuri Shinbun* launched an anti-*yakuza* campaign (mentioned in Raz 1996: 251) and in 1960 the *Chūgoku Shinbun* started to address the *yakuza* problem and to publish some courageous articles (Kitazawa 1988: 57).

Researching the *yakuza*

Here I have to make a brief comment about journalism covering the *yakuza*. The serious national daily newspapers are heavily dependent on police (and public prosecutor) sources, which they usually reproduce without critical reflection.[4] The dailies habitually support the police in their efforts to disseminate a negative picture of the *yakuza* and to create sentiment in favor of repressing them. However, the *yakuza* have their spokesmen too: the *gokudō* journalists.[5] These reporters write almost exclusively about *yakuza*, mostly in so-called *jitsuwashi*, magazines carrying stories about sex, crime, and showbiz-gossip (Herbert 1992: 85ff.; Adachi 1987; Raz 1996: 60ff.). These journalists tend to present a 'positive' image of the *yakuza*, by quoting them extensively in their own argot and giving them the opportunity to promote their own cause, ideology, and lifestyle. *Gokudō* journalists are well informed but are likely to report only the 'official' *yakuza* version of events. Some of them I use as sources myself, such as Yamada, Ino, and Mizoguchi, but they have to be read carefully for possible bias. Mizoguchi became more and more critical of the *yakuza* in the 1980s. He paid for that when he was violently attacked and stabbed by *yakuza* in June 1990.[6] The serious press has an ambivalent role: it does not simply publish items based on police sources, but it sometimes acts as a moral entrepreneur, putting pressure on the police to act tough on crime.

The reader will find some scattered remarks pertaining to my sources in this paper. Let me quickly indicate some of the main points. *Yakuza* are by no means mysterious or unfathomable. The police present long accounts of their activities and astonishingly precise statistics, surveys, and data in the annual police 'White Paper,' the *Keisatsu Hakusho*. Lengthy studies of *Yakuza* can regularly be found in the police research journal, *Keisatsugaku Ronshū*. Journalists specializing in *yakuza* affairs report frequently on new developments, internal power shifts and *yakuza* rituals.[7]

I also draw on an extended period of fieldwork in the late 1980s and the beginning of the 1990s. I had several *yakuza* contacts in Kamagasaki, the day laborer area of Osaka (also mentioned in the chapter by Gill). The outstanding one among them was a *wakagashira hosa* ('assistant young leader,' cf. Kaplan and Dubro 1986: 132) from a Yamaguchi-gumi affiliated syndicate. He took a fancy to me and took me along on his 'evening tours.' I was able to observe various transactions first hand, such as cashing in protection money or troubleshooting. In return he showed me around as his 'international asset.' This seemingly earned him further prestige and was his reward for disclosing stories and insider information to me. *Yakuza* tend to instrumentalize non-*yakuza* and also to stage an impressive show for them. However, they loosen up over a longer period of contact, notably after a drink or two. In the late 1990s I happened to make some new acquaintances among younger low-ranking *yakuza* in Shikoku. They readily talked about recent hardships regarding the new law and corroborated the developments described in this paper. In particular the existence of front companies and the trend not to join the *yakuza* officially seem to be well established and strengthening. Usually I chose to conduct 'soft interviews' without interference from technology (tape recorders and the like) as a method of information gathering. Talks were always transcribed immediately after they were held.

Let me also comment briefly on terminology. Since the 1960s, the police – and consequently the press as well – have called the *yakuza* '*bōryokudan*,' which literally means 'violent group.' As Bourdieu repeatedly notes, the categorization and labeling of a social phenomenon is a symbolic battle with consequences for the perception of what is conceived of as social 'reality.' The language of persons with authority (e.g. politicians) itself exerts power. They can even call things into existence by naming them in a particular manner (Bourdieu 1984: 65–66). The labeling of the *yakuza* as a 'violent group' is as intentional as it is partly unjust. It is unjust because it picks out one – admittedly important – element of the *yakuza* lifestyle, namely violence, and transforms it into a generic term. It therefore becomes a pseudo-explanatory, reductionist general label which functions like a stigma and overshadows the whole existence of the *yakuza* (Raz 1996: 241–42). It is intentional in the sense that it is designed to deprive the *yakuza* of their romantic Robin Hood image. This is associated with the term '*yakuza*' itself, which carries positive connotations of popular heroes and protectors of the weak. This heroic image can be found in popular culture from Kabuki, movies, and books to *jitsuwashi* journalism (Raz 1996: 39–81).

Controlling the *yakuza*

In 1956 the police declared their intention to conduct more extensive investigations into the *yakuza* in order to obtain the intelligence necessary for systematic control. From 1958 onwards, new departments for the investigation of *yakuza* were set up, beginning with one of the Metropolitan Police Headquarters (*Keishichō*) in Tokyo. Public concern about the *yakuza* was heightened and the annual number arrested rose from roughly 9,000 in the 1940s and 1950s to over 58,000. Despite these efforts, the number of *yakuza* gangs (5,200) and their members (around 184,000) reached an all-time high in 1963 (Worm 1988: 73).

In 1964 the police drew up a new program for the control of *yakuza* (*bōryokudan torishimari yōkō*). They announced what they called 'Strategy 65,' a set of guidelines for countermeasures against the *yakuza*. Its two main pillars were: *chōjō sakusen*, i.e. the apprehension of bosses and executives (*kanbu*) and *shikingen no kaimetsu*, meaning destruction of the *yakuza*'s sources of income (Asakura 1987: 233). Since then the three basic declared aims of the police have been the arrest of gang members, control of funds, and seizure of weapons (e.g. Keisatsuchō 1978: 38ff.). This is repeated in police reports like a ritual incantation. The slogans pertaining to this threefold strategy are periodically renewed. Yet another refers to the police clampdown on *hito*, *kane*, and *mono*, i.e. people, money and goods (Keisatsuchō 1989: 71), more or less the same as the 'Strategy 65' guidelines. In the 1990s a similar list was condensed into: '3 L-*katto*' – *katto* standing for the English 'cut' and 'L' for 'lifeline.' This meant that the police were intent on cutting down on *yakuza* staff (through arrests), goods (i.e. weapons), and income (Yamada et al. eds 1994: 260). Although since the late 1980s the police have undeniably taken a tougher line against the *yakuza*, it can still be argued that they are not interested in the total 'crushing' of organized crime, but rather in keeping it under control.

Earlier police efforts to clamp down had marked side-effects.[8] Altogether there were three 'summit strategies' (*chōjō sakusen*) launched in order to get hold of the top leaders of *yakuza* gangs. The first was initiated in 1965–67 and resulted in mass arrests and the disbanding of big syndicates. However, it was only formal coalitions between gangs that were dissolved. The coalition member organizations themselves were not dismantled. Big horizontally connected syndicates such as the Kantō-kai, Honda-kai, Tōsei-kai, Sumiyoshi-kai, Matsuba-kai and others were officially declared dissolved. But they were soon reorganized, especially once their leaders had been released from prison. The main effect of the second *chōjō sakusen*, in 1969, was that small gangs which relied exclusively on traditional income sources – and which were therefore obsolete anyway – were broken up. The big syndicates that survived diversified their portfolios and consolidated their business. A third concerted attempt to arrest gang members and their bosses in 1975, mostly on charges of illegal weapon possession, resulted in the grouping of *yakuza* gangs into stronger conglomerates (*keiretsuka*), an oligopolization of the underworld, and nationwide expansion by the three biggest syndicates. One of the main side effects was their introduction of a franchise system. The bosses are paid regular fees by all affiliated gangs and are therefore practically insulated from day-to-day activities, especially from 'dirty' work.[9] This insulation of the top executives was a defensive measure against police attempts to arrest the bosses.

The functions of organized crime

In this rough outline one can already see that *yakuza* react quickly to moves by the police. They do not just vanish because of intensified persecution and/or prosecution. Organized crime exists due to structural preconditions in almost any given society. At a micro-sociological level Raz suggests that the *yakuza* represent a variation on the core traditional culture and values of the Japanese (Raz 1996: 42). In fact *yakuza* send out two sets of signals, both exclusive ('we are outlaws,' etc.) and inclusive ('we have the real Japanese spirit,' etc.). He describes vividly the obsession of *yakuza* with posing and performance, their way of 'stigma management' (Raz 1992; cf. Goffman 1963). Raz subscribes to a Durkheimian view of criminality as being functional for society: it fosters cohesion and (moral) solidarity among its members by defining (rather arbitrarily) the boundaries between 'normal' and 'deviant' behavior (Raz 1996: 225–26). A functionalist macro-sociological viewpoint also provides a possible interpretation of why the *yakuza* are almost an accepted institution in Japanese society, despite official condemnation. They are deeply embedded in Japanese society, in which they function in several ways: economic, social, legal, and political.

The economic reason for the continued existence of the *yakuza* is obvious: as a business they satisfy the demand among 'ordinary' people for illegal goods (e.g. drugs) and services (e.g. prostitution, loan sharking, debt collection).

Socially, the *yakuza* offer an alternative career structure and avenue to success for members of Japanese society who suffer from disadvantage and discrimination. Among those with highly restricted opportunities are school dropouts. According to one police survey (Keisatsuchō 1989: 38), 80 percent of novice *yakuza* did not complete high school, compared with 2 percent of the population as a whole. Juvenile delinquents are another source of *yakuza* recruits: more than 60 percent of recruits have a 'history of delinquent behavior,' and 46.2 percent of those have been involved in severe criminal acts including murder, assault, or intimidation (Hoshino 1980: 43). People of Korean and Burakumin origin are also more likely than most to join the *yakuza*. Although no reliable data exist, it is well known that these two excluded minorities are greatly over-represented in *yakuza* syndicates, especially in western Japan.[10] According to an unofficial police estimate, around 10 percent of Yamaguchi-gumi members are of Korean origin, while up to 70 percent of them may have a Burakumin background (Kaplan and Dubro 1986: 145).

The legal role of the *yakuza* has developed out of loopholes in the Japanese judicial system. Not only is the number of lawyers hopelessly small, but also court proceedings take an enormous length of time until a judgment is handed down. The police also refuse to deal with civil disputes, and so *yakuza* are often hired instead of lawyers to solve them by negotiating out-of-court settlements.[11]

The link between politicians and the *yakuza* at the national level became weaker after the uncovering of the involvement in the Lockheed scandal (1976) of Kodama Yoshio (1911–1984), the great fixer and mediator between mainstream politicians, *yakuza*, and ultranationalists.[12] In the 1960s and 1970s *yakuza* were mobilized for strike-breaking and as an 'anti-communist force' (Ino 1992). On at least one occasion, the late Kanemaru Shin, at one time deputy prime minister of Japan, used *yakuza* to quell campaigns by rightists against himself.[13] Former prime minister Takeshita Noboru was also accused of using *yakuza* during an election campaign in 1987.[14] I do not have the space to discuss in detail the connections between conservative politicians and the *yakuza*, who were once seen as a stabilizing factor within Japanese society. But it can reasonably be argued that up to now the *yakuza* have enjoyed a certain degree of 'political protection' – even though it was usually ultraconservative politicians who made use of the *yakuza* rather than the other way round (Ino 1992: 259f.).

There may well be other factors as well behind the fact that the *yakuza* are a well-established institution in Japan. As long as society as a whole does not change so drastically as to render the *yakuza* superfluous, the law and law enforcement can only set boundaries to limit the activities of the *yakuza*, but they will not make them disappear. It can well be argued that the existence of organized crime (complete with names and addresses as in the case of the *yakuza*) might be better for society than disorganized crime *en masse*. I contend that this is also the tacit understanding of the authorities in Japan. In the following I want to demonstrate the effects that lawmaking can have on organized crime in some detail, using the 1992 legislation as an example.

The effects of legislation

The anti-*yakuza* law of 1992 is officially called *Bōryokudan'in ni yoru Futō na Kōi nado no Bōshi ni kansuru Hōritsu* ('Law Pertaining to Unjust Activities by *Yakuza*'), but it is also abbreviated to *Bōryokudan Taisakuhō*, or simply *Bōtaihō* ('*Yakuza* Countermeasures Law'). The *yakuza* used to call it simply 'the new law' (*shinpō*). In order to enact a new law, legitimation and some sort of moral project are necessary. The problems that were troubling the police in the years before the new law took effect can be seen from the annual Police White Paper (*Keisatsu Hakusho*) on public security (or insecurity) for 1991. One perceived threat was the invasion of the *yakuza* into the lives of ordinary citizens and their inroads into the business community. Rising figures for so-called 'violent interventions in civil affairs' (*minji kainyū bōryoku*) were presented, comprising things like debt-collecting, money-lending, bill-discounting, bankruptcy affairs, real estate disputes, and out-of-court settlement of traffic accidents etc. (see e.g. Keisatsuchō 1991: 116). Since the end of the 1980s more than

20,000 such interventions had been coming to the attention of the police annually, though only an estimated one-tenth of them actually led to an indictment (Yamada et al. eds 1994: 211).

Another problem stressed in the White Paper was that of *jiage* deals. *Jiage* literally means 'land raising' and refers to the practice of forcing up prices of real estate and the forceful eviction of recalcitrant tenants from land or premises needed for new projects. During the years of the bubble economy *yakuza* were often employed by real estate companies to intimidate occupants. Ample remuneration and the acquisition of knowledge concerning land speculation enabled the *yakuza* to set up real estate firms themselves.

A further area of operations seen as dangerous was corporate racketeering, the operations of the infamous *sōkaiya*.[15] Police also spoke of a general *yakuza* intrusion into economic systems, of an 'economic mafia,' and of illegal profiteering disguised as legal through so-called 'front companies' (Gill's chapter gives an example of this from the construction industry). The investment of *yakuza* income in legal spheres of business such as real estate and securities also made the police nervous. The 1992 law can be seen in part as a response to this advance of the *yakuza* into the world of high finance.

Organized crime making inroads into legal business is a well-documented transnational tendency. It is described extensively by Arlacchi (1986) for the Italian mafia in general, and by Gambetta and Reuter (1995) for the Sicilian mafia and U.S. Cosa Nostra. Granting protection, settling disputes, and monopolizing some of the shadier areas of business are seen internationally as well-established features of organized crime. Reputations both individual and generic, and brand images suggested by names such as 'mafia,' '*yakuza*,' or 'Yamaguchi-gumi,' are the most important assets in this 'industry of protection' – the title of the first chapter of a compelling study of the mafia by Gambetta (1993).[16]

The *Bōtaihō* permits a Public Safety Commission to designate a *yakuza* gang as one subject to the measures contained in the Law when certain pre-conditions are met. Members of the *shitei bōryokudan* ('designated underworld gangs') then become the 'object' of *chūshi meirei*, injunctions to stop certain 'improper' activities (*futō na kōi*) as specified in the Law. In case of recidivism, an order to prevent recurrence (*saihatsu bōshi meirei*) can be issued. The activities that can thus be prohibited include demanding undue donations, protection, or hush money; collecting debts at high interest rates; demanding the improper waiver of an obligation; private arrangements for compensation of traffic accidents; requests for improper loans; claims for money or goods on a false pretext, and so on. One can easily see from this list that the 'new' areas of profiteering were the main targets of the new legislation. Besides these, coercion or enticement in recruitment of juveniles, hindering someone from leaving the gang, and forcing someone to slice off his little finger (*yubitsume*, a common penalty or gesture of apology for blunders), have also become objects of the new law.[17]

Another widely discussed measure is the ban on the use of *yakuza* offices for three months (extendable to six) if and when gang wars break out. This provision can be seen as a concession to pressure by the public to clamp down on *yakuza* more severely, especially in times of gang warfare. A long feud broke out in 1985 after the murder of Takenaka Masahisa, the boss of the Yamaguchi-gumi, and the secession of a group calling itself the Ichiwa-kai. It lasted until this latter group was 'destroyed' and Watanabe Yoshinori, the current Yamaguchi-gumi boss, was chosen in 1989. Several non-*yakuza* bystanders were killed both during this feud and during the attack on the Yamaguchi-gumi's so-called 'Number Two,' Takumi Masaru, on 28 August 1997, and this cost the *yakuza* a lot of sympathy with the public.[18] Mizoguchi goes so far as to allege that the new law was drawn up with the Yamaguchi-gumi as its principal target (Mizoguchi 1992: 246).

Just one year and one month after the *Bōtaihō* came into force, a revision of the law was enacted. This shows how quickly legislators had to react to new developments and their need to constantly fine-tune their legal instruments. In the revision a range of further 'economic' actions came under the scope of *chūshi meirei*, such as compensation for losses in securities dealing, manipulation of shares, the loan business, remuneration for clearing real estate or premises, and obstruction of auctions. The stipulations concerning recruitment of juveniles became stricter: handing out pocket money to juveniles or compelling them to get tattooed also became liable to prosecution (*Asahi Shinbun* February 27 1993: 1).

The latest revision took effect on October 1 1997. Here, I believe, it can be clearly shown that legislation and police work are mainly reactive rather than proactive. *Chūshi meirei* were up to this date servable only on individual full-fledged gang members. This led to the practice of gang members working alternately on the same victim. To prevent this dodging of ordinances, the new revision made them servable on the superior or boss. They can also be served on non-*yakuza* if they are 'associate members,' or if a non-*yakuza* is directed by a *yakuza* to commit acts forbidden by the *Bōtaihō*. This is a reaction to the growing 'periphery' of *yakuza* syndicates, in which legal companies 'fraternize' with *yakuza* (so-called *kigyō shatei* or 'corporate brothers').[19] Debt collection was also made more difficult by the new provisions (BTHKS 1997).

The *yakuza* response

But of course the *yakuza* also watch closely every step the law enforcement agencies take, and they react accordingly. As soon as the debate on the new law started, the *yakuza* began to organize study meetings with lawyers in order to become familiar with it. The Yamaguchi-gumi issued a circular to its directly affiliated gangs, ordering them to transform themselves into joint-stock companies. By February 1992 half of them had achieved this goal. Already in 1991 more than 1,000 Yamaguchi-gumi offices had had their emblems (*daimon*) dismantled, while many gangs had also removed their membership lists, their articles of association, photos of former *oyabun* (bosses) and other such paraphernalia. All this was intended to help camouflage the fact that the premises were being used as *yakuza* offices. Some smaller gangs at the lower end of the hierarchy simply moved to a new place where the police could not track them down. There were internal notifications strictly forbidding fraternization with police officers, saying that visits by policemen should be declined and that no information should be given, even in the case of arrest. All this indicates a refusal to cooperate with the police. At the same time control of information within the Yamaguchi-gumi was tightened. Important information was kept in the upper echelons of the hierarchy, contacts by fax were discouraged and the use of public telephones recommended (Yamada et al. eds 1994: 186ff., 210, 243, 253).

The statistics on *yakuza* membership show some interesting characteristics. Between 1991, the year before the *Bōtaihō*, and the end of 1996, total membership of the *yakuza* fell by 11,000. During these five years the number of formal members (*kōsei'in*), fell by 27.9 percent, resulting in a rise of the proportion of associate members (*jun-kōsei'in*) in the total *yakuza* force from roughly 30 to 42.4 percent. Many full members retired, taking on the status of associate members, as which they were not covered by the *Bōtaihō* – a trend that was countered by the Law's revision of October 1997. In 1996 there were 46,000 active members of 3,120 gangs, surrounded and aided by 33,900 'associate' members, putting the total *yakuza* numbers at 79,900. Around two-thirds of them were organized under the big three syndicates: the Yamaguchi-gumi, Sumiyoshi-kai, and Inagawa-kai. Twenty-four gangs were designated as *shitei bōryokudan*.

According to the police an average of 220 gangs a year were being dissolved in the mid-1990s (the numbers are given in Bozono 1998: 79–80, and Keisatsuchō 1997: 183). Nevertheless, this 'decrease' in the number of gangsters and gangs is still within the range of 'natural' fluctuations, given the poor overall economic situation. As a matter of fact the Yamaguchi-gumi quickly banned more than 1,000 of its members in the year of the new law. It tried to get rid of members who had become a burden, such as drug addicts, those in debt, and 'under-performers' who were not fulfilling their duties. This is a reversal of a long-standing expansionist policy: instead of expansion at all costs the new line stresses quality rather than quantity, the aim being to reduce overall members and 'nurture an elite' (Yamada et al. eds 1994: 258, 270). The fall in the number of registered *yakuza* can therefore be interpreted as a rational decision by the management of an enterprise deciding to reduce staff during a period of economic recession, rather than as a glorious success for the police.

The Yamaguchi-gumi has also been cutting down on expenses. The internal money flow is restricted and the monthly burden of payments alleviated. The Yamaguchi-gumi is organized in the form of a pyramid. At the top is the 'boss of bosses' with an executive committee and advisers, forming the governing board, which consists of some twenty bosses. Watanabe, the Yamaguchi-gumi don, has about 100 'fictive children' (*kobun*) or direct subordinates.

Thc board and the *kobun* form the mother organization and they are called *chokkei kumichō* (directly affiliated bosses). They are at the same time the leaders of locally active organizations. These groups in turn have further gangs affiliated to them in up to three further organizational tiers. Money flows from the bottom to the top, i.e. the affiliated groups pay monthly royalties for the use of the name Yamaguchi-gumi, a kind of licensing or franchising fee that is called *jōnōkin* by the police. *Yakuza* simply call it a 'membership subscription.' The groups at the lowest end pay just ¥10,000 a month. The gangs of the *kobun* of Watanabe paid ¥850,000 per month, and the members of the board paid ¥1,050,000. The subscriptions of the *kobun* were lowered by ¥200,000 in the spring of 1994 and lowered again to a monthly fee of ¥500,000 with effect from January 1998. From the beginning of 1998 the monthly dues of board members were also reduced, to ¥700,000 (*Asahi Shinbun*, evening edition, December 19 1997, p. 15). These are austerity measures, so to speak. It is also said that the Yamaguchi-gumi is trying to save money by holding simpler, less expensive ceremonies. The bosses have also changed their ostentatious life-styles. Watanabe is even said to be speaking about 'honorable poverty' as a new motto (Yamada et al. eds 1994: 290 and 309). This too can be perceived as an adaptation to economically bad times.

Ways of generating revenues are also being adjusted to the needs and necessities of the long recession. Here some examples of how quickly the *yakuza* can adapt to new developments can be seen. During the height of the so-called 'bubble economy,' *yakuza* were involved in the overheated financial and real estate market, mostly in *jiage*-transactions. This meant that they harassed landowners or tenants until they vacated the object of speculation that they were occupying. Ironically the *yakuza* are now increasingly involved in the opposite kind of activity. It is they who occupy pieces of land, houses, or business premises that are to be sold off because they were used as collateral for loans. The borrower has defaulted, and in order to get its money back the bank or housing loan company wants to sell the collateral. The *yakuza* are obstructing this action and disrupting foreclosure auctions, using the same means and the same savvy with which they formerly evicted tenants.[20]

Another business opportunity – typical in times of recession – is intervention in the liquidation of bankrupt firms. The police have established a special new task force to deal with debt collection – a field in which the *yakuza* have become increasingly conspicuous in recent years (Keisatsuchō 1997: 184). One can see here that *yakuza* are highly flexible, innovative, and aggressive entrepreneurs. However it is mostly the big syndicates with their personnel, know-how, and capital, which can do big business. Small gangs are still dependent on traditional income sources. It seems that a polarization has developed between the business elite and the rank and file, or as an in-house police researcher put it, between the 'kings and beggars' (Uchida 1990: 41).

Whether because of the recession or the impact of the new law, there has even been a rise in cases of burglaries and robberies involving *yakuza* (*Asahi Shinbun* November 12 1997: 13), kinds of crime that they have traditionally despised. *Yakuza* have also moved into fields that used to be spurned as insufficiently lucrative. Since the 1990s they have become increasingly involved in human trafficking of Chinese nationals, most of them men. The trafficking of women from South East Asian countries has been organized by *yakuza* since the 1960s, but cases of smuggling male would-be workers into Japan were rare, even during the bubble era.[21] The surge in cases of illegal alien smuggling also indicates closer ties between *yakuza* and Chinese gangs abroad as well as those operating in Japan.[22]

Conclusion: *yakuza* on the defensive?

Before and after the *Bōtaihō* was enacted, the press launched an extensive information campaign, naturally with strong support from the police.[23] At the same time new centers for combating *yakuza* were founded all over the country. These centers now handle around one third of the over 30,000 annual complaints and requests for advice stemming from the new law, the rest being dealt with by the police (the number of consultations is more than eight times higher than the number of *chūshi meirei* issued annually concerning unlawful activities prohibited by the *Bōtaihō* – an indication that only a fraction of complaints are actually met with sanctions). One of the effects of the information campaign can be seen in the changed consciousness of the public. *Yakuza* complain of fewer requests for their services from ordinary citizens: this is not only due to the recession, but also due to the fact that more people now think it is wrong to employ *yakuza* for their own purposes or to solve civil disputes. The new law also encourages them to go to the police. Owners of restaurants or bars refuse payment of protection money or resist being indirectly 'taxed' by *yakuza* through being forced to buy overpriced goods, e.g. New Year decorations (Yamada et al. eds 1994: 275ff.). The *yakuza* are therefore more isolated and cut off from their former clientele. This trend, together with the tarnishing of their image, has been a blow to the yakuza. It came as a shock and the 'psychological effect' of the *Bōtaihō* may be stronger than the actual legal procedures connected with it, as Yamanouchi Yukio, scriptwriter, lawyer, and former legal consultant to the Yamaguchi-gumi has suggested.[24] Another problem the *yakuza* face is that the average age of gang members is rapidly rising. Recruiting has become more difficult (Hōmu Sōgō Kenkyūjo 1989: 349). The image of *yakuza* has been tarnished and youngsters seem to avoid them because they see the job as too demanding, dirty, and dangerous. These trends can be summed up in the catch-phrase *yakuza-banare* ('parting from the *yakuza*'), which Yamanouchi repeatedly used when I interviewed him.

The *yakuza* are on the defensive right now, but they are also restructuring their organizations and adopting counter-measures. The biggest gangs for instance hold so called '*gokudō* summits' in order to avoid conflicts and especially open gang warfare, because this would damage their image in the eyes of the public and consequently also damage business. Almost all concerted police actions against *yakuza* have been made in direct or indirect response to some long-lasting gang feud or other. In the case of the *Bōtaihō* the unprecedented scale of the war between the Yamaguchi-gumi and the Ichiwa-kai was described as the main motive for the new legislation by a representative of the police (Iwahashi 1998: 2). *Yakuza* know this and there have been several Yamaguchi-gumi internal notifications seeking to stop unnecessary disputes (Yamada et al. eds 1994: 254ff.). These moves are also reactions to the new public mood. Maybe it can be generally said that the *yakuza* have been cut down to their pre-bubble status. They will adjust to the new situation and the result will be a new equilibrium. But it is hard to assess which has actually hit the *yakuza* worse: the new legislation, or the recession. When the latter is over, it will be seen how far the *yakuza* will recover. They will certainly not just vanish: there are still too many reasons for their existence. The mere rewriting of laws will not remove organized crime from Japan, for it is far too pervasive, evasive, and innovative.

10 Houses of Everlasting Bliss: Globalization and the Production of Buddhist Altars in Hikone

Carla and Jerry Eades, Yuriko Nishiyama, and Hiroko Yanase

Introduction

Hikone is an attractive town on the eastern shore of Lake Biwa, Shiga prefecture, in the Kansai region of central Japan. One of the first sights which visitors see on arrival at the town's station is a large billboard advertising the main industries of the city: industrial valves, women's lingerie, and *butsudan*, or Buddhist altars, which are still one of the most prominent items of furniture in many households throughout the country. Hikone is one of fifteen areas designated by the Ministry of International Trade and Industry (MITI) for the production of these goods.[1] The city hall's publicity literature stresses the city's culture and history, the latter symbolized by Hikone Castle, its best-known landmark. The traditional crafts involved in *butsudan* production fit well with this image of tradition.[2]

Butsudan are intriguing items for several reasons. Firstly they bring together, at the highest level of excellence, many of the major surviving craft traditions in Japan: cabinet making (*kiji*), temple architecture in miniature (making the *kuden* or 'palace'), wood carving (*chōkoku*), lacquering (*nuri*), painting with lacquer and gold dust (*makie*), the application of gold leaf (*kinpakuoshi*), and various types of metal work (*kazari kanagu*). The assembly of the finished product from all these items (*kumitate*) is itself regarded as a separate skill.[3] Secondly, although these are in many ways deeply 'traditional' items, their production and sale is still a significant part of the local economy. A top-of-the-line *butsudan* made in the production area by MITI designated artisans can cost in excess of 20 million yen (approximately U.S.$200,000), and even 'cheaper' items at the bottom of the range will routinely cost around 3 million yen (approximately U.S.$30,000).

Tradition, of course, on closer inspection seldom proves to be pristine and unaltered from ancient times (Hobsbawm 1983), and the manufacture of *butsudan* is no exception. It has to be 'staged' to some extent for its authenticity to be established. This is indeed what happens in the Shinmachi area of Nanamagari, the street which winds through the center of the main district of Hikone concerned with the *butsudan* trade.[4] Old buildings, many dating from the Edo period (1600–1868), serve both as workshops and salesrooms for the industry, with advertisements and shop signs replete with Buddhist symbols and Edo-period calligraphy. The name of the largest firm on the street, *Eirakuya* ('House of Everlasting Bliss') complements its image as a company selling large and very expensive *butsudan* made in Hikone itself using traditional techniques. This excellence is reflected in the awards which the company often wins at the nationwide trade shows mounted by the *butsudan* industry.[5] Other large *butsudan* firms project a slightly different image. Their large showrooms display items that cover the entire price range. Increasingly, the cheaper *butsudan* and their components come from the companies' large mechanized factories and workshops in Hikone and elsewhere in Japan, or from overseas, including Taiwan, mainland China, and Vietnam.

In other words, the Buddhist altar industry, like the rest of the Japanese economy, is being affected by globalization and the regional economic integration currently taking place in East Asia. In general the manufacturers and dealers have to keep an eye on their costs and profit margins, as well as providing goods at prices that can be afforded by ordinary families. Their response is the increasing use of non-traditional production techniques, and/or components imported from neighboring countries where the labor costs are much cheaper. Yet they are still selling something which their customers regard as quintessentially 'traditional' and 'Japanese,' so the origins of these goods and the ways in which they are produced are discreetly masked by the images and language of 'tradition' which figure prominently in their publicity literature, photographs, and videos.

Another player in the game is MITI, which has its own interest in the maintenance of traditional skills and standards of production as a resource in the national economy. It has introduced a system of certification, classifying *butsudan* according to the extent of local content and the quality of artisanship. These standards are enforced by the Hikone Butsudan Jigyō Kyōdō Kumiai (Hikone Buddhist Altar Manufacturers' Cooperative Association – hereafter referred to as 'the Kumiai'), whose membership includes thirty businesses, and forty-five officially designated 'traditional artisans.' The Kumiai carries out regular inspections of items on request, and brands them with the appropriate mark of quality. However, as we shall see, the forces of globalization mean that the rules themselves have to be flexible in wording, in interpretation, and in enforcement. As Brian Moeran has pointed out in relation to the ceramics industry in Kyushu (1997), craft production in Japan involves complex decisions concerning manufacture and negotiation between artisans, merchants, consumers, and critics. For better or worse, beneath the surface of the formalized main-tenance of 'tradition,' both products and modes of production in the *butsudan* industry are gradually changing.

This paper therefore discusses the present state and the possible future of the Hikone *butsudan* industry, including production, the craft skills involved, the impact of globalization, the politics of certification, and the maintenance of quality. While the data presented here are drawn from a single industry in a single location, they do illustrate many of the tensions and paradoxes existing in craft industries throughout Japan, which owe their survival and prosperity to the successful staging of authenticity and tradition within a period of rapid economic globalization.

Hikone and *butsudan* production

The modern history of Hikone dates from the battle at nearby Sekigahara in 1600, which established Tokugawa Ieyasu's control over the country and marked the start of the Tokugawa shogunate. One of Ieyasu's generals, Ii Naomasa, particularly distinguished himself in the battle and was rewarded with the Hikone feudal domain, consisting of the lands along the eastern side of the lake. The construction of his castle began in 1603 and was completed

Figure 10.1 A typical Hikone butsudan

Photo by courtesy of Eirakuya Corporation.

by his successors over the years that followed. The central tower of the castle, one of only four original castle towers surviving in Japan, is designated as a national treasure, and is the main focus of the town's tourist industry.[6] During the Edo period, one of the routes from the farms into the city, known as Nanamagari, developed as a merchants' quarter to supply farmers' needs. It was here that *butsudan* production and sales first began, and it is here that many of the workshops and sales outlets in the local industry are still located (Ogura 1996: 13–14). Unfortunately there are few local records remaining to establish the reasons that led to the rise of the industry more precisely. Due to the structural weaknesses of the Hikone castle moat system and periods of heavy rain at the end of the nineteenth century, the Nanamagari area suffered repeatedly from severe floods. Company records were lost together with Buddhist images and texts. *Butsudan* floated, turned upside down, and sank (Nomura ed. 1977: 43), taking the wealth of many of the merchants with them.

Some accounts say that the production of *butsudan* in their modern form started in the early seventeenth century, when the Tokugawa shogunate attempted to stamp out Christianity (Boxer 1951; Elison 1973). At that time, documents were issued to show which temple each person belonged to, and installing a *butsudan* in the house was further proof of Buddhist affiliation. Ogura, however, argues that it is more likely that, at this early stage in the Edo period, proof of affiliation lay in organizing memorial ceremonies for the ancestors, which were performed by temple priests. Later, toward the end of the Edo period, *butsudan* became popular as a focus for these rituals within the household (Ogura, 1996: 15). Gradually people came to associate ancestor worship with Buddhist ritual, and the *butsudan* came to provide a setting for both.

Today's *butsudan* looks rather like a free-standing European wardrobe (see Figure 10.1). It consists of a layered base, a back and sides, and a layered top, forming a cabinet with two sets of doors in front. The decoration and range of items inside the cabinet varies slightly between different sects of Buddhism. Generally, in the lower part, there are a number of decorated drawers and compartments that are used for the storage of such things as Buddhist sutras. Above these there are platforms where offerings and the traditional five altar implements (two candlesticks, two incense burners, and a flower vase) can be placed. There is a central platform, the inner altar, on which a statue of the Buddha or a painted scroll can be put, and this in turn is usually surrounded by a complex of pillars supporting a decorative roof canopy in the shape of a miniature palace (the *kuden*). The pillars are decorated with elaborate metalwork, while the roof canopy is modeled after the intricate wooden superstructure of a Japanese temple. In front, above the inner doors, which consist of a wooden lattice with embroidered silk screens, there is a carved transom depicting natural scenes or motifs from Buddhist mythology. The set of solid wooden outer doors is usually covered with plain black lacquer to match the plain exterior. This contrasts all the more dramatically with the blaze of ornate gold decoration that is revealed when the doors are actually opened. The layout of the furnishings within the *butsudan* varies between the various sects of Japanese Buddhism.[7]

Partly because of its proximity to Hieizan, a mountain to the east of Kyoto on the border with present-day Shiga Prefecture which is a focal point for the Tendai sect, and partly because of its long farming tradition, Shiga people mainly follow Jōdoshinshū, the 'Pure Land' sect of Buddhism.[8] As ordinary people became wealthier and moved up the social ladder during the Edo period, they acquired their own Buddhist images and held prayer meetings in their houses (Fukushima 1981). As a result, when *butsudan* became increasingly popular during the middle-to-late Edo period, some people had the money needed to invest in the ornate gold *butsudan* that are now thought of as being typical of Jōdoshinshū. Much later, during the high-speed growth period of the 1960s, farmers selling off land built big houses and bought large *butsudan* to give due thanks to the ancestors. Therefore when people talk about the 'Hikone style' of *butsudan* they are referring mainly to the rather large, ostentatiously gilded styles which are popular amongst members of the Jōdoshinshū sect.[9]

Many of Hikone's *butsudan* merchants started their careers as artisans, most often as lacquerers or cabinetmakers who probably went to Kyoto to learn the craft. The work that they could not do was farmed out to other artisans clustered in the Shinmachi area of Nanamagari, and gradually the *butsudan* companies developed. Associations of merchants and artisans formed and disbanded either together or separately, depending on the needs of each group and the fortunes of the industry, but the present-day Kumiai was established in 1974. The formation of an association with both artisans and merchants as members was stipulated as a requirement for the 1975 MITI designation of Hikone as a 'Traditional

Handicraft Production Area,' specializing in *butsudan*. The criteria for the production of the higher grades of *butsudan* and procedures for the certification of artisans were also laid down at this time.

Generally it takes ten years to become a fully-fledged artisan. After working for a period of about twelve years an artisan can take an examination to become an officially registered 'traditional artisan' (*dentō kōgeishi*). The higher grades of *butsudan* are produced by these registered local artisans using a specified set of traditional methods, and their products are officially examined and certified as being of the required standard by a committee from the Kumiai.

However, alternative means of production have had to be found over the years. Originally this was because the demand for *butsudan* outstripped the production capacity during the period of high-speed growth in the 1960s. Merchants have continued to look for and use cheaper alternative methods of production to maintain their profit margins in the face of the decline in demand caused by the economic recession that set in after the collapse of the bubble economy in the early 1990s. Of course the finished products made using these cheaper methods cannot be designated as 'traditional handicraft items' (*dentōteki kōgeihin*), but the producers note that many people today, thanks to their 'reduction in religious spirit,' neither know nor care about that. The high and low quality items look the same superficially, even if the price tag is vastly different. It is said that these days the shop clerks in many of the larger *butsudan* shops are seldom sufficiently well informed to explain the differences. The Hikone merchants emphasize that only family-run businesses can fully explain to customers exactly what they are getting for their money and why one product is better than another. The companies in Hikone are largely divided into two groups: those that specialize in the most expensive and highest quality items, and those that concentrate on cheaper products which look similar but which are not made using traditional skills. The tendency in Hikone is still to turn out large, ornate *butsudan* similar to those that were popular in the earlier economic boom periods in the 1960s and 1980s, though some people say that this is at the cost of innovation and, perhaps, the long-term survival of the industry in the city.[10]

In the next section we describe the production of *dentōteki kōgeihin* together with the special skills that make a *dentō kōgeishi*. In the final section of the paper, we discuss recent changes in the business, which appear to be signaling the slow but steady demise of the traditional artisans, whose interests naturally diverge from those of the merchants. Even the merchants who are still producing and selling traditional items are more and more forced to cut corners through cheaper production techniques and/or the importation of cheaper components produced abroad, largely at the expense of the local artisans, who find themselves increasingly underemployed. Among the artisans, rumors and resentment in relation to the current situation in the *butsudan* market are rife, and they have devised various ways of coping with, or resisting, these developments.

Butsudan production: the seven crafts (*Hikone butsudan nanashoku*) [11]

The production of high-quality *butsudan* involves coordinating the skills of a number of different artisans. In the case of the larger producers, the different stages of production are carried out in their own factories, usually with some subcontracting to small craft workshops. Among the smaller makers and dealers, their part of the actual production, often including lacquering and final assembly, is carried out in their own workshops, with the other six crafts being farmed out to fellow artisans. The larger firms issue glossy catalogues and maintain Internet sites with details of their product range. It is also possible, however, for clients to go to smaller dealers and specify the precise details of the *butsudan* required, and even, in a few instances, their preferred artisans. The dealer then contacts the artisans and organizes the production and assembly of the required goods. Many of the highest quality *butsudan* are currently produced to order in this way, while for low budget items, clients are more likely to buy a standard model from the showroom of one of the larger companies.

Here we discuss the actual process of traditional production in each of the crafts, followed by the ways in which the artisans and merchants are finding it possible to reduce costs in response to the economic recession of the last decade.

Cabinetmakers (*kijishi*)

The *kijishi* is responsible for making the main cabinet of the *butsudan*, consisting of the top, base, sides, and backboards and the two sets of doors, in addition to inner parts such as platforms, doors, drawers, pillars, and the inner altar. His first step is to go to the customer's house and measure the *butsudan* space and make three special rulers (*tsue*), one for each of the three planes. These rulers provide the basic measurements for each of the constituent parts of the *butsudan*, so if there is a mistake in the rulers, it will be reflected throughout the entire piece. The next job is to select the wood, depending on the requirements and budget of the client or dealer. Red wood, toward the center of the tree trunk, is preferred because it is hard and not easily attacked by insects. The most important varieties include zelkova (*keyaki*), Hokkaido zelkova (*sen*) and Japanese cypress (*hinoki*). Both *keyaki* and *sen* have beautiful grains and are used for the front surfaces of the *butsudan*. They are especially valuable if burled, but are too expensive for all but the very highest quality items. These woods are therefore often veneered onto cheaper wood, a good quality product usually having a 3 mm thick layer of veneer. Cypress is used elsewhere in the cabinet because it resists both decay and insects. On the best quality *butsudan* all parts are finished using hand planes, and *kiji* artisans may possess over 200 different kinds of these tools.

When assembled, the pieces are held together by tenon joints or bamboo pegs rather than nails. This is a distinctive feature of Hikone *butsudan*, allowing them to be taken apart easily for cleaning and repair (*sentaku*) in the future. This is a complex process, which involves the complete dismantling of the parts, cleaning, re-gilding, re-lacquering, and reassembly. The normal life of this type of *butsudan* is up to two hundred years, and *sentaku* is carried out every thirty to fifty years, at a cost equivalent to 10–15 percent of the original price of the *butsudan*.

Kuden makers (*kudenshi*)

The woodworking artisan known as the *kudenshi* makes the model palace (*kuden*), which fits inside the upper part of the *butsudan*.

This often features a statue of the Buddha, and is thus the focal point of the interior design. It consists of the roof canopy, the complex system of beams and blocks beneath it, supporting pillars, and sometimes a base. The roof and beam system is close to being a scale model of that of a real Japanese temple (cf. Brown 1989: 101–09). Of the two main styles of *kuden*, the free-standing type is more expensive to make because it can be taken out and so has to have the same intricate work on the back as on the front. The other style, fixed permanently into the *butsudan*, does not have to be finished at the back. The designs of the roof, the complexity of the beam network and the number of pillars are all based on the design of the main temple of the particular Buddhist sect after which the style of *butsudan* is named. The main materials used are Japanese white pine, (*himekomatsu*) and Russian red pine (*benimatsu*). These woods are used most commonly because they are resinous, so that they are flexible and easy to carve. The *kudenshi* works with much smaller pieces of wood than the *kijishi*, and the final assembly is much more intricate.

Wood carvers (*chōkokushi*)

The *chōkokushi* is the artisan who makes the carvings on the *butsudan*, the main one being the front transom, which is visible when the outer doors are open. There are other smaller pieces inside the *butsudan*, on the side and back walls, between the pillars of the *kuden*, and on the inner altar. Central motifs include flowers, birds, and heavenly beings, surrounded by branches, buds, clouds, etc. It takes about six weeks to do all the work for a high-quality *butsudan*. The selection of materials is very important. After the timber has been cut into boards, as with the other crafts, the artisan dries it for at least three years. In Hikone *butsudan* carvings are usually covered with gold leaf, so often they are made with Japanese white pine, which is stable after drying, or red pine, which is comparatively cheap.

There are three styles of carving used to create the impression of varying degrees of depth and three-dimensional effects. The first type is where a design is carved on a single, thick board. In the second type, involving two layers of carving, background designs such as leaves and clouds are carved on the underneath board, while the central motifs are carved on the upper board. The layers are connected using bamboo pegs. The third type is where a top layer is added, the layers being separated by wooden blocks to produce an even more three-dimensional effect. Sometimes the wood blocks are slanted a little so as to give a sense of depth or motion such as flowers swaying in the wind, birds flying in the sky, or heavenly beings dancing.

Lacquerers (*nurishi*)

The *nurishi* is responsible for lacquering almost the entire surface of the *butsudan*, inside and outside, including those parts that will eventually be covered with gold leaf. When the *butsudan* arrives at the lacquerer, it will be completely disassembled and then reassembled after the individual parts have been treated. Lacquering can be divided into three main processes. The first is the base coating, which includes preparation of the wood and then filling and grinding it to get a completely flat surface. The second stage consists of the application of three layers of lacquer: a base coat, a middle coat, and, after wet grinding, a final coat. Third comes the finishing process, which varies depending on the quality of the item and whether or not the lacquered area will be covered with gold leaf.

The lacquer usually found on the door frames, some inside parts, the pillars, and on the outside of the *butsudan*, is the highest quality, highly polished black lacquer (*kuro roiro*). Where the lacquered parts are to be covered with gold leaf they may not be given a final polish. Another style, typical of the Hikone *butsudan* industry, is where the grain of the wood on some inside surfaces and parts of the doors is stained so that it shows through a clear lacquer coating. This is very attractive, especially where expensive wood with a beautiful grain is used.

Lacquer picture artisans (*makieshi*)

Makie literally means 'sprinkled pictures,' i.e., designs made by sprinkling gold dust onto the tacky surface of a picture painted with lacquer. The *makie* artisan draws these pictures on small door and drawer fronts and sometimes on the inner doors (*shōji*) of the *butsudan*. All *makie* artisans have their own design specialties, including landscapes, moon pictures, or flowers and birds. Autumn flowers or peonies are popular.

For *butsudan* the technique involves painting a layer of either clay or a lacquer and iron oxide (*bengara*) mixture onto the lacquered board as a base, and then applying gold powder to the half-dry surface with a silk pad, thus giving a textured effect. After the picture is finished it may be coated with a layer of lacquer and polished. This type (*migaki makie*) takes longer to do and is therefore more expensive than the unpolished kind. But it has the advantage that it can be cleaned and will not lose its beauty over the years.

Gilders (*kinpakuoshishi*)

The *kinpakuoshishi* applies gold leaf to the inside walls and doors of the *butsudan* as well as other parts, such as the shelves and platforms, the *kuden*, the carvings, ceiling, pillars, and the lattice-work of the inner doors (*shōji*). The thickness of gold leaf is about 0.1–0.2 microns, and a large *butsudan* requires 1,700 pieces. The gold leaf comes in stacks sandwiched between layers of specially made paper.

This technique requires first a thin base layer of special lacquer (*oshi urushi*) to act as an adhesive. As soon as the *urushi* is sufficiently dry and tacky the artisan applies the gold leaf with leafing chopsticks, pressing it gently against the tacky board surface. The paper falls away after the leaf has stuck to the surface. The gold leaves must be applied in the same direction or else the shine varies subtly between leaves. As each leaf sticks it wrinkles, and the artisan blows on it gently to smooth it out. Air bubbles disappear as the air seeps out through the surface of the leaf. Finally, the abutting surfaces are rubbed gently with teased silk wadding, pressing the air bubbles out completely, making it flat, and making the joins invisible by rubbing away the overlaps.

Decorative metal artisans (*kazari kanagushi*)

The metalworking artisan makes fittings to decorate all the doors, drawer fronts, pillars, and the fronts of platforms. About three hundred and fifty pieces are required for a large high-quality Hikone *butsudan*. There are two types of metal artisans. The *jibori* artisans use heat to soften the metal, so that thicker metal can be used, and the patterns are produced using carving, embossing, and punching techniques. The *kebori* or *ukibori* artisans do not use heat, so the metal must be thinner. It is not carved, but only punched and embossed. Both brass and copper are used, with thicknesses of between 0.4mm and 3.5mm. Brass is used for weight bearing fittings, such as door hinges, and copper is used for the purely decorative pieces. After the internal fittings are completed they are gold plated while external ones are covered with lacquer and fired to harden them and increase durability. Designs include flowers and birds, with a background pattern resembling fish roe to give them 'life.'

Coordinating production and final assembly

After each stage in the production process the *butsudan* cabinet with its added components is returned to the merchant, who then passes it on to the next artisan to add his contributions. Sometimes orders are sent by fax to the next artisan who therefore has little idea either of the appearance of the emerging whole or of its quality. The dealers tend not to have a single theme in mind, and seldom exchange ideas with the artisans. Neither do they give any credit to the artisans, if and when the finished *butsudan* wins an award at an exhibition.

Naturally the artisans are not happy with this. One artisan commented, 'I think we should make *butsudan* where people are aware of what skills are involved' – for example having the names of the artisans written on the certificate guaranteeing the quality of an item. 'These days, artisans are threatened by imported items. Initially many shops are started by artisans, and as the shop takes off, they want to push forward the "shop" image. They are more interested in profits, and de-emphasize the role played by the artisans.' Increasingly the artisans are finding themselves underemployed, while a growing proportion of *butsudan* are being produced using cheaper techniques or imported components, or are even being imported ready-made.

The response to social change and economic recession

The discussion of the various production processes given above is basically that of the traditional methods used in the highest quality *butsudan*. However, interviews with artisans and dealers suggest that the industry is under considerable pressure from a number of quarters, and many people are seriously concerned about its long-term future.

A number of these factors relate to demand. The most important and most obvious of these is the recession in the Japanese economy, which has led to a slump in consumption and rising unemployment since the collapse of the bubble economy in the early 1990s. Because *butsudan* are essentially luxury items, the purchase of which can be put off if necessary, many dealers report that their sales are a fraction of what they were a decade ago.

Second, the slump in sales of Hikone *butsudan* is exacerbated by changes in the Japanese family and housing patterns. Traditionally, the *butsudan* was inherited by the eldest son and his family, the 'main household' (*honke*), though on occasions another household within the extended family might also acquire a *butsudan* as a 'branch' household of the family (*bunke*). However, looking after the *butsudan* is increasingly seen as an expensive chore. The rapid process of urbanization since the Second World War means that many people now live in small city apartments rather than large rural houses, and there is simply no room for a large traditional *butsudan*. During the period of high-speed growth in the 1960s and the bubble economy in the 1980s, demand did increase for a while as newly-rich families invested their rising salaries, their investment income, or the proceeds from land sales in expensive *butsudan*. During the 1990s, however, the market contracted.

The sharp and rapid decline in the Japanese birthrate during the same period means that there are now fewer children available and willing to take on *butsudan* maintenance. Every generation or so the *butsudan* should ideally be sent back to the dealer for *sentaku*, and this renovation can be very expensive. Many younger people moving house or selling up their parents' house take the opportunity either to exchange the *butsudan* for a smaller model, or to do away with it completely.[12] One of the worries within the Hikone industry is that, unlike some other production areas, the Hikone artisans and dealers are simply not producing the smaller and less ornate designs which are required by contemporary lifestyles. Dealers see a loss of interest in traditional religion among younger Japanese as a further factor affecting sales.

Even if dealers can do little about the long-term decline in demand and the social and economic reasons for it, they can at least attempt to maintain their profit margins in a number of ways, by using cheaper production techniques and by bringing in cheaper imported components from other parts of Asia, mainly Taiwan, China, and Vietnam. Similar craft traditions linked to Buddhism exist there, and levels of skill and workmanship are not necessarily any lower than in Japan, but labor is of course much cheaper. In some cases, completed *butsudan*, already lacquered and gilded, are being imported from China ready for sale in Japan. Sometimes materials are sent abroad for manufacture and assembly in whole or in part, and then shipped back to Japan. The situation in each of the crafts is broadly as follows.

The wooden frame (*kiji*) will eventually be covered with lacquer and gold so that the customers may never know what is underneath. They may be getting plywood instead of solid cypress or zelkova, and unless they enquire (and Japanese consumers tend not to) they will not know that. It is not unheard of to apply paper with a printed grain to the surface instead of real wood veneer, and then to put clear lacquer on top. When making the various parts, computerized machines may be used to do up to eight jobs at a time.

Carvings were actually the first items to be imported for use in *butsudan*. This was done initially to keep up with demand during the period of high-speed growth in the 1960s, rather than as a means of keeping down costs. They have become increasingly common over the last twenty years. The first imported carvings came from Korea, but as they became too expensive the middlemen turned to Taiwan and now, increasingly, they look to China and Vietnam. These days a carved front transom imported from China is a quarter the cost of one made in Japan, so it is easy to see why they are used in these times of recession.

The merchants explain that the carvings are just as good as the Japanese ones, and that the reason they use them is that there are so few artisans working these days in Japan. However, this does not entirely square with the apparent underemployment among the artisans, some of whom are sitting at home and making goods which remain in their workshops unsold, just to keep busy. If they are lucky, some of them can find other outlets for their work, such as restoration work on temples, shrines or festival floats.[13] Some of them attempt to expand their range, by producing secular art for the general market. But the artisans say generally that their workload in *butsudan* production is between a half and a third of what it was ten years ago. Significantly the number of qualified *dentō kōgeishi* carvers at present is smaller than the number of qualified artisans in other crafts. Carvers experienced competition from imports early on, while the other artisans have felt the impact of the recession more recently.

If a complete butsudan is imported, the lacquer work (*nuri*) will have already been done. But sometimes the complete frame is brought from abroad with only the base coat already applied. The rest is done in Japan. Many shops no longer use real lacquer on cheaper goods at all. They formerly used a natural cashew that appeared on the market about thirty years ago, and now they use a synthetic cashew 'lacquer' or even polyurethane. These can all be applied either by spray or by dipping in a vat. Sometimes a layer of real lacquer will be applied by brush or spatula over a layer of sprayed 'lacquer' and the piece is then sold as a 'genuine' Japanese lacquered *butsudan*.

The same cost-cutting methods are used with the lacquered baseboards for the *makie* paintings. In addition, the *makie* designs may come in the form of ready-made plastic pictures on a plastic backing which can simply be peeled off and stuck on the work, or as a stencil covered with a fine mesh which can be painted over with a few brush strokes. But hand-drawn *makie* pictures, like carvings, have also started to come in from China, Taiwan, Korea, and even Vietnam. Often the designs themselves are actually Japanese, as one artisan described: 'Trading companies teach them how to make the items and then they import them at maybe half the cost. They send out photocopies of the finished picture or sometimes the actual boards done by local artisans.' Generally people in the trade say that they can tell the difference between the local and imported items. In part this is because the materials themselves look wrong: 'the gold is very shiny and doesn't have a refined feeling.'

The copying of their work abroad is an important issue for the artisans. Sometimes when their work is displayed at exhibitions they are worried that the designs will be photographed, copied, and sent away to be mass-produced. One artisan described the production process in Taiwan: 'I actually went to Taiwan and saw the factory. The work is done by assembly line. The person who wipes the board does only that. The person who draws the lines does only that. The person just draws the same line time after time. The person who applies powder does only that. Moreover they make dozens and hundreds of pictures of the same pattern. They can stare into space while they are working. There are stacks and stacks of boards with the same designs piled up in the workshop.' The response of some artisans has been to try and produce designs which are either difficult to copy because of the skill required, or not worth copying because of the low cost.

Imports have also become significant at the stage of gold leaf application. 'Now completed *butsudan* come in from China. Leaf is already applied and they are ready for sale. Someone from Japan teaches the people [in China] how to apply [the leaf] and has local people do the work.' Costs can be cut in other ways as well. In the case of the most expensive gold leaf, each piece is cut individually, but another, cheaper type of leaf can be used, where the makers cut it in a stack of more than a thousand pieces, interleaved with paper, at less than half the cost. Additionally, on lattices such as are found on the inner doors or the ceiling, 'machine leaf' may be used. Here, a thin layer of gold colored aluminum paint is sprayed onto a cellophane backing to be ironed on to the surface of the wood. Sometimes yellow lacquer is used as a base so that when the gold is applied any imperfections in the gilding will not show.

As far as decorative metal fittings are concerned, pressed and electroplated goods produced in Japan appeared on the market some twenty or thirty years ago. In both of these techniques a prototype made in the traditional way is used as a model. 'The difference between the hand-made fittings and "pressed" goods is that the machine punches the whole shape and pattern at one time so there is no variation,' explains one craftsman. Electroplated fittings are made of pure copper, but they are softer and lighter than hand-made ones. Sometimes a few touches are added by hand to machine-made fittings at the end of production so that it can be claimed that they are 'hand-made.' The artisans differ in their accounts of whether pressed and electroplated goods come from abroad, but certainly hand-made fittings do come from China. The merchants take the fittings to China, get them copied, and then send them back to Japan: 'Ten artisans do one stage of the process. For each artisan at each stage the process is simple and they can make many copies efficiently, but it has no soul!'

Conclusion: thinking locally, producing globally

As can be seen from the above discussion, even this most 'traditional' and 'authentic' of Japanese craft industries has not been immune to the effects of globalization of production during the post-war period, or the 'Heisei Recession' since the end of the Japanese bubble economy. Global economic forces, together with the long term Japanese social trends of secularization, urbanization, the declining birth-rate, and changes in house design have resulted in considerable fluctuations in the demand for *butsudan* over the years, rising during the periods of high-speed growth and the bubble economy, and declining sharply since.

After Hikone's designation by MITI as a Butsudan Production Area in 1975, the industry underwent a period of great expansion during which the local shops increased the number and size of their sales outlets. They also modernized or built additional factories within Hikone, in other parts of Japan, or even abroad. The artisans built new houses, new workshops, or extensions to their existing houses. Some of them branched out into selling *butsudan*, only to be discouraged by pressure from the existing dealers. Gradually a small number of dealers have gained control of more and more of the market, so that at present there are three or four major dealers operating alongside many more very small businesses. Even in the bubble economy period, some of the smaller businesses were selling only about twenty-five *butsudan* a year, compared with around 800 for the larger companies. In order to keep up with demand, the dealers found cheaper alternative forms of production and sources of components, purchasing them overseas or producing them in their own factories there. These alternatives are now keeping some of the dealers going during the prolonged recession, even though many of the artisans and smaller merchants, some of whom are artisans themselves, are underemployed.

Despite the show of solidarity between merchants and artisans on occasions such as the annual exhibitions at local and national level, or the '*Butsudan* Experience' days organized recently in the city to increase interest in its main traditional industry, it is clear that the interests of the artisans and the merchants, as well as those of the large-scale and small-scale merchants, have increasingly diverged as a result of the post-bubble recession. The big dealers who had the capital needed to set up their own factories abroad have moved into mass production, taking over an increasing share of the wholesale business at the expense of the smaller firms. This process is not complete, in that all the dealers, both large- and small-scale, are still ostensibly involved in both the wholesale and retail businesses. They all say that they deal in both cheaper items and high-quality traditional items, even if, in the case of small businesses, they only sell one high-quality item every one or two years. However, the domination of the market by the larger dealers may become more marked in the future.

The industry in Hikone as a whole, however, is also still concerned with the maintenance of standards, to protect the high quality which they see as the hallmark of the Hikone *butsudan*. Although the national recession has reduced demand, at the same time MITI has been fairly successful in controlling supply. The number of MITI-designated *butsudan* production areas is still fairly limited (fifteen in Japan as a whole), and the producers are therefore trying to attract a national as well as a local clientele. If differences in technique and materials are difficult for the layman to spot, one way to ensure value for money is to be able to guarantee the quality of the workmanship and the quality and origin of the materials in the finest and most expensive items.

Recently the Hikone Kumiai decided to lay down quite strict specifications for the production of traditional Hikone *butsudan*. They specified three levels, depending on the quality of materials and traditional handicraft skills employed, the highest being *dentōteki kōgeihin*. The rules stipulate that *butsudan* of the highest quality have to be made by local artisans, using the kinds of traditional techniques described above, and that the materials should come from the locality, or at least from within Japan. These *butsudan* are examined by the Kumiai and given a brand, a stamp and a certificate of authenticity issued under the auspices of MITI. The use of imported components is not allowed in the case of these high-quality items. Though metal fittings can be machine-made, everything else must be produced locally using traditional local materials. A certain proportion of the work on the highest grade of *butsudan* must be carried out by registered *dentō kōgeishi*.

Even with the highest quality of goods there is some room for latitude however. For example, according to the leaflet on certification issued by the Kumiai, natural wood is 'preferred' but not absolutely stipulated and chemical 'lacquer' is 'allowed' in some places even though it is not as good as real lacquer. In practice, therefore, inspection and certification are political processes involving negotiation between the Kumiai inspection committee, who sometimes 'forget to brush up on the rules,' and the merchants – who, of course, are also members of the Kumiai. Otherwise, as one informant noted, 'no one would pass!'

What about the future? Given the importance of *butsudan* in Japanese social and religious life, it is probable that at least some demand for then will continue, even though the number of official Production Areas may eventually be reduced, and even though much of the production will be of smaller items. The change in patterns of housing, from large traditional houses to smaller apartments, means that many people who want *butsudan* want smaller, simpler, and cheaper ones that require less space, or which can even hang on the wall. Even though the large, expensive, and very ornate *butsudan* that Hikone is so famous for are increasingly unsuitable for today's market, so far the local industry has been slow to develop alternative products.

Demand will also continue to be extremely sensitive to the fluctuations in the Japanese economy. As one artisan said, 'it's not like a car that you replace every few years. Once you have a *butsudan* it should be good for some 200 years…And even if the economy picks up, ours will be one of the last sectors to recover, because it is not an indispensable item in people's lives.'

The market for these goods will probably be increasingly dominated by just a few large wholesaling and retailing firms, as has happened in Hikone recently. With the integration of the East Asian economy, it is also likely that an increasing percentage of the content will come from abroad, with producers continuing to turn to cheaper labor markets, such as inland China, Vietnam, or Indonesia, as wage levels in other areas rise. It is difficult to see MITI standards and certification protecting Japanese production, simply because the high-priced items to which they apply will form an increasingly small proportion of sales. Indeed, the whole concept of 'local production areas' will become increasingly anachronistic as production moves offshore, and as marketing comes to be dominated by regional or national rather than local firms.

The smaller dealers may be able to maintain a niche for themselves in the market in the medium term, but perhaps not in the longer term. It is interesting to note that the three or four largest firms in Hikone have presidents who began their careers in marketing rather than as artisans. The smaller dealers running small family businesses are usually artisans themselves. When they get a one-off order for a high-quality *butsudan*, they are in a position to be able to do some of the most laborious and expensive work themselves, thus reducing costs and enabling them to continue to compete with the big companies. High-quality, high-price *butsudan* may continue as a niche market, holding a small percentage of the total trade, but even these dealers may increasingly have to look for their skilled artisans offshore, as the importance of the production area continues to decline.

The future of the artisans themselves is the most problematic of all. The power in the industry will increasingly lie with those who have capital, i.e. the larger companies rather than the small dealers and artisans. A small number of skilled artisans will be retained by the big companies, for repair, restoration, and the finishing of imported goods, in addition to turning out a small number of high-quality items for discerning clients for whom money is no object. Others may turn their skills to non-*butsudan* work, while yet others may simply leave the trade. Already there is a crisis in recruitment to the ranks of artisans, where young people are often actively discouraged by today's artisans. Unless the state takes over and institutionalizes the training process, the skills may gradually disappear, despite the best efforts of MITI and the local organizations to protect them. Even in this most traditional and authentic of Japanese industries, the forces of globalization will be difficult to resist or reverse in the twenty-first century.

11 A Mountain of Problems: Ethnography Among Mount Haguro's Feuding *Yamabushi*

Andreas Riessland

In accordance with this volume's leitmotif, this paper is about socio-cultural change. It takes a look at Mount Haguro, one of Northern Japan's traditional religious centers, and at the various social, economic, and political developments that have created, and still go on shaping, the very unique religious environment on and around this mountain. Yet the main focus of this paper is not on the changes at Mount Haguro as such. It is rather on the question of doing research within such an environment, and on the influences that its changes can have on the research situation.

This paper is about change as an obstacle to social research, as one of the incalculables in ethnographic fieldwork. It is about the unsettling experience in the field when one realizes that certain changes in the research situation – sudden, unforeseeable events, or gradual changes such as growing emotional involvement with the field – have altered one's position in such a way that a successful continuation of the research project becomes questionable. It is also concerned with a question that has bothered field researchers ever since Cushing's troubled encounters with the Zuni in the 1870s (Cushing 1967 [1882–83]), namely how they should interact with those they set out to investigate, and how far they should permit themselves to become involved in the processes they witness in the field.

Much of this long and controversial discussion in the social sciences is reflected in the substantial body of literature on fieldwork problems, on professional ethics and responsibilities, and on the fieldworker's 'unending dialectic between the role of member (participant) and stranger (observer and reporter)' (Hughes 1960: xi). What many of these publications have in common is that though they give extensive coverage to the many questions concerning the researcher's potential influences on the field, they dedicate relatively little attention to the other half of this equation (and one of themes of this article), the question of how the field may influence the researcher (Sjoberg 1967; Barnes 1979; Cassel and Wax eds 1980; Bulmer ed. 1982; Beauchamp 1982).

The background of this article is my experience with a group of religious ascetics known as the Haguro *yamabushi*, at Mount Haguro, on the Japan Sea side of Yamagata Prefecture in Northern Japan. Every year in late August, two groups of these ascetics, affiliated with different religious organizations, convene at this mountain and undergo a prolonged ascetic retreat known as the *Aki no Mine*, or 'autumn peak.' In the summer of 1995, one of these two *yamabushi* groups admitted me as a participant in their *Aki no Mine* at Kōtakuji temple on Mount Haguro. When I joined the group in Toge village at the foot of Mount Haguro, I expected a purely spiritual event, but soon our retreat developed an unforeseen political dimension when it turned out that the two religious organizations at Mount Haguro, after decades of apparently peaceful coexistence, had become entangled in a heated controversy over a planned road on the mountain.

This article is an anatomy of this conflict of beliefs, a portrait of the competition between two religious organizations over their common spiritual heritage. It looks at the two rivals' long and troubled relationship, at their conflicting interests, dogmatic incompatibilities and the still rankling memories of past injustices, and it tries to show why at Mount Haguro, even a seemingly unrelated matter such as a planned road can become a potent issue in the competition between two rivals, powerful enough to make one of them abandon one of their most coveted ritual principles. In addition, it is a portrait of my own situation in this conflict, highlighting how the events at Mount Haguro, in which I had intended to be merely a bystander and observer, began to involve me personally in a way which was obviously beyond my control, so that in the end I found myself in a virtual no-win situation, forced into a decision between personal engagement and professional interests.

The events of the past still play an important role in Mount Haguro's religious life. Accordingly, this article gives ample space to the history of the troubles at Mount Haguro, tracing them back to the specific point of their beginning, when a single administrative decision by the first Meiji government in effect created the Haguro rivalry, as a lasting troublesome after-effect of a political situation that has long since disappeared. In this respect, this paper may also serve as a reflection on continuity and *lack* of change, as illustrated by the remarkable resilience of this conflict, which, after more than 120 years of social and political change, still troubles Mount Haguro's rival *yamabushi* groups.

The *yamabushi* of Mount Haguro

The term *yamabushi*, 'those who sleep on the mountain,' is a generic term referring to the practitioners of Shugendō, an arcane religion whose central tenet is the practice of ascetic exercises on particular sacred mountains (Miyake 1989, 1996). Shugendō is a syncretistic belief that combines esoteric Buddhist teachings with Japanese indigenous traditions of mountain veneration, but it also draws from a multitude of other sources such as Daoism, numerology, and geomancy. As a religious phenomenon, Shugendō is somewhat eccentric. It has no central founder figure or object of veneration, there is no religious genealogy, and each one of the various *yamabushi* orders has its own cosmology. Moreover, Shugendō has no religious establishment as such, as all *yamabushi* orders are, in some way or other, attached to other religious groups. Most are affiliated with Buddhism's esoteric schools, Tendai or Shingon. Of the two *yamabushi* groups at Mount Haguro, one is linked to the mountain's large Shintō shrine, the Dewa Sanzan Jinja, and is itself strictly Shintō. The rival 'Mount Haguro Shugendō Main Chapter' (Hagurosan Shugendō Sōhonbu) at Kōtakuji, on the other hand, has close ties with the Tendai Buddhist sect. In accordance with their religion's esoteric character, Shugendō's followers treat their spiritual teachings as secret knowledge, open only to the initiated, and their unwillingness to reveal their knowledge to outsiders has ensured that, up until the present day, relatively little has been published about the spiritual life of the *yamabushi*.

Today, Shugendō plays a very marginal role in Japan's religious environment. Yet prior to its prohibition in 1872, this religion was one of the most vital influences in the spiritual life of Japan's population, and the numerous references to *yamabushi* in Japanese pre-modern literature, as well as the many mountain temples and shrines in Japan that still carry traces of onetime Shugendō practice, bear witness to the spread and the popularity that this religion once had. Particularly in Japan's rural areas, the population often depended on the services of mendicant or resident *yamabushi* for their spiritual needs, and with their popularity as pilgrimage destinations, the great Shugendō centers in Honshu, Kyushu, and Shikoku developed into wealthy and influential religious institutions. Towards the end of the Edo period, an estimated 170,000 *sendatsu*, or ordained Shugendō priests, were affiliated with the various rival *yamabushi* organizations (Nakayama 1930: 425). For the northwest of Japan, the center at Mount Haguro was the most important, both as a place of pilgrimage for lay people and as a practice ground for ascetics.

The priests and ascetics of Mount Haguro followed a ceremonial calendar which demanded regular and prolonged retreats on Mount Haguro and the neighboring Mount Yudono and Gassan (the 'Three Dewa Mountains,' sacred to Haguro Shugendō), to perform the elaborate rituals and the strict regimen of ascetic exercises which, it was said, would enable them to achieve outstanding spiritual powers. Of these retreats, the *Aki no Mine* was the most significant, for it was not only the most excruciating exercise, initially lasting up to 75 days, but it also served as the *Shusse no Mine*, or 'promotion peak' which decided the individual member's position within the Haguro *yamabushi* hierarchy.

Lasting a mere seven days, today's *Aki no Mine* is physically much less demanding than its 75-day predecessor, but as for the complexity of its rituals and its role in determining hierarchy within Haguro Shugendō, it has lost little of its significance. Both in its function and in its choice of symbols, the *Aki no Mine* is an exemplary model of an initiation rite, a *rite de passage* by which the individual is transported from a less exalted stage of existence to a higher one. In the act, the individual has to pass through an extended liminal phase during which the actual change is accomplished. In the *Aki no Mine*, every symbol, every ritual, and every exercise serves to mark this liminality. The abolition of customary concepts of space and time, the prohibition of certain everyday terms, the fasting, the ritual seclusion at Kōtakuji temple, the many acts and symbols relating to death, conception, gestation and rebirth, the various performances that symbolize one's way through the ten (or, according to interpretation, the lower six) Buddhist realms of being, the *saitō goma* fire ritual in which both the participants' bodies and their earthly desires are symbolically burned away – every single element of the *Aki no Mine* serves to underscore its exceptional and out-of-this-world character, and the other-worldly, vulnerable state of being of its participants.[1]

This is, in short, how the literature on Haguro Shugendō sums up the meaning of the *Aki no Mine*, and as part of my own mental research kit, I found these explanatory models very helpful during my participation in it while I tried to make sense of its many complex rituals and ambiguous symbols. These explanations were further supported by the *sendatsu* and the veteran *yamabushi*, who also portrayed the *Aki no Mine* as a rite of passage and emphasized its importance as a liminal space. So with the explanations of both outside observers and insider participants in unison, I had little reason to doubt that for the Haguro *yamabushi*, the *Aki no Mine* did indeed happen in a world outside of this world, in a time beyond time, and that for the duration of their seclusion, participants moved in a different reality.

Yet on the third day of our retreat, our blissfully secluded existence at Kōtakuji was suddenly interrupted by the intrusion of an utterly non-spiritual, profane matter which instantly brought us back into the world which we had, I thought, left behind. On the morning of that day, we were called together at the temple's main hall, but instead of the expected prayer session we were treated to an impromptu lecture by one of the *sendatsu* about the prefectural government's plan to build a new road up Mount Haguro. The purpose of this new road, he said, was to make Dewa Sanzan Jinja more easily accessible for tour buses, but the worrisome part was that the planned new route would bring the road significantly closer to Kōtakuji temple, and it would seriously impede, if not utterly terminate, the *Aki no Mine* of the Kōtakuji *yamabushi*. Therefore, several members of the Kōtakuji *yamabushi* community had founded the Kōtakuji o Mamoru Kai (Kōtakuji Protection Association), an initiative with the declared goal of creating publicity for their plight and thereby generating enough political pressure to effect a cancellation of the road plans. His lecture was followed by a lengthy discussion among the *Aki no Mine* participants about this matter, and afterwards those of us who were interested were invited to join the *sendatsu* in a visit to the proposed building site. Cars stood ready outside the temple precincts, and most of us did indeed make use of this officially sanctioned chance to leave the temple, not so much to inspect the proposed road as to escape the confinements of the *Aki no Mine* and stretch our legs for a while. Consequently, the overall mood during our visit to the site had more in common with a high school outing than with the political event it was supposed to be. After about an hour, we were back at Kōtakuji, where the strict regimen and routine of the *Aki no Mine* embraced us again.

In hindsight, this episode left me somewhat perplexed. With our leaders' permanent emphasis on the serious and sacred nature of our endeavor, how was it possible that a matter of such profane nature was permitted to enter the domain of our solemn seclusion? We were supposed to be somewhere deep in limbo, passing through the various realms of being while our newly conceived and vulnerable selves, cocooned in the womb of the mountain, were to direct all their energies toward the difficult task of being reborn. So how could this matter be of any concern to us while we were, in a spiritual way, not even of this world? Of course, the new road plans were of crucial importance for the Kōtakuji *yamabushi* community, but wasn't there room for all this after the conclusion of the *Aki no Mine*? And how come the other *gaijin* (foreign) participant and I seemed to be the only ones who worried about these questions?

In the following days, the two of us repeatedly tried to raise this matter with our fellow participants, but in response we got very little beyond the customary defense against obstinate children and *gaijin* anthropologists, a thoughtful drawn-out 'Sō desu ne...' ('Yes, I see...') which successfully terminates any discussion before it can even begin. Toward the end of the *Aki no Mine*, though, we had a chance to discuss this matter with Shimazu Kōkai, the *daisendatsu* (the nominal head of Kōtakuji's *yamabushi* organization), with the *sendatsu* who, as the spokesman of the Kōtakuji o Mamoru Kai, had briefed us about the road plans, and with several other members of the Kōtakuji o Mamoru Kai.

Asked about the nonchalance with which rules that we had believed absolute and binding were disobeyed during the *Aki no*

Mine, the *daisendatsu* answered that he was indeed aware of violations of rules, but that he saw little merit in enforcing an overly strict regimen. On the contrary, he often made a conscious effort to overlook such transgressions. Of course, he said, certain essential rules were beyond dispute, but apart from these, the matter of obeisance or disregard of the rules was in the hands of the participants themselves. To illustrate his attitude, the *daisendatsu* pointed out the mandatory fasting and its rather liberal interpretation by some participants ('As eating involves chewing, candies are permissible, as long as I do not chew them'), which contrasts starkly with the attitude of others who continue to abstain from food long after the mandatory fasting period has ended. Ultimately, he said, it is up to the individual members and their conscience to decide how strictly the rules are adhered to.

Yet the case of the Kōtakuji o Mamoru Kai lecture, he said, had been different. This went clearly beyond individual responsibility, it concerned the whole community, and it did indeed constitute a serious breach of the *Aki no Mine* ceremonial agenda. Consequently, the decision whether or not to permit the lecture had been made in a far from nonchalant manner, and those involved in this decision had given their go-ahead only because of the vital importance of this matter for the Kōtakuji *yamabushi* community as a whole, and only after it was clear that no alternative date before or after the *Aki no Mine* could be found. Yet even then, he said, the decision had been far from unanimous.

The *sendatsu* and the other members of the Kōtakuji o Mamoru Kai agreed with the explanations of the *daisendatsu*. For them, to request permission for staging a lecture during the *Aki no Mine* would have been utterly out of question, had it not been for the gravity and the urgency of the matter at hand. This extraordinary situation called for an extraordinary response, and in their eyes this was a far from ordinary matter: the troublesome road plans, they were convinced, were no brainchild of an incompetent or insensitive road planning department in far-off Yamagata City, but the direct result of the politicking going on over at Dewa Sanzan Jinja. For them, this new road was nothing more than yet another attempt by the leadership of the Shintō organization to elbow Kōtakuji out of the religious business at Mount Haguro. Of course, they were quick to assure us, no one among them was keen on an open confrontation between the two groups, but if the Jinja was going to push ahead with the planned road, the Kōtakuji *yamabushi*, or at least those in the Kōtakuji o Mamoru Kai, were not going to stand idly by.

These remarks made me realize that until then, I had seriously misinterpreted the relationship between the two religious institutions on Mount Haguro. That there was rivalry between the two *yamabushi* organizations was common knowledge in the Haguro area, but from what I had heard and read until then, this rivalry seemed to be nothing but the vague aversion found in any competitive situation, a dislike that might show through in the odd sarcastic comment and in the marked indifference that the two groups displayed toward each other, but nothing more. If anything, this religious competition seemed more likely to enhance Mount Haguro's particular appeal than to cause any serious disturbance.

In view of the antagonism between the two institutions, my own situation in this local power struggle also started to look more precarious than I had been aware of. My participation in the *Aki no Mine* was, after all, the first time that I had become closely involved with the Kōtakuji *yamabushi* group. Until then, most of the events I had attended at Mount Haguro had been organized or co-sponsored by Dewa Sanzan Jinja. Much of the support for my research had also come, directly or indirectly, from the Jinja. My host and main contact in the area was a Shintō *yamabushi*, and almost everyone else I knew around Mount Haguro was in some way affiliated with its Shintō institutions.

These close ties with the Shintō side were at least partly responsible for my relative ignorance about the conflict. During my prior stays at Mount Haguro, there had never been any talk of rivalry between the two groups. In my interviews with the representatives of the Shintō establishment, no one had ever mentioned this topic. Most of the Jinja-related publications and exhibitions about Mount Haguro's religious life were conspicuously silent about the existence of a rival *yamabushi* group (in return, many academic publications on Haguro Shugendō largely ignore the Shintō *yamabushi*; see below), and when I questioned my personal acquaintances about the relationship between the two groups, they would speak about it only in very general and noncommittal terms. In short, the religious quarrel at

Mount Haguro was a matter that was not talked about, in particular not with an outsider such as myself.

At Kōtakuji, the situation was completely different: the conflict between the two rivals was openly discussed, and my presence apparently did not cause anyone to hold back in their very outspoken, and at times very angry, criticisms of the Jinja's actions. Partly, the Kōtakuji members' willingness to discuss their troubles in public and without any restraints was because they were aware that any public attention in this matter was to their advantage. The management of Dewa Sanzan Jinja had a vital interest in keeping rumors about the quarrels at Mount Haguro at bay, for any bad publicity was likely to damage the business side of their religious enterprise. For the much smaller and less well-connected Kōtakuji group, on the other hand, this susceptibility of the Shintō organization to bad publicity was exactly why they tried to raise this matter in public.

But their frankness toward me was also due to the insider status that I enjoyed in their group. Participation in the *Aki no Mine* had designated me as a regular member of Kōtakuji's *yamabushi* community, with the same rights and obligations as any other member. My acceptance into the group had been formally marked by the bestowal of a new name,[2] and from now on, I would be identified through my affiliation with the Kōtakuji *yamabushi* group.[3] The group's concerns had become my concerns, and this meant that there was no further need for the other members to hold back in their opinion about their opponents.

Consequently, I got a much closer look at the religious rivalry of Mount Haguro during the *Aki no Mine* than during my former visits to the area. With the Kōtakuji *yamabushi*, I was able to speak about topics that formerly I had thought too sensitive, and the background details which I was given so freely helped me to fill in several of the blank spaces that had until then hampered my understanding of the two rivals' relationship. The picture that emerged from these conversations was far from the simplistic 'Kōtakuji spirituality vs. Dewa Sanzan Jinja business acumen' equation which some of Kōtakuji's more hot-headed members propounded. It was rather the tangled story of two religious groups who find themselves saddled with a common spiritual heritage, of two organizations whose similar interests and contrary philosophies keep them in permanent conflict, and of a political decision 130 years ago whose reverberations are still felt today.

The divided faith of Haguro Shugendō – a short history[4]

The origins of the conflict on Mount Haguro go back to the year 1868, when the reform-minded Meiji government proclaimed, through its *jinbutsu bunri* edict, a new policy of strict separation between Shintō and Buddhist religious establishments. One outcome of this policy was that the religious institutions at Mount Haguro became the target of a successful reform effort by the government's bureaucrats – successful inasmuch as it almost completely annihilated the Shugendō tradition of Mount Haguro.

Judging from its present-day appearance – a pilgrimage place and tourist destination of mainly local importance – one wonders what it was about this picturesque little place deep in the hinterland of Upper Honshu that attracted the full brunt of the government's reform zeal. But if one looks at the historical development of the Haguro Shugendō community, it becomes clear that from the Meiji bureaucrats' point of view Haguro did indeed pose a threat that needed to be taken care of.

Building on a long tradition of mountain veneration in the region, the Dewa Mountains had, since the Nara period (710–794), been popular both as a pilgrimage destination and as a place for the practice of religious austerities. With the growing stream of pilgrims and ascetics, the doctrine and religious practices of the Shugendō sects in the Kinki region must have been brought to this area, for since the Heian period (794–1185), the Dewa Mountains had been known as a place for the practice of Shugendō rites. Over the years, the local community of Shugendō followers began to develop its own traditions and create its own foundation myth, and it finally established itself as an autonomous Shugendō branch, named after the location of its spiritual and administrative headquarters, Mount Haguro. With their populist religion and the manifold spiritual services they had to offer,[5] Haguro Shugendō's mendicant priests and ascetics managed to attract a considerable following among the populace in the Kanto region, and consequently, the Shugendō organization at Mount Haguro became one of the most powerful religious institutions in northeastern Japan, with substantial wealth, and considerable religious and political influence in the region.

During the Edo period, the Haguro Shugendō branch achieved even greater prominence among the rival Shugendō sects, in particular after the government-enforced subordination of the *yamabushi* to the authority of two Shugendō branches linked to the Buddhist Shingon and Tendai sects. While this stripped practically all of Japan's many Shugendō associations of their autonomy, the community at Mount Haguro, with its many formal and informal ties to the Tokugawa clan and the Imperial Household, was one of the few to escape this subordination policy and to maintain its status as an independent and self-governed religious body. In due course, Mount Haguro was able to assert itself alongside the two Buddhist-affiliated umbrella organizations, and to claim the whole northeast of Japan as its exclusive sphere of influence.[6]

With the demise of the Tokugawa shogunate, the fortunes of the spiritual community at Mount Haguro took a turn for the worse. The new Meiji government, intent on dismantling the former administration's power network among the country's religious organizations, decided to implement a policy of strict separation between Buddhist and Shintō institutions and their respective properties and rights. In light of this new policy, Mount Haguro's *yamabushi* order – powerful, independent, and propagating a creed that was in open contradiction to the government's ideology of religious separation – simply was not tolerable.

Consequently, it was decided that the religious organization on Mount Haguro was to be brought into line. In 1870, the government decreed that Mount Haguro's largest establishment, the Haguro Gongen hall, should be renamed 'Ideha Jinja' and declared a Shintō shrine, and that its priests were to either reorganize along Shintō lines or leave. Yet this measure proved far from efficient – formally, the Haguro *yamabushi* complied, but apart from a few cosmetic changes, everything remained pretty much the same. Of course it was only a matter of time until the authorities realized that more drastic measures were required, and in 1873, on the timely death of the *bettō* (abbot) at Mount Haguro, they installed Nishikawa Sugao as the new head, a religious hard-liner whose declared goal was to dismantle this 'bulwark of Shintō-Buddhist mish-mash' ('*shinbutsu konkō no nejiro*,' Hayashi ed. 1993: 97).

Three years later, when Nishikawa was recalled from his office, the Shugendō establishment on Mount Haguro had practically ceased to exist: of the more than 100 temples, monasteries and other religious institutions on and around the mountain, only three had survived the purge unscathed. Fifty-one were now officially part of the newly established Shintō enterprise, and the remainder – more than sixty – had been destroyed. For Mount Haguro's community of several thousand *yamabushi*, the effect of this transformation had been equally hurtful. Some had decided to side with Mount Haguro's new management and had taken office in one of the many new Shintō shrines, others had regrouped under the umbrella of the Buddhist Tendai sect. The large majority of *yamabushi*, though, had secularized and turned to other sources of income.

Yet in spite of this serious blow to its spiritual center, the religious practice of Haguro Shugendō managed to survive, albeit on a greatly diminished scale. One of the driving forces behind its survival was the small group of Tendai-affiliated *yamabushi* who, now officially as Buddhists, continued to perform the old Shugendō rituals at the traditional places of worship, in defiance of Mount Haguro's new owners. Ironically, the management of Ideha Jinja (today's Dewa Sanzan Jinja) also had a vital interest in keeping the old tradition alive, to legitimize itself publicly as the true heir to Haguro's tradition. Consequently, the Shintō-affiliated *yamabushi* were also able to continue with the practice of the former rituals, albeit in a revised, strictly Shintō version, devoid of all Buddhist elements.

As a result, Mount Haguro now found itself host to two competing religious groups, each one laying claim to the area's spiritual heritage and each involved in its own version of their formerly common religious practices. Over the years, the chasm between the two organizations widened, and marked differences began to develop. In the 1940s, for example, Kōtakuji started to admit women as regular members in its *yamabushi* organization, while Dewa Sanzan Jinja continues to exclude women to this day. The *Fuyu no Mine* winter retreat on the other hand, with its close ties to the local *Shōreisai* (New Year) festival,[8] is conducted only by the Shintō *yamabushi*. Still, in the case of the *Aki no Mine*, the unwillingness of either group to surrender to its adversary this most meaningful of rituals has led to the probably unique phenomenon at Mount Haguro, that two fundamentally different religious groups both perform a ritual which, in its agenda, symbols, location, and duration, is an almost exact mirror image of the other group's version.

Even the new religious freedom of the post-war era brought no reconciliation between the two groups. If anything, the rift between them widened still further, with the 1946 decision of the Buddhist-affiliated group to officially change its name to 'Mount Haguro Shugendō Main Chapter' (*Hagurosan Shugendō Sōhonbu*) and thus renew its claim to be the sole heir of Mount Haguro's Shugendō tradition. Yet in spite of their conflicting interests, both groups generally managed to contain the mutual dislike between their followers, and apart from occasional bickering, no open hostilities between the two rivals were recorded over the years. Probably this relative quiet was due mainly to the small number of active *yamabushi* in both groups, as well as to the prudent compromise to begin the Shintō group's *Aki no Mine* one day after that of the Kōtakuji group, making sure that the two groups would steer clear of each other on the mountain. Ever since, the atmosphere between the two groups had been one of uneasy coexistence. Times of conciliatory moves by one side or the other alternated with attempts to publicly tarnish the rival group,[9] but the attitude encountered most often was one of marked indifference to the other side.

The division today

With the recent controversy over the planned road, though, the conflict at Mount Haguro has entered a new and more critical stage. The former occasional grumbles between the two groups over ritual authority and authenticity have given way to much more serious accusations – of unlawful interference in private business matters on the Jinja side, of strong-arm tactics aimed at the very core of its religious life on the side of the Kōtakuji organization – and with the involvement of local and regional governments, of law courts and the press, the conflict has taken on a much more public dimension.

This recent swing toward a more controversial course between the two groups is due only in part to the planned road and its potential consequences. Rather, the character of the groups as such has changed substantially over the years. In the early 1960s, when the first non-Japanese researchers participated in the *Aki no Mine*, the Kōtakuji group had around thirty members; today there are more than one hundred participants each year, and the total of all registered members in the Kōtakuji *yamabushi* organization is several times this number. The Shintō *yamabushi* group has also been attracting growing numbers of followers. Along with their growth in size, the two groups have also experienced changes in their composition. The relatively small groups of three to four decades ago had a much higher share of local members. Nowadays, however, many participants in the *Aki no Mine* are from outside the Haguro area; as such they can afford to be more openly confrontational and unwilling to compromise than the local members, who have to be mindful of local loyalties and social relations that cross denominational boundaries.

Naturally, both groups also have their share of moderate members who hope for a more conciliatory settlement (most prominently on the Kōtakuji group's side its nominal leader, the hereditary *daisendatsu*, Mr. Shimazu). Yet in view of the present emotionally charged situation, even these moderates are pessimistic about the chances of a reconciliation between the two rivals, not least because in their respective business philosophies, both organizations follow directly opposite agendas.

In accordance with the tradition of Shugendō, the Kōtakuji group is strictly esoteric. One of their central tenets is to keep their ritual and spiritual knowledge away from the eyes and ears of the uninitiated. Confidentiality is a crucial part of their religious life: instructions are usually embedded in repeated oaths of secrecy; all ritual performances (with the exception of one or two of minor importance) are closed to outsiders, permissions to document or publish any part of their spiritual life are given only with the greatest reluctance, and not much is advertised about their activities outside their own members' network. The result of this secluded existence is that apart from religious or academic specialists with an interest in such matters, hardly anyone outside the Haguro area has even heard about this group and its activities. According to the *daisendatsu*, this relative anonymity is very much in the group's interest.

At Dewa Sanzan Jinja, the attitude is quite the contrary. In their version of the *Aki no Mine*, the Jinja *yamabushi* also observe the rule of *komori*, or ritual seclusion, for the duration of their retreat. In actual practice, however, they are much less dogmatic in this than their counterparts at Kōtakuji. They are far more accommodating to outsiders' requests to witness their activities, and much of their *Aki no Mine* has been documented and published in print or on TV. What is more, they actively invite outside attention through events such as the public performance of one of Shugendō's most spectacular rituals, the burning of the *saitō goma* pyre, in front of Dewa Sanzan Jinja, witnessed by more than a thousand onlookers and several TV crews – a mere publicity stunt and a profanity, in the opinion of their Kōtakuji rivals.

The driving force behind these public performances is not so much the *yamabushi* group itself as the management of the Jinja, which hopes to boost the attractiveness of Mount Haguro as a tourist destination through such spectacular events. Dewa Sanzan Jinja is, after all, a thriving religious enterprise, and its executives are well aware that for Mount Haguro to remain an attractive choice in the mind of the potential visitor, it takes constant innovations and a well-functioning publicity machine. Consequently, Dewa Sanzan Jinja is permanently reinventing itself, with programs such as the recently introduced '*yamabushi* experience' (*yamabushi taiken*) weekends for tourists, or the new *miko shugyō*, five day, female-only adaptations of the all-male *Aki no Mine*. The Jinja was behind many of the celebrations in 1993 for the 1400th anniversary of the legendary 'opening' of the Dewa Mountains, and the local culture center at the foot of Mount Haguro has also profited greatly from the Jinja's support.

The result of the Jinja's many PR activities is that, for the average visitor to the area, Dewa Sanzan Jinja is by far the more prominent and visible representative of *yamabushi* culture. At Mount Haguro, not much hints at the fact that Dewa Sanzan Jinja may not be the sole inheritor of Haguro's religious tradition. The permanent exhibition in the culture center concentrates almost exclusively on the Shintō version of *yamabushi* culture, and in many official pamphlets and tourist brochures, too, it is only the Shintō side of events that is displayed. Consequently, many visitors and tourists are not even aware of the existence of a second, non-

Shintō *yamabushi* culture on Mount Haguro. In general, as was said before, the Kōtakuji *yamabushi* are little inclined to end their reclusive existence for the sake of greater media exposure, but for the efforts of the Kōtakuji o Mamoru Kai, the predominance of Dewa Sanzan Jinja in the public eye has proved one of the main obstacles.

In Toge, the community at the foot of Mount Haguro, the relationship between the two rivals is similarly lopsided. Both spiritually and economically, the local population's ties are much closer with the Jinja than with the Kōtakuji group. Shrine tourism supplies much of the income in and around Toge, and in one way or another, many households depend on the business created by Dewa Sanzan Jinja. Apart from the usual variety of souvenir shops and restaurants, the village also has thirty-three traditional pilgrims' inns known as *shukubō*, semi-religious institutions that are directly linked to the Jinja. As required by custom, the thirty-three heads of these *shukubō* are all certified *yamabushi* with the Shintō group, and many other locals are also members of the Jinja *yamabushi* organization. The links between Dewa Sanzan Jinja and the local populace are further reinforced through the second great event in Toge's ceremonial calendar, the *shōreisai* New Year's festival where Dewa Sanzan Jinja and its *yamabushi* take a crucial part in the ritual agenda. With the prominent position of the Jinja in both the spiritual and the secular life of the village, it is only natural that many people in and around Toge strongly identify with Dewa Sanzan Jinja and its concerns.

The Kōtakuji *yamabushi* organization, on the other hand, has hardly any power base in the local community. Mr. Shimazu, the hereditary *daisendatsu* of the group, is one of the few Kōtakuji *yamabushi* living in Toge, and as the resident priest of the two Buddhist temples there, he is the only member in the group with a say in the affairs of the village. Most other Kōtakuji *yamabushi* are in Toge only in the few days preceding or following the *Aki no Mine*, and even then they do not interact much with the local population. This, and their habit of publicly mocking their rivals' ritual conduct (see note 9), is probably the main reason why in the descriptions of the villagers, the Kōtakuji *yamabushi* sometimes come across as somewhat stand-offish and supercilious. Yet in spite of such occasional criticism, the general attitude in Toge toward the Kōtakuji *yamabushi* is one of genuine respect. People acknowledge the group's deep spirituality, and even the officials at Dewa Sanzan Jinja are quick to point out that both *yamabushi* groups are an indispensable part of the local tradition. In the ongoing controversy over the planned road, many people in Toge actually sympathize with the Kōtakuji group, including several Jinja *yamabushi* who privately confided in me that they understand their competitors' worries. Yet in practice, the Kōtakuji *yamabushi* group profits very little from such respect or tacit sympathy in the local population. To the frustration of the Kōtakuji o Mamoru Kai members, their door-to-door campaigns in Toge got them numerous expressions of personal sympathy, but hardly anyone in the village was prepared to openly go against the Jinja's interests and sign the group's formal letter of protest to the prefectural government.

Losing distance: the dilemma of emotional involvement

During the lecture of the Kōtakuji o Mamoru Kai representative early in the *Aki no Mine*, my immediate resolution had been to steer clear of Mount Haguro's politics for the sake of my independent researcher's position. By the end of the *Aki no Mine* though, this had proved impossible, for what had begun as a simple anthropological field project had taken on a dimension of intense personal involvement. With the completion of the *Aki no Mine*, I had become a member in more than one respect. Formally, I had passed the requirements to join the group. I had received my name (and thus my identity within the group), and I had begun to define my own position in the Mount Haguro religious environment first and foremost through my membership in the Kōtakuji *yamabushi* group. With this strong identification through the group, joining the Kōtakuji o Mamoru Kai seemed an almost inevitable next step. After all, the road posed a very real threat to the religious life at Kōtakuji, and a foreign researcher's name on the group's member list would certainly be a valuable asset in their struggle. But then again, was I really in a position to decide that supporting the Kōtakuji o Mamoru Kai was the right thing to do? Even among the Kōtakuji supporters in Toge village, many were rather critical of the Kōtakuji o Mamoru Kai and its firebrand rhetoric. Then again, from the viewpoint of professional ethics, wasn't my task as an anthropologist to keep my notions of right and wrong to myself, to stick strictly to the role of the participant observer, and not to become involved in such a way that my facilities of objective observation might be impeded?

Actually, no. The academic discussion is just as undecided on this point as I was, and there are as many opinions favoring involvement as there are against it. Jarvie, for example, argues that keeping one's own sensitivities and moral judgments from interfering with the events in the field is clearly the wrong course of action. Not only, he says, are such notions of cultural relativism doomed to fail in practice, but they are also detrimental to one's research, and dishonest toward those in the field: 'As well as being a scientist [the anthropologist] is a member of the society he came from and will return to and should avoid giving a misleading impression to his hosts either by words or deeds' (Jarvie 1982: 71). Observers in the field are outsiders by definition and, in the eyes of those they investigate, they will never be full members of the group. Therefore, he argues, there is nothing to justify the assumption that acting in accordance with one's own emotions and moral values will harm one's position in the field: 'There is no reason to think the host people will not respect [the fieldworker] more for this than for attempting to curry favor by pretending to go along with things that in truth offend, horrify or disgust him' (Jarvie 1982: 71).

Prus on the other hand, in his exhaustive discussion of emotionality in ethnographic research, strongly advises against letting one's personal sense of morality or humanism govern one's actions in the field. For him, to keep a nonjudgmental, nonpartisan position in the field is as much a matter of professional ethics ('these people didn't invite me to study them. And, even if they did, studying them and judging them are two different things') as it is a question of risk management. Any partisanship by the researcher carries the danger of becoming 'emotionally entangled in... a situation that may subsequently jeopardize one's project (and possibly one's well-being)' (Prus 1996: 194).

For Gans, the question of emotional involvement in the field is related not so much to ethics as to pragmatism and to the psychological dynamics in the field. He agrees with Jarvie that, as a participant observer, the anthropologist 'can never participate totally because he cannot ever internalize the norms and values of another culture' (Gans 1982: 55). But, he claims, total avoidance of emotional involvement in the processes in the field is similarly beyond the researcher's capabilities: '[People in the field] treat him as a person even if he treats them as subjects of study, and if he wants to remain in the group, he is obligated to participate behaviorally and to express feelings of interest' (Gans 1982: 55). What causes the researcher's emotional involvement, though, is not so much this external pressure (which demands practical, not emotional, compliance) but the internal pressure, the researcher's own wish not to alienate, the desire to be accepted, the need to belong.

According to Gans, the researcher's answer to this tension between personal emotional needs and actual position at the margin of the group is compensation through identification:[10] 'If he cannot be truly a part of the group, he can at least adopt some of their values and beliefs so as to satisfy his feelings for belonging' (Gans 1982: 60). This tendency, he claims, is further supported by the researcher's operative division into an emotionally involved 'participant' identity and a detached 'observer' identity, which makes the research situation inherently an act of deception: 'He pretends to participate emotionally when he is not; he observes even when he appears not to be doing so... In short, psychologically, the participant observer is acting dishonestly...' (Gans 1982: 60). Feeling guilty about this dishonesty, claims Gans, the researcher then tends to counterbalance this perceived guilt through a strong emotional identification with the people in the field.

The great drawback of Gans' theories is that in practice, they are virtually impossible to verify. What is more, they build upon a dichotomy that presupposes a clear-cut separating line between the marginally placed researcher on one side and a largely homogeneous group on the other. What, then, if this dichotomy is not tenable? At the *Aki no Mine*, for example, how much more marginal was the position of the two non-Japanese participants than that of the numerous other eccentric and unusual characters among the forty first-time participants? And how much of my growing identification with the Kōtakuji *yamabushi* was due to any subconsciously compensated feelings of marginality or guilt?

Personally, I suspect that much of my emotional involvement had to do with the character of the *Aki no Mine* itself, a ritual whose social function in the *yamabushi* community is integration, and the creation (or reconfirmation) of group identity. For close to nine days, I had spent almost every waking minute in the company of the same group of people. Several times during the *Aki no Mine*, we had come close to our physical and emotional limits, but such points of extreme stress had been contrasted by periods of similarly extreme elation. The experience of our collective effort, of sharing the rigid regimen and the physical hardships of the *Aki no Mine*, of having to overcome our habitual egotism for the sake of the group, had indeed created a strong feeling of community, of mutual dependence, of belonging. This inward fixation of the group was further supported by the fact that almost all of the *Aki no Mine* had occurred in perfect seclusion from the rest of the world – apart from ourselves and our fellow *yamabushi*, we had no one else to depend on. Passing through the *Aki no Mine*, I had undergone an initiation, and while I had remained largely insensitive to its spiritual dimension, my detached researcher's attitude had been no match for the emotional intensity of the experience and its powerful group dynamics. As I said before, endorsing the Kōtakuji group's position in the quarrel with Dewa Sanzan Jinja was an almost inevitable consequence – not to support the Kōtakuji o Mamoru Kai, and not to endorse its objective, the protection of Kōtakuji temple and its environs, seemed like disloyalty to the group.

What complicated the matter in this case, though, was that I also had obligations toward the representatives of the Shintō side. There was, for one, the fact that I had received substantial support in my research from Dewa Sanzan Jinja and the institutions close to it. I also had to be mindful of those among my informants and personal acquaintances who were Jinja *yamabushi*. For them, the fact that I had taken part in the *Aki no Mine* over at Kōtakuji was of minor importance. But from our conversations I knew that getting myself involved in the local conflict about the road was an altogether different matter. A political statement such as publicly siding with the Kōtakuji o Mamoru Kai and going against Dewa Sanzan Jinja might not only compromise our mutual relationship, but also reflect on their own personal standing within the local community. In short, it was clear that any involvement on my part in the local conflict might have serious consequences for my personal network on and around Mount Haguro, and apart from damaging several valuable friendships, it might also jeopardize any future research that I intended to do outside the Kōtakuji group.

Conclusion

In the end, my professional concerns prevailed, and I did not put my name behind the Kōtakuji o Mamoru Kai. Not sure how much longer I could maintain my precarious position with one foot in each camp, I even contemplated terminating the whole research project, but fortunately this proved unnecessary. As for the Kōtakuji o Mamoru Kai, they did indeed manage to put a hold on the plans for the road, and the planning office at the prefectural government is finally considering what would have been the best solution all along, an alternative route that enables the tour buses to reach Dewa Sanzan Jinja comfortably, without coming too close to Kōtakuji. As a result, the tensions at Mount Haguro have somewhat abated, and at least for the time being, the two groups have returned to their former course of quiet yet wary co-existence. Ultimately, though, little has changed in their competitive situation. Given their conflicting interests, the next clash between the two rivals at Mount Haguro is probably just a question of time.

As for the question of how and to what degree this experience inhibited my research, the consequences were, in hindsight, less momentous than I had anticipated at the time. My reluctance to support the Kōtakuji o Mamoru Kai was never held against me, and my acquaintances from both sides are still on speaking terms with me. To some extent, the whole event even proved to be beneficial, for it was only through my participation in the *Aki no Mine* and the lecture of the Kōtakuji o Mamoru Kai representative that I learned about the tense relationship between the two rivals. Yet psychologically, the experience has left its mark, and my contacts around Mount Haguro have become less uninhibited than they had been before the *Aki no Mine*. With my participation in the *Aki no Mine*, I have become located in the local competitive environment, and I am no longer a neutral entity.

My personal dilemma also remains unresolved. From a strictly rational point of view, there are more than enough reasons why, at that time, not to become involved more deeply in the struggle at Mount Haguro had been the right decision. Yet there remains the nagging feeling that by refusing to support the struggle of the Kōtakuji *yamabushi* to protect their temple, I had somehow shirked my responsibilities as a group member and had, for the sake of my own interests, gone against 'my community.' Involving myself in the controversy, though, would have likely resulted in a similar dilemma toward my personal contacts on the Shintō side.

Ultimately, it can be argued, I had brought this problem upon myself, by not sticking to the position of the disinterested researcher and not avoiding any emotional involvement with those in the field. But such discussions about professional ethics are of little help here, for as we saw, the opinions among social scientists on how to act and react in the field are far from unanimous, and the case for intervention can be argued just as plausibly as that for strict non-intervention. Moreover, the question that the researcher has to face in the field usually is no simple dichotomy of whether to become emotionally involved or not, but rather a question of how deep this involvement should go. The whole idea of participant observation is built around personal interaction with those in the field, and the researcher's emotional involvement is an inevitable part of this interaction. In the case of the *Aki no Mine*, this involvement was further supported by the event's essential character as a communal experience, conveying to its individual members a group identity, and a self-definition through and within the group.

For the first non-Japanese researchers at Mount Haguro, the question of emotional involvement was clearly much less of an issue. In 1963, when Carmen Blacker and Byron Earhart participated in the Kōtakuji *Aki no Mine*, the rivalry at Haguro was still a predominantly local affair between two small groups, both of which had strong ties to the local community and neither of which could afford to let this conflict get out of hand. In addition, with the much smaller scale of the religious enterprise on Mount Haguro, much less was at stake for the two competitors. Altogether, the rivalry between the two organizations was of such little consequence for the religious life on Mount Haguro that both researchers could well afford to disregard it and either, as in Blacker's account (1992), simply ignore the existence of a rival group of *yamabushi* or, like Earhart (1970: 53), treat this matter in a few dismissive sentences.

With the changed situation of today, though, such an easy negation of the whole issue is not possible anymore. The growth in size of both organizations, the increasing involvement of outsiders with no fear of repercussions within the local community and little inclination to surrender what they see as their group's vital interests for the sake of local peace, and the considerably greater financial stakes – all these factors have made it increasingly difficult to participate in Mount Haguro's religious life while steering clear of its conflicts. The polarization between the two factions forces everyone involved to take sides, for association with one faction inevitably means being associated with their position in the conflict. The posture of the disinterested and disassociated researcher, difficult to maintain at the best of times, has become utterly untenable.

12 Received Dreams: Consumer Capitalism, Social Process, and the Management of the Emotions in Contemporary Japan

John Clammer

Introduction

The difficulties which social theorists have encountered in attempting to characterize the nature of Japanese society and culture does suggest that here is a civilization whose cultural fault lines run in unexpected directions when compared with the other industrial civilizations of the world. In essence this is not a new problem in the social sciences: anthropologists in particular have long struggled not only with the issues of representing 'alien' cultures in terms intelligible to their readers, but also with the more fundamental question of locating quite different cosmologies and their attendant social logics in the total universe of thought. Many of the societies in relation to which these theoretical conundrums have been addressed have been small in scale and remote in space or time. But not so Japan, whose economic presence, cultural influence, technological dominance, and social example have made it arguably the major challenger to Western hegemony, material and spiritual, in the contemporary world.

But despite Japan's enormous influence and visibility in the modern international system, it can also safely be said that there is little consensus among those who make it their business to understand or explain Japan about the fundamental principles of interpretation that might be applied to this society. Major cleavages still exist amongst Western Japanologists, for instance between those who favor a political economy/bureaucratic model (e.g. Chalmers Johnson, 1982, 1995; Karel van Wolferen 1989) and those who favor a culturalist approach (e.g. S.N. Eisenstadt 1996; Donald Keene 1998). Furthermore, despite some important recent attempts to break free of them, especially via the route of postmodernism, old models inherited from the past – for instance the 'vertical society' model of Nakane Chie (1970) or the 'moralist' model of Ruth Benedict (1946) – continue to exercise considerable influence and are still widely debated despite the enormous empirical and theoretical flaws that they contain. Clearly some fresh paradigms are needed for the revitalization of Japanese studies, and in particular of the anthropology of Japan, but where are they to be sought?

A central problem with many of these 'classical' approaches to Japanese society, and with many of their more recent successors, is that they are static in nature. They concentrate, that is, on structural characteristics of the society and culture and on sets of classificatory principles which are supposed somehow to 'capture' the reality that actually constitutes Japan, whether that reality be seen through the prism of, say, the 'Japanese self' or notions of 'inside' (*uchi*) and 'outside' (*soto*) (Bachnik and Quinn eds 1994). What they fail to 'capture' is that Japanese society, especially in the post-war period, has undergone tremendous changes and continues to do so. Social change in a society of such a scale is of course itself a highly complex phenomenon, encompassing as it must forces of globalization; Japan's encounter with the 'Other' represented by the flood of foreign workers who have come to reside for varying periods of time in the country; political and economic shifts; and, perhaps pre-eminently, the emergence of the new consumer society, the society in fact of hyper-consumption, which is now the dominant mode of everyday life, the matrix in which almost all contemporary Japanese live out their existences and which in a sense comprises those existences.

How then is one to begin to explore this complex change, clearly essential if Japan is to be characterized in any accurate way? A number of avenues, which on deeper exploration prove to be related in unexpected ways, suggest themselves. The first is that category of works known collectively to Western scholars (for whom it is largely a target of hostile criticism) as *nihonjinron* or 'theories of Japaneseness.' (Western scholars often fail to take into account the large internal variations within this literature, a failure which might itself be seen as a new form of 'Orientalism.') While the wilder reaches of *nihonjinron* have been attacked (most notably in English by Dale 1995) as ultranationalist absurdities, this unremittingly hostile approach deflects attention from the equally important fact that it also represents a genuinely indigenous discourse. As such, it may be read as an attempt to salvage Japan from the ravages of a 'universalist' history which proves on closer examination to be in actuality a homogenizing and Westernizing one in which other voices (Asian or African ones for instance) play at best a supporting role. What has not always been noted in studies of *nihonjinron* are the calls for cultural (which is not necessarily culturalist) analysis, something which points many Japanese commentators toward a view of Japanese society as one not dominated by the pervasive rationalism of Western social thinking. Cultural criticism (not just nationalist braying) is in fact very much alive and well in Japan (for example in the works of Karatani Kōjin, Asada Akira, Ōe Kenzaburō or Yoshimoto Taka'aki).

This cultural criticism in fact contains implicitly a number of theories of social change since the essence of *nihonjinron* is precisely the attempt to place Japan in a different historical frame from both the West and the rest of Asia and so to provide an alternative explanation of Japan's emergence as a distinctive civilizational form (Sugimoto 1999; Yoshino 1997).

At the same time the internal unity of Western social theory has been breaking up as modernist, rationalist, knowledge-based systems (Marxism, structuralism, and structuration theory for example) have been challenged by feminist, post-structuralist, and postmodernist tendencies. These in turn have in part been fueled by social movements such as the so-called 'New Age' movement, which has drawn much of its epistemology from Asian philosophical and religious systems, a trend which is now spreading into serious academic disciplines and especially psychology, particularly through a serious engagement with the implications of Buddhism (e.g. Pickering, 1997). One of the most significant elements in this whole broad tendency has been the attempt to formulate a 'post-rationalist' understanding of culture and society in which a much more somatized approach to human social reality is taken. Since the publication in 1984 of Bryan Turner's seminal book *The Body and Society: Explorations in Social Theory*, this has included a flood of works on the body in society and culture, and, extending quite logically from this and in part through the rediscovery of the work of Norbert Elias, to the parallel recovery of the place of the emotions in human social activity (e.g. Elias 1995). The current interests of the so-called 'cultural turn' in Western social theory turn out to be surprisingly like those of indigenous (and rather older) Japanese social theory. Indeed this confluence has triggered the translation and publication in the West of hitherto little known Japanese contributions on similar issues (e.g.Yuasa 1987, Nagatomo 1992). One of the most significant things about this literature is precisely its relating of, or merging of, the social and cultural into a single unified field, something still rare in Western social analysis, and as such it has the potential to correct, or even subvert, mainstream Western socio-cultural categories.

A third source of renewal in Japanese studies has undoubtedly been the expansion of interest in popular culture, inspired partly by an upsurge in interest in the subject internationally. Until recently a marginal and peripheral field, the study of popular culture, itself linked to the expansion of cultural studies generally, has moved to center-stage. The realization has belatedly dawned that what people actually do in their everyday lives and the nature of their cultural consumption (be it in music, literature, food, art, media, fashion, religion, tourism, or material artifacts) constitutes the fabric of those lives and is also enormously revealing about deeper grammars of behavior and thinking, including of course the emotions. A good case can be made indeed that the analysis of popular culture reveals most quickly and clearly social change in action, since it is precisely there that it is most rapidly registered (Martinez ed. 1998). The concerns of much *nihonjinron,* and of broader strands of Japanese cultural criticism, resonate with post-structuralist varieties of Western social theory and popular culture studies in significant ways. It is my contention here that this resonance is generating fresh paradigms in Japanese studies, ones that do indeed reveal the deep grammar of that society more effectively than most. Common to all these potential sources of renewal is a largely unsignalled emphasis on changes in subjectivities which both indicate and are themselves examples of social change – changing self-perceptions, shifting interfaces with the material and spiritual worlds, and the reformulation of social relationships and cultural identities. These changing identities collectively constitute, I would argue, the basic substratum of cultural change and are consequently of necessity involved in the formulation of any coherent theory of social change. The forms of modernization theory which have tended to dominate more critical and theorized versions of social change studies of Japan (for example McCormack and Sugimoto eds 1988), and even their postmodern variants (Sugimoto and Arnason eds 1995) have sadly neglected all these potential approaches to Japanese society. In so doing, they have entirely occluded the question of what the experience of modernization actually means to those who have lived through it and how this experience has transformed the sense of self and of identity. This issue has actually been grasped more accurately by historians than by sociologists (e.g. Gordon ed. 1993).

The logic of emotions

A major trend in social theory, then, has been away from the rationalist and structural-functionalist models that have dominated sociology since Parsons and anthropology since Malinowski, toward a more somatized understanding of human social experience, of which the possession and expression of emotions is a central part. However, while the sociology and anthropology of the body have expanded in leaps and bounds, parallel developments in the cultural analysis of the emotions remain at a much more tentative and programmatic level, although more developed in anthropology than in sociology. This is perhaps not surprising given that the body is, quite literally, more graspable, and that the study of the emotions in general has been beset by culturalism, psychologism, and biologism to an extent that few other features of human life have been. It is actually in philosophy that the most analytically sophisticated work on the emotions has occurred, both in general philosophy and, very recently, in the comparative study of Asian philosophies (e.g. Marks and Ames eds. 1995). Its analysis in relation to both the cultural sciences and to actual life (as opposed to text-based philosophical and religious systems) in contemporary Japan is however very limited. This chapter is intended as a very modest contribution to this formative field.

A wide range of writers concur that the emotions do indeed play a dominant role in the structuring of (or are themselves expressions of) Japanese culture, whether in particular fields such as literature, aesthetics, film, comics, or religion; in the context of particular cultural sites or events as varied as Noh drama, the tea ceremony, karaoke or suicide; or in the ordering of social responses, such as attitudes to outsiders. Authors both popular (e.g. Iyer 1991) and technical (e.g. Wawrytko 1995) have noted the specific affinities (different, that is, from other cultural locations) of sex and religion, of language and silence, of images and reality, of reason and feeling in Japan. They show how these affinities add up to a specific language of the emotions or a culture of feeling deeply at variance with, say, the neighboring Chinese or Koreans, with whom there are otherwise such profound cultural links. Likewise certain broad emotional themes – the preponderance of nostalgia being a very good example – stand out as cultural themes requiring deeper analysis, particularly as they are indicators of the ways in which people are managing change and integrating it back into a world-view which is itself perpetually under construction.

But while the introduction of the study of the emotions into social science discourse is itself a very positive move, simply to assert this does not develop the argument very far. What also needs to be done is to demonstrate how such a study might be undertaken and how, in this particular case, it contributes to the understanding of social processes (which are by definition dynamic in nature) in contemporary Japan. The thesis that I will advance here is that such a study can best be undertaken not by analyzing emotions as things-in-themselves, or in their aestheticized expression, but by relating emotions as sociocultural processes to their economic context. This should not be done in some simplistic base/superstructure model, but by seeing emotions as continuously interacting and mutually modifying forces, the interplay of which actually constitutes much of the fabric of everyday life. This approach, I would suggest, both provides a mechanism to uncover the fundamental structures of that everyday life and advances beyond the point so far reached by the majority of anthropological approaches to the study of emotions. So before entering Japan proper, it is necessary to take a very brief excursion into the territory of the anthropology of the emotions.

The study of emotions in anthropology has largely concerned itself with one of three groups of questions. The first is that of the relation between language itself (and in particular poetics) and the expression (or 'politics') of emotions in different cultures (e.g. Lutz and Abu-Lughod eds 1990). The second is that of the language of emotions – the ways in which they are categorized, talked about and used as post-event explanations of behavior and as a language of motives for those about to undertake some course of action. Concepts (familiar of course to Japanologists through the work of Ruth Benedict) such as shame, guilt, or embarrassment do not necessarily have the same semantic range or motivational force in all cultures (e.g. Lutz 1988). The third is to link emotions with the currently fashionable preoccupation with selfhood (e.g. Shweder and LeVine eds 1995), a concern that historically grew out of the older 'culture and personality' approach once popular in North American anthropology.

This third variant in particular has produced the insights that emotions are culturally shaped and that however much they may have physiological correlates (rapid pulse or other forms of excitation for example), they cannot be understood in purely biological terms; and, vitally, that they are not free floating states or entities, but are about, and only make sense in terms of, relationships (Levy 1995: 222). So far, so good. But on closer examination, the category of 'culture' being employed here turns out to be largely an amalgam of religion, traditional values, and kinship. To be given greater explanatory power, it needs to be expanded, as it should be, to include the economic, and specifically to include everyday economic activity – that is to say consumption.

The political economy of emotion

The contemporary Japanese economy is of course a capitalist one, albeit with its own distinctive characteristics. Its distinctiveness and ubiquity have led at least one commentator to suggest that modern Japanese capitalism *is* contemporary Japanese culture (Sakakibara 1993), a view with which in large measure I would concur. Normally a 'culture' and its associated economy are kept analytically distinct, a dualism that persists despite the criticisms that have been directed against it (by Habermas for example) in mainstream Western social science. The relationship between beliefs and economies has been endlessly explored in connection with the origins of capitalist systems in both the West (Weber 1987) and the East (Rodinson 1974), and also with the shaping of the non-Western industrial and trading economies. The prime example of the latter is the debate about the role of Confucianism in the rise of Japan and the 'Tiger' economies of East Asia (e.g. Tu ed. 1996). But in all these cases, note that a rationalist model is at work – beliefs as quasi-philosophical systems with alleged sociological consequences are at the core of the explanatory system being proffered, the assumption being that it is beliefs, even if abstractly or conventionally held, that provide the motivation for action. At the root of this model is a conception of the human actor as rational and as motivated by systems of thought, a conception which is precisely the target of the attempt to broaden the basis of social explanation to recognize that in practice emotions usually precede reason in decisions for action and that emotions are so powerful precisely because they are the primary springs of action and at the same time are non-rational.

The extent to which pre-existing emotional patterns (not patterns of belief, which themselves stand in a complex relationship to emotions) may have shaped the emergence of capitalist or proto-capitalist economic processes and institutions is an almost entirely unasked question in history or historical sociology. In turn it can be assumed that the spread of capitalism in its local variants has contributed to the shaping of emotions in its areas of influence through the creation of new needs, desires, and self-images, and the necessity of their satisfaction through particular patterns of consumption and display (cf. Miller 1994).

This is true of all societies – Nuer passions fluctuate in tune to the rising and falling of the Nile and to the movements and fortunes of their cattle, even as Trobriand emotions fluctuate with the health of their gardens. What distinguishes contemporary Japan is not any difference in principle, but the fact that it is an intensely capitalist society: one saturated with consumption as the primary way of life, the altar on which almost all other energies, preoccupations, and social functions are sacrificed. If emotions are indeed shaped in response to everyday realities, and that reality is largely composed of the consumption nexus, then it will be consumption and the means by which consumption is made possible (work) that mould ever changing subjectivities. In fact (although I will not completely do so) it might even be better at this point in the argument to dispense with the term 'emotion' altogether given its psychological and biological connotations, and instead speak of these changing subjectivities. However, 'subjectivity' is a concept rather different from 'emotion': it contains the emotions, but can also refer to other elements of identity such as gender, race, or sexual preference.

We must also pay attention to the fact that, certainly in the modern industrialized world, identities are constructed and maintained largely through relationships to material things – their consumption, display, and exchange and the symbolic charges with which they are invested (Dittmar 1992). The challenge then, building on older approaches in economic anthropology, is to formulate not so much a new political economy of the advanced capitalist countries as a new cultural economy: one which sees the cultural and economic as aspects of each other, but which also sees the social actor as an embodied being, motivated by emotional drives and concerned primarily with relationships and identity maintenance. Contemporary cultural studies suggest that the field of socio-cultural analysis requires restructuring in such a way that the concepts of the economic, political, and social are entirely rethought as to their internal contents and configurations and to their relationship with each other, a relationship much more seamless than previously supposed. As postmodern theorists such as Jean Baudrillard have suggested, the old analytical categories of production dominating consumption, of the base controlling the superstructure, of classes forming the primary social structure of the advanced capitalist societies, no longer have the theoretical validity that they once did in explaining the principal modern social formation – the society of consumption (Baudrillard 1970). Japan is arguably the most developed example of that society anywhere in the world.

Consumption and subjectivity in Japan

Japan is a society that has whole-heartedly embraced capitalism, yet it has changed and modified capitalism to its own distinct social ends. This can be seen in any number of ways: the taking of elements from other economies and cultures and transforming their size, symbolism, and use to suit Japanese needs (Tobin ed. 1992); the intensely material life of Japanese teenagers, yet the synthesizing of that materialism with an overarching concern for social harmony and generational continuity (White 1994); the 'socialist' characteristics of Japanese capitalism and the rhetoric of social utility which pervades it (Kenrick 1990); the characteristics of Japanese advertising and the modification of images necessary to sell foreign products in the Japanese market (Moeran 1996a); and, what concerns us primarily here, the shaping of emotions and subjectivities. Consumer capitalism creates new subjectivities. It does so by shaping taste, identity, and lifestyle options; by creating needs, desires, and images of things, services, places, and foods; and through its impact on concepts of the perfect body via ideas of diet, health and fitness, body shape, color and decoration. It operates most powerfully through media and advertising, and in so doing profoundly influences the emotions associated with subjectivities. This list could of course be extended to include changes in ideas of sex and gender (the pre-war invention of the 'modern girl' and her subsequent transformations associated with changing concepts of fashion and entertainment); of technology (the emergence of *pachinko*, the cinema, TV, and most recently electronic games centers and 'virtual reality' centers); of the contents of popular culture including *manga* (comics) and popular music; or of sport, with the literal invention of soccer as a Japanese mass sport in the late 1980s (the 'J League'). All of these quite obviously represent commercial interests on a grand scale and all have extensive effects on the subjectivities and life-styles of those exposed to them.

Advertising itself quite obviously lies at the core of consumer society – it is the primary mechanism through which knowledge of new or revitalized products is disseminated, tastes created, fashions popularized, 'ideal' appearances formulated. But it is not the only mechanism, and the Japanese media are pervaded by 'information,' sometimes in the form of quasi-advertising advice, for example on makeup, diet, or body-shape, but also in the shape of other advice on almost every imaginable aspect of life. Such advice is furthermore stratified in terms of the gender and age of the target audience, and although such advice is particularly associated with magazines for women and teenage girls (Skov and Moeran eds. 1995) it also occurs in magazines for men and youths (in well known titles such as *Brutus* or *Tarzan*), for senior citizens (for example in the magazine *President*), and in general consumer magazines such as *Goods Press* or *Mono*. This 'information' ranges across such subjects as what to wear on particular occasions, appropriate makeup and accessories, places to go, how to behave on dates, dietary advice, health (both in general and in relation to particular complaints such as skin problems), hair care, how to eat particular dishes (especially foreign ones which may be unfamiliar), sex, new music, books, movies and videos, and hobbies and sports. There is also information on where to seek yet further information if more detailed or specialist advice is needed or desired. Many women's magazines (for example the well-known fashion magazine *More*) carry pictorial advice in the form of paired photos of the same woman before and after a particular application of makeup, hair-do, or change of fashion, it being made quite clear which is the approved version. Others contain information that reveals how little young modern Japanese women actually know about the more traditional aspects of their own culture. For instance, a recent edition of *Hanako*, a magazine which circulates widely among young working women, devoted its main feature to the question of where to drink good coffee, Chinese tea, and Japanese tea; but it also contained a column on how to brew Japanese green tea in the correct way if making it yourself – surprising advice indeed in a tea-drinking culture.

The somatization of the emotions in contemporary Japan

In any capitalist society, what is fashionable, consumable, healthy, and appropriate is largely constructed by the capitalist system itself and changes as that system itself evolves and expands. The mass consumption society in Japan is itself a recent (post-1950s) phenomenon, which will presumably continue to undergo constant modifications and adjustments in the future. Subjectivities are formed as a consequence largely around consumption of appropriate goods and services and participation in prescribed activities. Identities are in other words largely formed through consumption, and things, places, and activities that formerly fell outside the consumption nexus are rapidly assimilated into it once they are discovered by the system as exploitable new fads. But it may have escaped attention that these subjectivities are formed largely through the shaping of the body. It is precisely through care of the body that emotions are structured and expressed and identities are formulated. Discussions of the 'self' in recent Japanology (e.g. Rosenberger 1995) have largely overlooked this, even in those cases where work and its attendant physical regimes are the focus of analysis (e.g. Kondo 1990).

Seen from this perspective, the emotions are not some kind of free-floating force, but are grounded in somatic experiences out of which they are formed and through which they are expressed. Body politics consequently become the central analytical unit of cultural investigation. At least since the Heian period, Japanese culture has stressed both the emotional (often glossed as 'aesthetic') and the significance of bodily practice (through self cultivation involving meditative practices, the tea ceremony, judo, and aikido, the culture of the bath, and many other traditional and modern forms). Hence there is a hidden or alternative history of the culture waiting to be written from a somatic perspective.

The significance of some forms of biopolitics has already been recognized in the role which the state in Japan plays in controlling medicine (for example its only recently lifted ban on the Pill as a permitted method of birth control), education, diet (through control over permitted imported foods), and the calendar (the designation of certain days as 'health-sports day,' 'marine day,' 'respect for the aged day,' and so forth). The power of the media is equally strong, not just through advertising, but as Anne Allison has argued (1996) also through *manga*, the ubiquitous comics of Japanese popular culture, which play a major role in shaping conceptions of sexuality, violence, and the imaginary. However, the links between leisure and fantasy, the boundaries between normalcy and transgression, the relations between images and commodities are not just however somehow 'different' in Japan, but are both made that way and reinforced by cultural and economic forces. If the state is one of these, the media and advertising industries are clearly other key actors, as we have already suggested, creating subjectivities, creating and then 'solving' problems and doubts, and making it very difficult to find other reference points, especially in a culture which valorizes conformity, in the sense of membership in a valued in-group. Self-cultivation, the traditional mode of character formation, still continues, but is pursued increasingly through practices of consumption: fashion, commercialized sports, diet, and hobbies.

This is not necessarily to argue that Japan is exactly the same as other advanced capitalist societies. Even as Japanese capitalism itself has its own distinctive features, so too do the subjectivities that it shapes. One of these we noted above, where Merry White found that the highly material pursuit of identity by Japanese teenagers did not undermine the high levels of generational solidarity and horizontal sociality (civility in other words) traditionally (and correctly) associated with Japan. Another is the active incorporation of a relationship with nature. This can involve simply marketing strategies ('ecological' clothing, 'green' industries), participation in nature through tourism (domestic tourism in particular stressing on the whole nature over history, unlike say British domestic tourism where the opposite is true), a preoccupation with gardens and plants, or literal bodily immersion in nature in the *onsen* hot spring sub-culture, to name some of the main ones.

Norbert Elias, the major theorist to date of the relationship between emotions, culture, consumption, and the civilizational process (e.g. Elias 1978–82) and a writer who thinks primarily in terms of the West, sees a contradiction between nature and civilization as the basic fault line. Quite the contrary argument can be made about Japan, where nature and culture, far from being separated spheres as in the thinking of Lévi-Strauss, interpenetrate and constantly inform each other, not only at the level of philosophy and religion, but in expressions of everyday life, including advertising, architecture, the seasonality of fashions, colors, and interior decorations. The argument of Daniel Bell in *The Cultural Contradictions of Capitalism* (1976), that modernist rationality was increasingly being overwhelmed by a culture of instincts (a precursor of postmodernity), sounds quaint when placed in the context of the development of Japanese capitalism. This has created a mass culture in which aesthetic standards still predominate and a consumer democracy in which the legitimacy of hierarchical standards of social ranking and authority are still maintained largely undiminished (Clammer 1995), in which hedonism at play and asceticism in the workplace coexist, and in which a bourgeois capitalism in the sense of a conservative mercantile class has arisen – but without the religious, moralistic, and sexually repressive attributes historically associated with that class in the West.

To suggest, then, that capitalism shapes emotions through the management of the body, while true, is also subject to the principle of comparative variability. Japanese capitalism indeed profoundly shapes subjectivities, but does so in distinctive ways. One is through the modification and transformation of foreign objects, images, and body practices (Japanese baseball for example, is played very differently from its North American parent, as many players from both sides have testified in what is now a minor literature). Another is through the creation of cultural categories, or rather perhaps through the dissolution of cultural categories familiar to other cultures, such as nature/culture, death/sexuality, sexuality/violence, silence/communication, or the old pairs familiar to readers of Ruth Benedict – *uchi/soto*, *tatemae/honne*, *giri/on* – to name some of the most famous. This means too that patterns of protest and social movements take correspondingly different forms – many being to do with the protection of nature and few, given the high standards of Japanese products, having to do with consumer protection. Other social movements take the form of alternative modes of production and consumption. The mushrooming organic food movement in Japan is one of the most conspicuous instances, and one of the most interesting. It is a reaction to food additives, pollution, and soil destruction, and simultaneously an attempt to create new forms of consciousness outside the hegemony of the capitalist ideological system; and yet, as it grows in popularity, it is in danger of succumbing to or adopting precisely the capitalist methods that it so abhors. While the state, and to a great extent capitalism itself, prefer (to use Foucault's language) docile, disciplined bodies occupying their allotted places in social space, the primacy of a somatized rather than a rationalized frame of discourse also allows dissent to take place easily within that same frame. Non-conformity is easily signaled in Japan by choice of clothes, hairstyle, accessories, and body language. The high level of visuality of Japanese culture (signaled today by the national obsession with photography; the quality and volume of images in Japanese print media; and the saturation of the entire culture with television and televisual images, internet, video outlets, *manga*, virtual reality centers, art galleries, and movie houses) makes the shaping of subjectivities through such means easy, while also ensuring that dominant images can be contested with other subversive images. Culture wars in Japan are as a result fought largely as, quite literally, symbolic contests, contests of images, tournaments of beauty.

The conception of the self then in contemporary Japan is profoundly linked to consumption (Clammer 1997), but this linkage is mediated in interesting ways – notably through the preoccupation of Japanese capitalism with being the major contemporary source of cultural nationalism and the primary shaper of what it is to be Japanese (understood not mainly as genetic inheritance, but as cultural and bodily practice – not just as language, but as a particular way of speaking that language, not just as food, but as particular foods prepared and presented in specific ways, and so on through the cultural repertoire). Other mediating factors include the concern to protect rather than destroy sociality, to reduce rather than increase alienation, and to minimize the risk to society rather than intensify it.

Body and self are thus united, as consumption builds that self through bodily practices, and as the body becomes, in Foucault's terms again, the site of intervention by outside forces – the state, capitalism and its agencies, cultural others. The soul, the site of intervention in medieval Catholic Europe, for example, is no longer the object of concern (in Japan it rarely was), but insofar as it is considered relevant it is seen as being expressed through the body. Examples of this would include the pragmatic and this-worldly contemporary Buddhism of groups such as Sōka Gakkai, and the *hinokishin* principle of the neo-Shintō new religion Tenrikyō, in which selfless physical service to the handicapped or deprived is seen as the mechanism for overcoming negative karma.

The self furthermore cannot really consume alone, since consumption is to do with identity and solidarity and must as a consequence take place in the context or company of others. Michel Maffesoli has argued that the major principle of social structure in advanced capitalist societies is the 'neo-tribe,' a group or quasi-group formed around consumption of particular goods or services. Constituted of strangers whose unity is only achieved through common participation in consumption, it dissolves as soon as fashion or fad moves on, in which case the members disperse and reform in new temporary groups centered on a new interest or type of product (Maffesoli 1996). This is clearly a rhetorical overstatement, at least as applied to Japan, given the continuing ties of work, neighborhoods, voluntary associations, merchants' guilds, and social movements. Nevertheless, it does capture the temporary nature of shifting interest groups and does underline the 'materiality' of most contemporary relationships, which are based on shopping together, eating together or consuming services together, something as true for many adults as it is for Merry White's teenage informants. And since Japanese culture is based as much on self-control as it is on desire, the individual's relationship to consumption is modified by a kind of discipline or self-discipline which modifies the materiality of social bonds (gift-giving, still an extensive and seasonal activity in Japan, being an excellent example). The 'internal psychic world' which Campbell sees as displacing the simple sensuality of the pre-modern hedonist with a world of the imaginary and emotional (Campbell 1987: 70) is consequently to be conceived rather differently in Japan, since the social bond is still primary.

This is not to imply that the Japanese do not enjoy rich interior lives or possess individuality (as some have suggested). Rather I would argue that in Japan the emotional and imaginary were always very much present, but have been modified by modernity, and that additionally, interiority is subordinated to sociality. This makes the adoption of, or historical adaptation to, the construction of identity through consumption really quite easy since in Japan the social bond has always been marked by material relations, which is not to say at all that it is reducible to them. The study of the emotions then takes us back to the body, not understood in terms of biology, but in terms of the social body as the site of the most fundamental cultural politics. This is significant at many levels, not least from the point of view of an influential theory of the postmodern emotions that suggests that we are now living in a 'postemotional' age, one characterized precisely by the collapse of feeling as the core element of culture. This thesis clearly needs to be addressed as it might pertain to Japan, since for at least some commentators, Japan is the quintessential postmodern society, the one that others will follow as modernity passes away. Seen from this perspective, Japan has a universal significance. And insofar as Japan is set on the difficult path of defending and keeping alive a particular social model – of relationality, risk reduction, and bonds between the social and the material – its management of these in the face of globalization and its accompanying pressures of social change, and its attempts to keep this balance, are of profound sociological interest.

Postemotional society or postmodern emotionality?

The theory of the 'postemotional society' has been popularized by the Yugoslav-American sociologist, Stjepan Mestrovic, in a book of that title (Mestrovic 1997). In that book he argues, quite rightly in my view, that in a rationalist-dominated social science universe the emotions are the major element that have not yet been subjected to systematic study. But he then goes on to argue that contemporary late modern society is characterized by 'postemotionality' – a condition in which prepackaged emotions predominate, a thesis built on the assumption that society has become 'mechanized' and that this process includes the mechanization of the emotions (1997: 1). In the pages that follow a jumble of examples of what Mestrovic calls 'quasi-emotions' – including 'niceness,' 'curdled indignation,' nostalgia, the manipulation of the emotions in regard to famines and international events in Africa, the former Yugoslavia and other trouble spots, and the simulational theories of Jean Baudrillard – are listed. All of these quasi-emotions allegedly lead to a 'happy consciousness' in which reality is scripted, controlled, and rendered risk free. The absence of emotional empathy, the unwillingness to become involved and the triumph of 'McDonaldization' lead to a society that in Mestrovic's understanding is divided by ethnic, gender, and life-style splits and dominated by the 'cult of the machine' (1997: 146). This bleak depiction, characterized by a curious mixture of naivety, insight and empirical confusion, is paradoxically written with great passion – but then sociologists have always been famous for denying to the masses qualities that they consider only themselves to have. What the book does raise are interesting comparative theoretical questions. These include the question of whether the spread of standardized routines in specific contexts ('McDonaldization' – cf. Ritzer 1996) can in any way be generalized to a characterization of a society as a whole, especially one like Japan where artisanal and craft production are still common and where very small businesses still predominate, contrary to the common image of Japan as an economy and society dominated by huge corporations. Furthermore Japan is a society in which even McDonald's itself is tempered with highly courteous and friendly service, and in which even the mechanical is quite literally given a human voice – as anyone who has used Japanese ATMs, automatic toll-booths, and other conveniences will recall. Secondly it does again raise the question, made fashionable by Ulrich Beck (1986), of the 'risk society,' in which modernity has created technological, economic, and environmental risks of an unprecedented order. Mestrovic's belief is that the citizens of advanced industrial countries manage this by withdrawing emotionally while maintaining (via TV and other media) a cognitive knowledge of such risks (wars, technological disasters, stock market fluctuations). His model excludes sociological responses to such risks (community solidarity, networks of cooperation and self-help, intentional communities, and political and economic management of such risks at the national governmental or even international level), and also assumes that only one variety of emotional response is possible. Not only does the 'groupism' of Japan suggest that sociological mechanisms for the management of risk are indeed in place, but the argument that modernity can create only a single, negative set of subjectivities is contradicted by the whole Japanese experience and the self-reflection that it has occasioned (Clammer 1995). The 'postemotional' thesis oddly is a theory that simply reproduces at an emotional level the same faults that Western modernization theory created for itself and the world at the economic and political levels. Mestrovic's theory is, paradoxically, a rationalist theory of the emotions, one which itself reproduces the dynamics of modernity in the guise of a critique of it.

The purpose of postmodernity, whatever its other shortcomings might be, is presumably the challenging of such monolithic, rationalist beliefs. I do not wish here to enter the complex territory of the debate over the extent to which contemporary Japan is a postmodern society. However, a case can certainly be made that Japan's path into the world society of the turn of the century has been markedly different from that of other major capitalist economies. For the most part the reasons for this have been sought in economics itself and in underlying institutional patterns, whether sociological or political, but rarely in the patterns that themselves underlie economics and institutional arrangements.

Today's Japanese society contains a complex set of accommodations and resistances to contemporary capitalism and the culture that it generates. Some of these come from 'traditional' sources – the Left and religion – while others come from within the culture of consumer capitalism itself, precisely because such capitalism is itself a paradoxical and internally contradictory creature. The critic Naoki Sakai has suggested that the will to represent everything, to bring everything into 'presence' is the defining characteristic of modern subjectivity (Sakai 1989: 119). Japan, I would suggest, stands in opposition to this principle. The 'hiddenness' of symbolism in much Japanese advertising, the mutability of reality embodied in many forms of Japanese Buddhism, the nature of traditional aesthetics and its contemporary transformations, the nature of the Japanese language itself – all these create fields of ambiguity. Within those fields, different or even quite contradictory interpretations can be given of the same symbolic vocabulary, or a new vocabulary can be created out of existing or emerging symbolism (as in the conventions of *manga* art for example). Advertising, which is often seen as the manipulation of the masses by capital, needs reinterpretation in this context. As Marilyn Ivy puts it, 'That Japanese producers would throw their money into commercials which negate themselves and involve the viewer in a game of complicity reveals the strategic extremes to which capital must go in order to embody the desires of the consumer' (1989: 38).

The extreme informational nature of Japanese society has led Karatani to suggest that Japanese capitalism has in fact surpassed Baudrillard's image of simulational consumerism and as such has created a wholly new discursive space in which transformations and combinations of symbolism, desire, social practice, and ideological formulations can occur which are unexpected from, for example, traditional Leftist or Rightist perspectives (Karatani et al 1984). The result, again in Ivy's words, is that 'In no other postindustrial nation is there more of a polarity between the ordering structures of capital and the accelerated flows of energy and innovation in consumerism' (Ivy 1989:44). This is in a society in which the codified hierarchies of the educational system and the bureaucracy (described in this volume by McVeigh) stand in a complex relationship to the 'liberation of desire' (Ivy 1989: 44) made possible by mass consumption.

Of course, the liberation of desire suggests the expression not just of material energies, but more significantly of emotional ones. For example, nostalgia, a seemingly reactionary response to the problems of late modernity, can in fact become a mechanism for the critique of that modernity, and consequently the media which are the major representatives of capitalism in the 'symbolic society' can in this respect become the agents of its subversion. The same can be said of memory and its revitalization with the passing of the Showa Emperor and the 50th anniversary of the conclusion of the War (Field 1993). The 'New Deal in emotions' (Hirschmeier, 1964: 202) – the non-economic motives which represented the 'liberation of desire' and the consequent upsurge of economic activity in early modern Japan – is paralleled by the libidinal economy of late capitalism expressed through consumption. The mapping of the emotions (e.g. Mita 1992, which attempts a history of nostalgia, joy, tears, folksongs, and other elements of popular culture) needs to be correlated with the evolution of Japanese capitalism, although not identified with it since, as we have suggested, they stand in a complex and sometimes contradictory dialectical relationship.

This question extends beyond emotions, since consumption creates not only new subjectivities in an emotional sense, but also new moralities. At each level capitalism is implicated: Japanese capitalism needs restudying in terms of its hidden history – that of its transforming impact on the human body, the emotions, aesthetics, sociality, and religion and morality. That however is a rather large project of which the present paper is merely an intimation. Suffice it to say that Adorno and Horkheimer's claim that civilization has two histories – the public, political one and an underground one that 'consists in the fate of the human instincts and passions which are displaced and distorted by civilization' (1979: 231), while correct in principle, is based on an argument that an alliance of Christianity and capitalism have made work virtue and the body and desire evil. How this might work out in a society dominated by Buddhism and Shintō and in which it is precisely capitalism that has brought the body out of the kimono and into nudity, and the emotions out of formalized suppression into the liberation of desire, is certainly a matter for much detailed further investigation. What cannot be denied is that the analysis of social and cultural change must be pursued at these levels too, at the levels of the deep grammars of life, and not simply through the study of macro-economic change or of particular institutions and activities taken in isolation, whether they be the media, fashion, gender, literature, education, politics, or industry. The frame that contains them provides the language that they must speak, and the discovery or recovery of that fundamental language is a primary task for cultural analysis.

Notes

Notes to Chapter 1

1 Following on from the pioneering work of Chalmers Johnson (1982) on the Ministry of International Trade and Industry (MITI), the 1990s saw the publication of a series of critical studies of the Japanese ministries, in both historical and contemporary perspectives. Examples of the genre include Miyamoto (1994), Johnson (1995), Gibney ed. (1998), and McVeigh (1998b) on the system in general; Kato (1995) and Hartcher (1997) on finance; McCormack (1996: 25–77) and Woodall (1996) on construction; Garon (1997) on home affairs; Sugihara (1997) on foreign affairs; and Schmid (1996) on justice.

2 For the literature on this period, including a number of biographies of the Meiji oligarchs themselves, see Eades (1999: 41–50, 67–75).

3 The 1990s saw the publication of a number of important studies of Japanese imperialism and colonialism, including Duus, Myers, and Peattie eds (1991) on China; Ka (1995) on Taiwan, Duus (1995) on Korea; Duus, Myers, and Peattie eds (1996) on the wartime Japanese empire; and Young (1998) on Manchuria.

4 For a guide to the literature on these periods, see Eades (1999: 41–50).

5 In addition to the references cited by Bishop, see also Brinton (1993), Hunter ed. (1993), Gelb and Palley eds (1994), Fujimura-Fanselow and Kameda eds (1995), Imamura ed. (1996), Morley (1999).

6 For a general survey, see the essays in Weiner ed. (1997). For recent studies of the Koreans in Japan, see Weiner (1994) on the historical background; Ryang (1997) on the North Korean

community; and Fukuoka (2000) on the experiences of Korean youth.

7 Gill (forthcoming 2001) is one of three major studies of casual labor in recent years, the others being by Fowler (1996) who concentrates on the narratives of the workers, and Stevens (1997) who focuses on the activities of welfare agencies.

8 There have been surprisingly few full-length academic studies in English of traditional crafts in Japan, the main recent exception bcing Moeran (1997).

9 The richness of the literature on consumption is largely due to the Curzon/Hawai'i *ConsumAsiaN* series, edited by Brian Moeran and Lise Skov. This includes volumes on women, media and consumption (Skov and Moeran eds. 1995); popular culture (Treat ed. 1996); advertising (Moeran 1996b); weddings (Goldstein-Gidoni 1997); and department stores (MacPherson ed. 1998). See also the general discussion by Clammer (1997) and the important study by Havens (1994) of the Tsutsumi family and the influence of their Seibu-Saison enterprises on consumption and leisure in Japan.

Notes to Chapter 2

1 The research for this paper was carried out as part of the project on 'Global Japan,' sponsored by the Institute for Cultural and Human Research, Kyoto Bunkyo University. It was also supported by funding from the Japanese Ministry of Education (Project nos.10041094 and 08041003), International Nikkei Research Project of the Japanese American National Museum (funded by the Nippon Foundation), the Ito Foundation, and the Ito Foundation, U.S.A. Their generous support is gratefully acknowledged herewith. I also wish to thank all the interviewees in Hong Kong, Bangkok, Los Angeles, and the San Francisco area for providing valuable personal data so willingly. My thanks are also due to Ms Mari Honda for her help in editing successive versions of the manuscript.

2 For details see e.g. Daniels (1988), Hosokawa (1969), Ichioka (1988), Kitano (1976), Takaki (1994), and Ölschleger (1997).

3 Japanese migrants arrived first in Mexico (1892), followed by Peru (1899), Chile (1903), Cuba (1907), Argentina (1907), Brazil (1908), Panama (1915), Bolivia (1916), Colombia (1921), Uruguay (1930), Paraguay (1930), and Venezuela (1931) (Konno and Fujisaki, 1994: 360–61).

4 In 1970 there were just 2,108 marriages in Japan between a Japanese husband and a foreign wife, against 3,438 between a Japanese wife and a foreign husband. By 1980 the proportions had been reversed, with 4,386 marriages between a Japanese husband and a foreign wife, against 2,875 between a Japanese wife and a foreign husband. Since then the former type of marriage has increased much more rapidly than the latter. By 1997 there were 20,902 marriages between a Japanese husband and a foreign wife, and 7,349 between a Japanese wife and a foreign husband. However, a different pattern emerges if we narrow the focus to marriages between Japanese and Caucasians. For example, in 1997 there were 1,374 marriages between Japanese women and men from the United States, and only 184 between Japanese men and women from the United States. Corresponding figures for 1970 were 1,571 marriages with American men and 75 with American women, showing that this has been a consistent, long-term pattern (Asahi Shimbun 1999: 62–3, citing Ministry of Health and Welfare statistics).

Notes to Chapter 3

1 While one does not want to overstate the degree of potential cooperation among the wide range of Japanese interests engaged in business abroad, a sound argument can be made that these entities represent a far more unified force on a global level than the corporations of any of the other countries in the so-called 'Group of Seven' (G-7) advanced industrial nations. The classic literature on the organization and management of large-scale private enterprises in modern Japan includes Cole (1971), Dore (1973), Rohlen (1974), Clark (1979), and Abegglen and Stalk (1985).

2 Much of my analysis below applies to large Japanese multinational corporations generally. However, the case in this

study is a first-tier, global-scale Japanese manufacturer, a 'household name' in electronics, and a key firm in the Nikkei index, the Japanese equivalent of the Dow Jones Industrial Average. Firms such as this have been closely watched for decades as gauges of Japan's economy. They are viewed as leaders in engendering and innovating 'typical' Japanese corporate practices. That said, I would be the first to acknowledge that the conceptual load that the categories 'typical Japanese corporate practices,' 'Japanese manufacturing' and 'Japanese techniques' have been made to carry must be questioned by those who study social relations in industry. I also acknowledge the distinctions between these large firms and the diverse set of medium and small Japanese firms that are often put forward to undermine generalized claims about 'Japanese enterprise.' For example it is important to recognize that at its peak fewer than one-third of Japanese employees were beneficiaries of the 'lifetime employment' system that is understood as typical of Japanese firms, as Bishop and Gill point out in Chapter 6 and 8. As for their forms of 'internationalization,' small- and medium-scale Japanese firms have had related but different histories abroad. Though thoroughly interesting, these histories will not be described here. For examples in the *butsudan* industry, see Chapter 10.

3 Hannerz' full quote is as follows: 'The macroanthropological project entails a strategic selection of research sites which would take ethnographers to those interfaces where the confrontations, the interpretations and the flowthrough are occurring, between clusters of meaning and ways of managing meaning; in short, the places where diversity gets, in some way and to some degree, organized' (1989: 211). Hannerz' interests would seem to overlap with those of Marcus in his call for 'multi-sited ethnography' (Marcus 1995: 95–117).

4 The English word 'internationalization' often appears in Japanese, transcribed in the phonetic *katakana* script as *intaanashonaraizeeshon*. The equivalent word in Japanese is *kokusaika*, written in Chinese characters. 'Global' and 'globalization' are also regularly used in Japanese, transcribed in *katakana* as *gurōbaru* and *gurōbaraizeeshon*.

5 'Internationalization' and 'globalization' continue to engage much media attention in Japan. In the headlines, however, they have had to compete with more personalized subjects; such as discussion of *karōshi* [death by overwork], and, later, 'the decline of Japan's lifetime employment system,' on which see the chapters by Bishop and Gill in this volume. Currently the Japanese media are full of reports of tearful apologies by corporate leaders whose financial institutions have failed.

6 An example of this from my research in Thailand was a speech by a visiting top manager from Japan, delivered in English translation to 300 Thai employees on the day shift and their twelve Japanese colleagues, to commemorate production of the ten thousandth automobile from the Thai subsidiary.

7 The model's deployment abroad is a different matter from its 'successful' installation. For a treatment of the Japanese model abroad as it relates to shop floor techniques and managerial communication patterns, see Sedgwick (2000).

8 The retrospective treatment of work experienced abroad as a personal 'sojourn' may relate to the frequent assumption that local work practices at the subsidiary abroad will, in the future, come to match practices in Japan – despite the contrary evidence readily available to Japanese managers.

9 In comparing Western and Japanese multinationals in Thailand, my data suggest that Japanese managers are far more aggressive in pushing their solutions to problems at all levels of overseas operations than are expatriate managers at Western multinationals. Though the situation naturally varies depending on particular conditions and the skills of local engineers in particular plants, in Western firms expatriate engineers made themselves available to assist their local (Thai) colleagues who were in the end responsible for their production lines, using what we might call an 'arm's-length' model of management. This matter is explored in greater detail in Sedgwick (1999).

10 Large Japanese corporations are, of course, not literally 'total institutions' as Goffman defines them; Japanese managers can physically leave them. What I am trying to preserve here

is a sense of these corporations as all encompassing. For a Western audience, the image of a 'total institution' is the appropriate marker. Our 'embodiments' of institutions – how we carry them in or with us – are most successfully described, of course, by Foucault. See Goffman (1961), Foucault (1963, 1975).

Notes to Chapter 4

1 Sincc in the data used for this paper the type of measurement varies from one survey question to the other, the degree of concreteness or 'object-relatedness' of a question is in fact the only criterion left for a distinction between values and attitudes.

2 Another possible way of developing personal value systems based on a value synthesis might be socialization conditions that actively favor such a synthesis. These kinds of socialization conditions have been reported for German country town society by Klages (1988: 133–38) and for Japanese schools by Ortmanns (Ortmanns 1994; Ölschleger *et al.* 1994: 165–221), based on a content analysis of Japanese school textbooks.

3 These kinds of processes have been described by the German sociologist Ulrich Beck for postwar West German society as 'accelerated waves of individualization' (Beck 1986: 121–60; 1994). Similar processes accompanying social change are also apparent in Japan, albeit in a different context.

4 Of course, this kind of approach rejects the assumption of the existence of a 'fundamental' or 'modal' value system typical for all contemporary Japanese, in the sense of the culture and personality approach in cultural anthropology. But this does not mean that the assumption of characteristics peculiar to Japanese values is rejected *in toto*.

5 It should be noted that not all values are affected by processes of change in consciousness. A considerable number of values are quite resistant to change and retain a very high (or very low) importance at the aggregate level.

6 The main prerequisites are that the variables are correlated with each other and that they are measured in interval scales.

7 Descriptions of the analyses can be found in Seimei Hoken Bunka Sentaa (1988: 99–104; 1992: 73–76).
8 The percentages for each of the value patterns refer only to respondents with a high score on the respective pattern. For instance in Figure 2, in 1976/77, 27 percent of the respondents scored high in relation to the 'synthesis of traditional and modern values,' while the other 73 percent had average or low scores.
9 Japanese researchers had already become aware of the pluralization of lifestyles and consumption styles during the second half of the 1980s, e.g. Hakuhōdō Seikatsu Sōgō Kenkyūjo (1985) and Akuto and Matsuda (1989).
10 It should be noted that the 1991 Japanese life values survey was conducted in the autumn, after the bursting of the bubble economy.
11 For instance, students with crew cuts are now less common than they were in the late 1980s. Similarly, with 'hair nudes' in every weekly magazine, it is difficult to remember the endless debates on the outlawing of pubic hair in publications.
12 Due to shortage of space, I am attempting here a condensed summary of the main characteristics of the new value patterns and value types. The description is based on the 1985 and 1991 patterns of hedonistic and materialistic values from the *Nihonjin no Seikatsu Kachikan Chōsa*, by the Seimei Hoken Bunka Sentaa; and the 'non-committed' value type from the 1991 *Nihonjin no Kachi Ishiki Chōsa* by the German Institute of Japanese studies, together with their 1996 and 1997 surveys. For details of these surveys and the resulting publications, see the Appendix to this chapter. More detailed descriptions of the value patterns up to 1991 and the value types in the 1990s can be found in Möhwald (1995: 12–31) and Möhwald (1998).
13 The disengagement from politics is not limited to these value patterns and types, but lack of interest, knowledge, and trust concerning politics and politicians can be seen more generally among younger Japanese. Compared with these value types and value patterns, the young individualistic and idealistic types display a strong inclination toward social engagement and voluntary activities, and an interest in social problems.

14 For a detailed discussion of change in Japanese attitudes toward gender equality and the structure of these attitudes, see Möhwald (1996).

Notes to Chapter 5

1 My thinking here is inspired by Huber's notion of Japan's 'strategic economy' (1994).
2 My thoughts expressed here about education policy, strategic schooling, and Japanese identity are explained in more detail in *The Japanese Ministry of Education: Strategic Schooling and the Construction of Japanese Identity* (under review). See also McVeigh (1998a, 1998b).
3 Six years of primary school, followed by three years of junior high school, three years of high school, and four years of university.
4 The humor in this ridicule rested in part on the fact that the characters for Amano's name can also be read 'Tennō' or 'Emperor' (Horio 1988: 147).
5 By 1960, these forces were organized as the Self-Defense Forces under a Defense Agency.

Notes to Chapter 6

1 'Workers at Small Firms Bear Brunt of Job Losses,' *Nihon Keizai Shinbun*, Saturday Nov 27 1999 (*http://www.nni.nikkei.co.jp/AC/TNKS/Search/Nni19991127D27JF894.htm*). Downloaded January 24, 2000.
2 I carried out a pilot study of 214 women who responded to questionnaires and/or took part in semi-structured interviews between 1996 and 1997. I also carried out further interviews with members of women's groups, trade unionists, and women in industries in the process of restructuring between October 1999 and February 2000. During that period I also conducted a focus group. This chapter will be illustrated with the views of these respondents.
3 In fact, the Ministry of Labor's 1990 Comprehensive Survey of the Conditions of Part-Time Workers defined the main criterion for inclusion in the survey as being 'treated as so-

called part-timers' rather than as regular employees. It went on to classify 'part-timers' who worked full-time hours as 'Part Timer B.' Many part-timers work long hours: in 1993 there were 5.65 million workers who were defined by their workplaces as *paato*, but who worked more than 35 hours per week (Wakisaka 1997: 144).

4. Nakura (1997:46), citing H. Shiga, 'Haken rōdō wa career o ikaseruka' [Can agency work promote one's career?], *Keizai Taikoku Nippon no Josei* [Women in Japan, the Economic Giant], 1990 (place and publisher not given).

5 'Top Court hits but backs mom's firing,' *Japan Times*, 29 January 2000, p.2.

6 The group, Women Working in Trading Companies, has issued reports criticizing the Japanese government's positive view of the changes wrought by the EEOL. The Letter to Japanese Women Circle issued a *Counter-Report to the Japanese Government's Second Periodic Report to the Convention on the Elimination of All Forms of Discrimination Against Women* in 1994. From January 21 to 24, 1999, three women working for companies in Osaka gave talks to the IWRAW (International Women's Rights Action Watch), attended the CEDAW convention, and lobbied UN delegates afterwards. In August 1999, the Japan NGO Report Preparatory Committee issued an alternative report to the Special Session of the UN General Assembly on 'Women 2000: Gender Equality, Development and Peace.' A group called Working Women's International Network explained to me their strategy of collecting signatures from overseas as well as in Japan in support of plaintiffs suing the Sumitomo Corporation for alleged sex discrimination: they argued that foreign pressure (*gaiatsu*) was important in campaigning for a global standard of labor rights.

7 By the end of November 1999, 77.3 percent of final year male students at four-year universities had received informal job offers compared to 68.8 percent of female students, while at junior colleges where 90 percent of the students are female, only 46.8 percent of students had received job offers. See 'Job prospects grim for grads amid recruiting cutbacks,' *Nikkei Weekly*, January 24, 2000, (*http://www.nikkei.co.jp/AC/*

TNW/Search/Nni20000124EE101AAA.htm) Downloaded January 24, 2000.

Notes to Chapter 7

Acknowledgments: The bulk of the research for this project was completed with the generous financial support of a Fulbright research grant. Additional support was received from the Institute for the Study of World Politics. I also want to express my gratitude to the entire staff of the Inter-University Center for Japanese Language Studies in Yokohama, for providing the linguistic preparation needed to execute a research project in Japan.

1 The list of such works is already substantial and continues to grow at a rapid pace. See for example, Ooms (1996), Ryang (1997), Sellek (1997), Siddle (1996), Taira (1997), Weiner (1997).

2 This phrase is often used in describing Japan as a mono-racial and mono-cultural nation. For a good discussion of the term and its history see Oguma (1995). The word '*buraku*' originally means simply a 'hamlet,' but it is also used as an abbreviation for phrases such as '*tokushu buraku*' – the 'special' hamlets in which people of outcaste status (the 'Burakumin') lived. The '*buraku* problem' is thus the problem of the status of the Burakumin.

3 *Uchi/soto* refers to inside/outside. It is a familiar concept in Japanese studies. For a general introduction to these concepts, see Bachnik and Quinn eds (1994). For a discussion of these concepts as they relate to discrimination, see Creighton (1997).

4 Information contained in this section comes from participant observation in Osaka during the outbreak of the incident and from a document prepared by the Buraku Liberation League (Buraku Kaihō Dōmei Chūō Honbu and Buraku Kaihō Dōmei Osaka Furengōkai 1998).

5 In 1975 several major Japanese companies were found to be in possession of books listing information (such as name, location, number of households, and major occupations) about more than 5,000 *buraku* areas. For a discussion of this

incident and related issues, see Buraku Kaihō Kenkyūjo 1989 (3): 201–213.

6 This term literally means 'integration' and is written using the characters for 'same' and 'harmony.'

7 Various status systems existed prior to the Tokugawa Era, but they are believed to have no connection to the contemporary *dōwa* issue. See Osaka Jinken Rekishi Shiryōkan (1994) for a concise summary of the various status systems that have existed at various points in Japanese history. Some within the *buraku* liberation movement implicate the Emperor system as part of the problem, arguing that it perpetuates status consciousness by sending the message that some people are above others. Although the topic rarely came up for discussion, each year on the Emperor's birthday, which is a national holiday, the local branch of the BLL in the *dōwa* area where I conducted fieldwork invited a lecturer to come to the community and discuss a human rights issue. In 1998 someone was invited to discuss the Nanking Incident, something which had become quite controversial with the publication of Iris Chang's *The Rape of Nanking* (1997).

8 Please note that 'Eta' is a highly offensive term and is used here only for historical purposes. There is no consensus about whether Burakumin descend exclusively from the 'Eta' class or whether their history can also be traced back to the Hinin class. The boundary between the two was likely crossed frequently as individuals negotiated social status (see Ooms 1996).

9 Concern about states of (im)purity is grounded in Shintoism as well. Some branches of the BLL continue to be active in campaigning against *kegare ishiki* (consciousness of impurity) as manifest for example in the practice of sprinkling salt over one's body before entering the home after attending a funeral for the purpose of purifying oneself. See Sumitomo and Itakura (1998: 100–112) for a general discussion of *kegare*. Miyata (1996) provides a more detailed academic inquiry into this topic.

10 Ninomiya (1933: 115–125) lists the types of social discrimination routinely encountered by former members of the class.

11 Neary (1989) provides a detailed analysis of the genesis and development of this organization.
12 See Neary (1997: 63–69) for a discussion of political tensions within the Suiheisha.
13 Part of this report has been reproduced in Buraku Kaihō Kenkyūjo (1981: 252–259).
14 The financial burden was divided between the national, prefectural and local governments in the ratio 20:10:70.
15 The SML paved the way for 'targeted areas' to receive money for improvement programs. The BLL argues that about 1,000 *mikaihō buraku* (unliberated *buraku*) communities exist which have not been recognized by the government and, consequently, have reaped no benefits from the passage of the SML.
16 This is a pseudonym for the actual community where research was undertaken.
17 Increasingly this has become a centerpiece of annual negotiations (*kōshō*) between the BLL and the prefectural and municipal governments of Osaka.
18 See Rohlen (1976) for an essay detailing how emotionally charged such confrontations can become. Although this is an exceptional case, it is well known in Japan and has made many teachers somewhat reluctant to deal with the *dōwa* issue at school. One informant who was a middle school teacher told me how she was denounced because one of the students in her class used a derogatory term to refer to Burakumin.
19 Building *taiko* drums and engaging in performing arts such as *Kabuki* are just two examples.
20 See note 5 above.
21 See Upham (1987) for a discussion of the legal history of the BLL's use of the tactic of denunciation.
22 Based on participant observation at a couple of denunciation sessions witnessed in Osaka, Japan in 1998 and 1999, my own impression is that they have limited effectiveness. The accused rarely speak candidly about their alleged discriminatory actions. The most common strategy employed by the accused to prevent a politically charged atmosphere from getting out of hand is to apologize profusely without even clarifying exactly why they are apologizing. Nevertheless, the tactic may

have some effectiveness because not only do the accused appear, but also they are typically accompanied by their immediate superior at work (in the case of an incident occurring in a company), and by the president of the company. Denunciation sessions tend to last between 2 to 3 hours. Several such sessions may be held before the issue is resolved to the satisfaction of the BLL. Denunciation sessions do not actually begin until after several *kakuninkai* or confirmation sessions are held to try to establish a record of facts to which all parties can agree. So at the very least, the person accused is responsible for causing a considerable inconvenience to superiors at work. This means that even if one is able to endure the pointed interrogations of the BLL, the odds of emerging unscathed are slim.

23 The full text of the poster read: *Konna sabetsu aru no? Nakusō, buraku sabetsu.*

Notes to Chapter 8

1 Fieldnotes, Sunday September 18, 1994. For evidence that the kind of practice described here is not very exceptional in the Japanese construction industry, see Woodall (1996).

2 The Japan Association for *Yoseba* (JASY; *Yoseba Gakkai*). JASY publishes an annual journal, *Yoseba*, which reached its 13th edition in 2000. Volume 3 of *Yoseba* (1990) includes an annotated bibliography of 100 *yoseba*-related books and papers in the Japanese language. During 2000 JASY was making preparations to publish a new bibliography, this time of 300 books and papers in Japanese. I myself contributed an appendix listing some 40 English-language *yoseba* books and papers, annotated in Japanese. Anyone wishing to delve into this goldmine of proletarian sociology, economics, history and literature, can contact JASY at the following address: C/o Matsuzawa Tessei, Tokyo Women's University, 2-6-1 Zenpukuji, Suginami-ku, Tokyo, Japan. E-mail: tessei@twcu.ac.jp. My own address is tpgill@iss.u-tokyo.ac.jp (English or Japanese) or tpgill@yahoo.com (English only).

3 Like *doya*, this term is a slang reversal: *basho*, standard Japanese for 'place,' is reversed to give *shoba*, and *dai*

(money, fee) is added. Some *tehaishi* will park their minibuses just outside the *yoseba*, to avoid paying *shobadai*. Others, who specialize in long-term contracts, will come to the *yoseba* in their minibuses at weekends, when the yakuza patrols are off duty, again to avoid paying *shobadai*.

4 Foreign manual workers in Japan are mostly illegal, and tend to avoid the *yoseba* districts because of the higher risk of arrest and deportation in these places with concentrations of casual workers. Kotobuki is something of an exception, because of its ethnic Korean landlord class and the continuing demand for strong young men to work at the Yokohama docks. Out of a general population of about 7,000, the foreign population peaked at just over 1,000 in the mid-1990s and was down to about 500 by the end of the decade, as the recession ate into job opportunities. In recent years the great majority of foreigners in Kotobuki have been Korean. There was a thriving Filipino community there in the late 1980s and early 1990s, described by Ventura (1992), but nowadays there are fewer than 100 Filipinos living in Kotobuki. The size and make-up of the foreign population changes very fast.

5 See for example *Asahi Shinbun*, July 6 1994, evening edition, p.17.

6 As far as I know, *ninpudashi* merit little more than a few fleeting references in the English-language literature on Japanese casual labor. JASY is of course fully aware of the institution and does discuss it in its Japanese-language publications, but not to anything like the same degree as the *yoseba*.

7 I know of no English-language account of this dramatic phase in Japanese labor history. There is a vividly-written Japanese-language account by Kamata Satoshi, which I wholeheartedly recommend (Kamata 1994 [1971]).

8 I have changed the widow's name and the first half of her company's name to protect my informant's privacy.

9 I say *around* Tennōji Park, because in 1990 the Osaka city government tried to put an end to this large park's traditional role as a center for homeless people by erecting a high fence around it, instituting an admission fee of ¥150 and closing the park down after dark. A lawsuit by pro-homeless activists

demanding that these moves be rescinded was defeated in court in 1993 (see Dohi 1999). Ever since then there have been rows of makeshift dwellings around the outside of the park.

10 One side effect of this has been a growing trend for homeless men in Tokyo to move to the neighboring city of Yokohama and try their luck with the more liberal regime there. With city finances coming under increasing strain, it is surely only a matter of time before this creates a diplomatic problem between the two huge cities.

11 The 1960s and 1970s saw numerous riots in all the major *yoseba*. Things quietened down after the economic recession following the oil crises in the mid-1970s, but there were major riots in Kamagasaki in 1990 and 1993. I have further detail in Gill (forthcoming 2001).

Notes to Chapter 9

1 '*Yakuza*' here signifies the individual mobster as well as Japanese-style organized crime.

2 The relevant term in almost every annual report, or 'White Paper,' is *kaimetsu*, the 'eradication' of the *yakuza*. For a recent example, see Keisatsuchō (1997: 183).

3 For this perspective I owe much to Pascha (1993), who analyzes *yakuza* using an operational economic approach.

4 This lack of reflection is often condemned, e.g. by Yamaguchi (1990: 102) and Katsura (1990: 39–40).

5 *Gokudō* is a term popular among *yakuza* to denote themselves.

6 On this incident, the publication of a book critical of the Yamaguchi-gumi, and value change in the *yakuza* world, see Herbert (1996b).

7 The most important anthropological work remains that of Iwai (1963), though there is also an outstanding more recent account in Japanese by Raz (1996). A well-researched journalistic account is available in English by Kaplan and Dubro (1986). It covers the history of the underworld as well as recent changes up to the middle of the 1980s. The most recent comprehensive study is the dissertation by Peter Hill (2000). I am grateful to the author for allowing me to read this

excellent study prior to publication, as well as for his insights and ideas. Other books I have used are cited and discussed below.

8 For the following I rely on the account by Ino (1992).

9 This money flow from bottom to top is called *jōnōkin*; I discuss it later in the chapter.

10 *Zainichi* Koreans are permanent residents in Japan of Korean origin, most fully described in the monographs by Ryang (1997) and Fukuoka (2000). An estimated 3 million Japanese are of Burakumin origin. In addition to Davis's chapter in this volume, see also Neary (1989, 1997).

11 These cases, classified by the police as *minji kainyū bōryoku*, are described in more detail below.

12 His career is described in detail by Kaplan and Dubro (1986: 41–123).

13 'Seikai to bōryokudan. Sagawa jiken no danmen 3. "Yami no hiyaku" takai daishō,' *Asahi Shinbun* (November 6 1992: 30).

14 'Seikai to bōryokudan. Sagawa jiken no danmen 1. Home-goroshi chūshi ni jōken,' *Asahi Shinbun* (November 4 1992: 22).

15 *Sōkaiya* are racketeers who blackmail corporations by threatening to disrupt the annual shareholders' meetings by asking awkward questions, though conversely they are also used by the corporations to 'manage' these meetings in some cases (Kaplan and Dubro 1986: 170–71).

16 Gambetta applies economic theory most cogently to explain the emergence and prevalence of mafia firms in Sicily. He makes several references to the *yakuza* and it would be a rewarding task to apply his theoretical framework to them, though this is beyond the scope of this paper. Structural analogies between mafiosi and *yakuza* abound, but so do cultural and other differences, which a more detailed study would have to take carefully into account.

17 For a detailed discussion of the new law, see Endo (1992).

18 A description of the backdrop to Takumi's murder and his biography can be found in Mizoguchi (1997).

19 The police prefer the term 'front company' (*furonto kigyō*). They are managed by relatives of *yakuza* or ex-*yakuza* or merely sponsored by *yakuza* and used for money laundering.

During the last five years well over 200 *furonto* per annum have been uncovered by police, through arrests resulting from legal infringements (Keisatsuchō 1997: 186).

20 For a case study see *The Daily Yomiuri* (May 27 1997). A racy description of a case in which two rival *yakuza* gangs were involved can also be found in Seymour (1996: 82–88). Seymour presents a lively, witty account of a three-month period spent hanging out with *yakuza*. He witnessed a remarkable range of activities, including an ammunition transaction, nocturnal shooting practice, traditional gambling, and even the rare import of cocaine and some violent beatings. However, some linguistic blunders of a very fundamental nature cast a shadow of doubt on the credibility of his study and the accuracy of his rendering of dialogues and stories, e.g. *hari-maki* instead of *haramaki* (p. 26) Shimizu no Jirōchō is made into Jinrochō (p. 26 and in the rest of the book), *des* is given instead of *desu* (p. 172), *shinjinue* instead of *shinjinrui* (p. 181ff.), Setaguya instead of Setagaya (p. 192) and *sensai* instead of *sensei* (p. 198 ff.).

21 See Herbert (1996: 28ff. and 64ff), where I underestimated the later involvement of *yakuza*.

22 See e.g. *The Daily Yomiuri* January 21 1997.

23 Cf. also the survey on the effects of the new law in its first year in Keisatsuchō (1993), which was extensively quoted in the mass media.

24 This was in an interview I conducted with him on December 9, 1997.

Notes to Chapter 10

Acknowledgements: This paper is based on research carried out by Carla Eades, Nishiyama Yuriko and Yanase Hiroko from 1996 to 2000. Quotations in the text are taken from interviews with local artisans and *butsudan* dealers, transcribed and edited by Nishiyama and Yanase. The paper was drafted by Carla Eades, with Jerry Eades supplying help with background literature, bibliography, and editing. We are grateful to members of the Hikone Butsudan Kumiai who gave so freely of their time in providing information about the industry.

Special thanks are due to Eirakuya who provided the photograph of a *butsudan* reproduced here. Unless stated otherwise in the text, opinions and interpretations expressed here are those of the researchers and not those of the Kumiai.

1 The Japanese Ministry of International Trade and Industry (*Tsūshin Sangyōshō*), often abbreviated to MITI in English or *Tsūsanshō* in Japanese, is well known from the work of Chalmers Johnson (1982) as having guided the Japanese economy to commanding heights during the period of the postwar economic miracle. However, it also has a remit to look after the interests of the medium- and small-sized businesses which make up the majority of Japanese enterprises, including local-level craft production as discussed in this paper.

2 On Hikone Castle and its changing meaning for the city, see Mock (1993).

3 The literature on *butsudan* in both Japanese and English is limited, perhaps surprisingly, given their ubiquity and cultural importance in the household. The main discussion in English of their use in ritual is still perhaps that given by Smith (1974), but there is hardly any discussion in English of their production. Important studies in Japanese include those by Nakae ed. (1977), and Nomura ed. (1977), which includes a brief section on Hikone. On production in the Hikone area see also Hikone Butsudan Kigyō Kyōdō Kumiai ed. (1996), and the relevant sections in vol. 3 of the official history of the city, *Hikone Shishi* (Hikone Shiyakusho 1987). Popular accounts of the use of *butsudan* in ritual in Japanese include Hanayama (1988). On contemporary trends in *butsudan* design, see Ekuan (1986)

4 The name, Nanamagari, refers to the seven bends in the road, which is in striking contrast to the grid layout that predominates in much of the rest of the city. 'Shinmachi' simply means 'New Town.'

5 These trade shows are held every two years, rotating between the production areas, and (until recently) resulted in lavish catalogues with photographs of the exhibits.

6 The others are Himeji, Inuyama, and Matsumoto. Most of the others were either demolished at the start of the Meiji period, or destroyed during the bombing of the Second World War.

On the layout of Japanese castle towns in general, see e.g. Yazaki (1973), Jinnai (1995, chapters 1–2), and Cybriwsky (1998: 54–62). On Hikone, see Mock (1993).

7 Standard Japanese textbooks on Buddhism often present diagrams of typical *butsudan* designs and layouts for a number of different sects. Useful concise accounts of the history of Japanese Buddhism are contained in Bowring and Kornicki eds (1993: 158–64), and the books by Picken (1982), Kitagawa (1966), and Reader (1991).

8 For more details on the rise of Jōdoshinshū see Ogura (1996: 15), Kitagawa (1966: 116), and Kashiwahara and Sonoda eds (1994: 161–64).

9 On the development of the Hikone industry, see Ogura (1996), Nomura ed. (1977) and the official history of Hikone, (Hikone Shiyakusho 1987, especially vol. 3: 306–14).

10 The Kumiai Newsletter of November 1999 reflected this pessimism, on the basis of the national exhibition held that year in Kagoshima. The writer made the point that though the Hikone *butsudan* on display were well made, they lacked the originality to be found in the work of the other production areas, which were trying harder to adapt their products to the modern market.

11 The descriptions of production in this section are compiled from interviews with informants, together with the relevant chapters in the books edited by Nakae (1977) and Hikone Butsudan Jigyō Kyōdō Kumiai (1996), and with the papers in Nomura ed. (1977). Assembly is not usually considered one of the seven traditional Hikone *butsudan* crafts.

12 Significantly, there is hardly any market in second-hand *butsudan*. In Hikone, most *butsudan* that are no longer required are collected by the Kumiai, exorcised by a Buddhist priest, and cremated along with their fittings at a ceremony held once or twice a year.

13 Many Japanese festivals, or *matsuri* (Ashkenazi 1993; Plutschow 1996), involve the use of portable shrines or elaborately decorated and carved floats called *dashi* which are pulled through the streets by the townspeople. Some of these are officially designated as national treasures or

important cultural properties in their own right, and therefore require skilled maintenance and restoration.

Notes to Chapter 11

1 For an exhaustive description and discussion of the various rituals in the *Aki no Mine* see Blacker (1992) and Earhart (1970).

2 At this stage I still had, like all other first-time participants, a provisional name, which marked me as a member on probation. The actual naming, marking the achievement of regular membership, followed after our 'rebirth' at the end of the *Aki no Mine*.

3 From then on, every new introduction in the Haguro area was accompanied by the information that I had gone through the *Aki no Mine* at Kōtakuji ('*tera de sanka shita*,' lit. 'He joined in at the temple.').

4 The data for this section are taken from Togawa (1950, 1954), Hayashi (1993), Earhart (1970), and my interviews with Mr. Shimazu Kōkai, priest at Shōzen'in and spiritual head of the Hagurosan Shugendō Sōhonbu, and with Mr. Hoshino Fumiharo, former vice director of the Ideha Bunka Kinenkan and member of Ideha Jinja's *yamabushi* organization.

5 These were mainly services of a ritual nature, such as rites of commemoration, divination, or exorcism, but they also included the sale of amulets, or guidance during pilgrimages. For an extensive list of rituals conducted by *yamabushi*, or *shugenja*, see Miyake (1989).

6 Some idea of the extent of this religious enterprise can be gained from Mizoguchi's comment (in Hori 1974: 142) that 'more than 90 per cent of the village shrines in mid-northern and northeastern Japan were served by Shugendō priests.' In his detailed account of the Mount Haguro religious organization in the mid-eighteenth century, Togawa (1950: 167–70) says that the number of Haguro-affiliated temples exceeded 4,000 in those days.

7 An administrative post, equivalent to a managing director.

8 Again, Earhart (1970) is the book to turn to for an accurate description of the ceremony as it is conducted today, the only

difference being that nowadays those parts taking place at night are floodlit for the benefit of the various TV crews present.

9 On the last day of the *Aki no Mine*, I accompanied several young members of the Kōtakuji group to their rivals' public performance of the *saitō goma* fire ritual, where their declared goal was to annoy the performers of the rival group with their loud comments on what they perceived as ritual bungles. Once they were satisfied with the stir they had caused, they left the scene in truly theatrical manner, with an extra loud (and for the shrine extra annoying) rendition of the Hannya Shingyō on the steps of Ideha Jinja. On a more positive note, the *daisendatsu* of the Jinja *yamabushi* recently advised his followers during the *Aki no Mine* to line up outside their mountain retreat and to show their respect to Kōtakuji's *yamabushi* by applauding their passing procession.

10 Gans speaks of 'overidentification,' a somewhat critical term which infers a dividing line between the 'right' amount of identification and 'too much' identification.

References

Abe, Y. (1994) 'Bases for educational reconstruction: March 8, 1946,' in E.R. Beauchamp and J.M. Vardaman, Jr. (eds), *Japanese Education since 1945: A Documentary Study* (Armonk: M.E. Sharpe), pp. 82–85.

Abegglen, J. C. and G. Stalk, Jr (1985) *Kaisha: The Japanese Corporation*, Tokyo, Charles E. Tuttle.

Adachi, S. (1987) 'Gokudō jaanarizumu wa shimin shakai no torankiraizaa da' [*Yakuza* journalism is the tranquillizer of civic society] in Ishii Shinji (ed.) *Yakuza to iu ikikata. Toshi no soko ni hisomu otokotachi no monogatari* [The *yakuza* way of life: tales of men lurking in the depths of the city] (Tokyo: JICC), pp. 242–51.

Adorno, T. and M. Horkheimer (1979) *The Dialectic of Enlightenment*, London: Verso.

Akuto, H. and Y. Matsuda (1989) *'Yutori' jidai no raifusutairu* [Lifestyles in the era of 'comfort'], Tokyo: Nihon Keizai Shinbunsha.

Allen, M. (1994) *Undermining the Japanese Miracle: Work and Conflict in a Coalmining Community*, Cambridge: Cambridge University Press.

Allison, A. (1996) *Permitted and Prohibited Desires*, Boulder: Westview Press.

Aoki, H. (1997) 'Nikkei kokusai kekkon kōryū sekai taikai,' [A world conference of ethnic Japanese in international marriages], *Kaigai Ijū* 576: 7.

Appadurai, A. (1990) 'Disjuncture and difference in the global cultural economy,' in M. Featherstone (ed.), *Global Culture: Nationalism, Globalization and Modernity* (London: Sage Publications), pp. 295–310.

Araki, T. (1998) 'Recent legislative developments in equal employment and harmonization of work and family life in Japan,' *Japan Labour Bulletin*, 37(4).

Arlacchi, P. (1986) *Mafia Business: The Mafia Ethic and the Spirit of Capitalism*, Oxford: Oxford University Press.

Asahi Shimbun (ed.) (1999) *Asahi Shimbun Japan Almanac 2000*. Tokyo: Asahi Shimbun-sha.

Asakura, K. (1987) 'Yamaguchi-gumi wa naze kaimetsu shinai no ka?' [Why doesn't the Yamaguchi Syndicate collapse?], in S. Ishii (ed.) *Yakuza to iu ikikata. Toshi no soko ni hisomu otokotachi no monogatari* [The *yakuza* way of life: tales of men lurking in the depths of the City] (Tokyo: JICC), pp. 230–41.

Ashkenazi, M. (1993) *Matsuri: Festivals of a Japanese Town*, Honolulu: University of Hawai'i Press.

Aston, G.W. (1972) *Nihongi*, Tokyo: Charles E. Tuttle.

Bachnik, J. and C. Quinn (eds) (1994) *Situated Meaning: Inside and Outside in Japanese Self, Society, and Language*, Princeton: Princeton University Press.

Barnes, J.A. (1979) *Who Should Know What? Social Science, Privacy and Ethics*, Harmondsworth: Penguin.

Baudrillard, J. (1970) *La Société de Consommation*, Paris: Gallimard.

Bauman, Z. (1998) *Globalization: The Human Consequences*, Cambridge: Polity Press.

Beauchamp, E.R. (1994) 'Introduction: Japanese education since 1945,' in E.R. Beauchamp and J.M. Vardaman, Jr (eds), *Japanese Education Since 1945: A Documentary Study* (Armonk: M. E. Sharpe), pp. 3–33.

Beauchamp, E.R. and J.M. Vardaman, Jr (eds) (1994) *Japanese Education since 1945: A Documentary Survey*, Armonk: M.E. Sharpe.

Beauchamp, T.L. *et al.* (eds) (1982) *Ethical Issues in Social Science Research*, Baltimore: Johns Hopkins University Press.

Beck, U. (1986) *Risikogesellschaft: Auf dem Weg in eine andere Moderne*, Frankfurt am Main: Suhrkamp. [Translated as *Risk Society: Towards a New Modernity*, London: Sage, 1994.]

.... (1994) 'Jenseits von Stand und Klasse?' in U. Beck and E. Beck-Gernsheim (eds), *Riskante Freiheiten: Individualisierung in Modernen Gesellschaften* (Frankfurt am Main: Suhrkamp), pp. 43–60.

Befu, H. and N. Stalker (1996) 'Globalization of Japan: cosmopolitanization or spread of the Japanese village?' in H. Befu (ed.),

Japan Engaging the World: A Century of International Encounter (*Teikyo Loretto Heights University Japan Studies,* vol. 1, no. 1), pp. 101–20.

Bell, D. (1976) *The Cultural Contradictions of Capitalism*, London: Heinemann Educational.

Benedict, R. (1946) *The Chrysanthemum and the Sword: Patterns of Japanese Culture*, Boston: Houghton Mifflin.

Benjamin, G.R. (1997) *Japanese Lessons: A Year in a Japanese School through the Eyes of an American Anthropologist and her Children*, New York: New York University Press.

Billig, M. (1995) *Banal Nationalism*, London: Sage.

Blacker, C. (1992) *The Catalpa Bow* (2nd edn), London: Harper-Collins.

Bourdieu, P. (1984) *Questions de Sociologie*, Paris: Les Editions de Minuit.

Boxer, C.R. (1951) *The Christian Century in Japan, 1549–1650*, Berkeley: University of California Press.

Bowring, R. and P. Kornicki (eds) (1993) *The Cambridge Encyclopedia of Japan*, Cambridge: Cambridge University Press.

Bozono, S. (1998) '*Yakuza* on the defensive,' *Japan Quarterly* 45(1): 79–86.

Brackett, D.W. (1996) *Holy Terror: Armageddon in Tokyo*, New York: Weatherhill.

Brameld, T. (1968) *Japan: Culture, Education, and Change in Two Communities*, New York: Holt, Rinehart & Winston.

Brinton, M.C. (1993) *Women and the Economic Miracle: Gender and Work in Postwar Japan*, Berkeley: University of California Press.

Broadbent, J. (1998) *Environmental Politics in Japan: Networks of Power and Protest,* Cambridge: Cambridge University Press.

Brown, A. (1989) *The Genius of Japanese Carpentry*, Tokyo: Kōdansha.

Brown, N. (1996) The *Nisetai Jūtaku* Phenomenon: The Prefabricated Housing Industry and Changing Family Patterns in Contemporary Japan, DPhil dissertation, Oxford University.

Bryman, A. (1995) *Disney and his Worlds*, London: Routledge.

BTHKS (Bōryokudan Tsuihō Hyōgo Kenmin Sentaa [Hyogo Prefecture Citizens' Center for the Expulsion of Yakuza]) (ed.)

(1977) *Bōtsui sentaa dayori* [BTHKS Bulletin] 11. Tokyo: Bōryokudan Tsuihō Hyōgo Kenmin Sentaa.

Bulmer, M. (ed.) (1982) *Social Research Ethics*, London: Macmillan.

Buraku Kaihō Kenkyūsho [Buraku Liberation Research Center] (1981) *Long Suffering Brothers and Sisters Unite! The Buraku Problem, Universal Human Rights, and Minority Problems in Various Countries,* Osaka: Kaihō Shuppansha.

.... (1989) *Buraku kaihōshi* [History of Buraku liberation] (3 vols.), Osaka: Kaihō Shuppansha.

.... (1997) *Konnichi no Buraku sabetsu: kakuchi no jittai chōsa kekka yori* [Buraku discrimination today: based on the results of a survey to assess conditions in each region], Osaka: Kaihō Shuppansha.

Buraku Kaihō Dōmei Chūo Honbu [Buraku Liberation League Central HQ] and Buraku Kaihō Dōmei Osaka Furengōkai [BLL Osaka Prefecture Association] (1998) *Anata mo shiraberarete imasu: sabetsu chōsa jiken no shinsō* [You too are being investigated: the truth about the discriminatory investigation incident], Osaka: Buraku Kaihō Dōmei Chūō Honbu and Buraku Kaihō Dōmei Osaka Furengōkai.

Caldarola, C. (1968) 'The *doya-gai*: a Japanese version of skid row,' *Pacific Affairs* 41: 511–25.

Calder, K.E. (1993) *Strategic Capitalism: Private Business and Public Purpose in Japanese Industrial Finance*, Princeton: Princeton University Press.

Campbell, C. (1987) *The Romantic Ethic and the Spirit of Modern Consumerism*, Oxford: Basil Blackwell.

Carlile, L. and M. Tilton (1998) 'Is Japan really changing,' in L. Carlile and M. Tilton (eds), *Is Japan Really Changing Its Ways?* (Washington D.C.: Brookings Institute Press), pp. 197–218.

Carney, L. and C. O'Kelly (1990) 'Women's work and women's place in the Japanese economic miracle,' in K. Ward (ed.), *Women Workers and Global Restructuring* (Ithaca: ILR Press, School of Industrial and Labor Relations, Cornell University), pp. 113–45.

Cassel, J. and M.L. Wax (eds) 1979 'Ethical problems of field-work,' *Social Problems* 27(3): 259–378.

Castells, M. (1996) *The Information Age, vol. I. The Rise of the Network Society*, Oxford: Blackwell.

.... (1997) *The Information Age, vol. II. The Power of Identity*, Oxford: Blackwell.

.... (1998) *The Information Age, vol. III. End of Millennium*, Oxford: Blackwell.

Chalmers, N.J. (1989) *Industrial Relations in Japan: The Peripheral Workforce,* London: Routledge.

Chan, S. (1993) *East Asian Dynamism: Growth, Order, and Security in the Pacific Region*, Boulder: Westview Press.

Chang, I. (1997) *The Rape of Nanking: The Forgotten Holocaust of World War II*, Harmondsworth: Penguin.

Clammer, J. (1995) *Difference and Modernity: Social Theory and Contemporary Japanese Society*, London: Kegan Paul International.

.... (1997) *Contemporary Urban Japan: A Sociology of Consumption*, Oxford: Blackwell.

Clark, R. (1979) *The Japanese Company*, New Haven: Yale University Press.

Clear, L. (1991) Education for Social Change: The Case of Japan's Buraku Liberation Movement, EdD dissertation, University of California, Los Angeles.

Coates, D. (ed.) (1990) *Shattering the Myth of the Homogeneous Society: Minority Issues and Movements in Japan*, Berkeley: Japan Pacific Resource Network.

Cole, R.E. (1971) *Japanese Blue Collar*, Berkeley, University of California Press.

Cook, A. and H. Hayashi (1980) *Working Women in Japan: Discrimination, Resistance, and Reform*, Ithaca: Cornell University (Cornell International Industrial and Labor Relations Report, no. 10).

Creighton, M. (1997) '*Soto* others and *uchi* others: imaging racial diversity, imagining homogeneous Japan,' in M. Weiner (ed.), *Japan's Minorities: The Illusion of Homogeneity* (London: Routledge).

Curtis, G.L. (1999) *The Logic of Japanese Politics: Leaders, Institutions, and the Limits of Change*, New York: Columbia University Press.

Cushing, F.H. (1967 [1882–83]) *My Adventures in Zuni*, Palmer Lake: Filter Press.

Cybriwsky, R. (1998) *Tokyo: The Shogun's City at the Twenty-First Century*, Chichester: John Wiley & Sons.

Dale, P.N. (1995) *The Myth of Japanese Uniqueness*, London: Routledge.

Daniels, R. (1988) *Asian America: Chinese and Japanese in the United States since 1850,* Seattle: University of Washington Press.

de Barry, B. (1985) 'San'ya: Japan's internal colony,' in E.P. Tsurumi (ed.), *The Other Japan: Postwar Realities* (Armonk: M.E. Sharpe), pp. 112–18.

Dearing, J.W. (1995) *Growing a Japanese Science City: Communication in Scientific Research*, London: Routledge.

DeVos, G. and H. Wagatsuma (eds) (1967) *Japan's Invisible Race: Caste in Culture and Personality,* Berkeley: University of California Press.

Dittmar, H. (1992) *The Social Psychology of Material Possessions*, New York: St. Martin's Press.

Dohi, M. (1999) 'The community design process at Kamagasaki, Osaka, Japan,' in *Democratic Design in the Pacific Rim* (Michigan: Ridge Times Press), pp. 228–40.

Dore, R. (1973) *British Factory, Japanese Factory: The Origins of National Diversity in Industrial Relations*, Berkeley: University of California Press.

.... (1986) *Flexible Rigidities: Industrial Policy and Structural Adjustment in the Japanese Economy 1970–1980*, London: Athlone Press

Duus, P. (1995) *The Abacus and the Sword: The Japanese Penetration of Korea, 1895–1910*, Berkeley: University of California Press.

Duus, P., R.H. Myers, and M.R. Peattie (eds) (1991) *The Japanese Informal Empire in China, 1895–1937*, Princeton: Princeton University Press.

.... (1996) *The Japanese Wartime Empire, 1931–1945*, Princeton: Princeton University Press.

Eades, J.S. (1999) *Tokyo*, Oxford: ABC-Clio (World Bibliographical Series, 214).

Earhart, H.B. (1970) *A Religious Study of the Mount Haguro Sect of Shugendō*, Tokyo: Sophia University.

Economic Planning Agency (1995) *Survey of Life Preferences of Japanese Citizens*, Tokyo: Economic Planning Agency (*http://jin.jcic.or.jp/insight/html/focus05/data/DATA006*).

Eisenstadt, S.N. (1996) *Japanese Civilization: A Comparative View*, Chicago: University of Chicago Press.

Ekuan Kenji (1986) *Butsudan to Jidōsha* [Buddhist Altars and Automobiles], Tokyo: Dharma Books.

Elias, N. (1978–82) *The Civilizing Process, vol. I: The History of Manners, vol. II: State Formation and Civilization*, Oxford: Basil Blackwell.

.... (1995) 'On human beings and their emotions: a process-sociological essay,' in M. Featherstone, M. Hepworth and B.S. Turner (eds) *The Body: Social Process and Cultural Theory* (London: Sage), pp. 339–61.

Elison, G. (1973) *Deus Destroyed: The Image of Christianity in Early Modern Japan*, Cambridge, Massachusetts: Harvard University Press.

Endo, M. (1992) *Kaidoku. Bōryokudan shinpō*, [Reading the new law on organised crime], Tokyo: Gendai shokan.

Field, N. (1993) *In the Realm of a Dying Emperor: Japan at Century's End*, New York: Vintage Books.

Foucault, M. (1963) *Naissance de la Clinique: Une Archéologie du Regard Médical*, Paris: Presses Universitaires de France.

.... (1975) *Surveiller et Punir: Naissance de la Prison*, Paris: Gallimard.

Fowler, E. (1996) *San'ya Blues: Laboring Life in Contemporary Japan*, Ithaca: Cornell University Press.

Fox, C.M. (1999) 'Changing Japanese employment patterns and women's participation: anticipating the implications of employment trends,' *The Manoa Journal* 3 (*http://www.soc.hawaii.edu/future/j3/fox.html*).

Friedrichs, J. (1968) *Werte und soziales Handeln. Ein Beitrag zur soziologischen Theorie*, Tübingen: Mohr.

Fujimura-Fanselow, K. and A. Kameda (eds) (1995) *Japanese Women: New Feminist Perspectives on the Past, Present, and Future*, New York: Feminist Press at the City University of New York.

Fujita, K. and R.C. Hill (eds) (1993) *Japanese Cities in the World Economy*, Philadelphia: Temple University Press.

Fukuoka, Y. (2000) *Lives of Young Koreans in Japan*, Melbourne: Trans Pacific Press.

Fukushima, S. (1981) 'Butsudanron nōto' [A note on the theory of Buddhist altars], *GK News* (Tokyo: Group Koike), December 1981: 12.

Furuta, M. (1998) 'Shokuminchi to dai-ni-ji sekai taisen,' [Colonies and the Second World War], in D. Yui and M. Furuta, *Sekai no rekishi 28: Dai-ni-ji Sekai Taisen kara Bei-So tairitsu e* [World History, 28: From the Second World War to the confrontation between America and Russia], Tokyo: Chūō Kōron-sha, pp. 124–90.

Gambetta, D. (1993) *The Sicilian Mafia: The Business of Private Protection*, Cambridge, Massachusetts: Harvard University Press.

Gambetta, D. and P. Reuter (1995) 'Conspiracy among the many: the mafia in legitimate industries,' in G. Fiorentini and S. Peltzman (eds) *The Economics of Organised Crime* (Cambridge: Cambridge University Press), pp. 116–36.

Gans, H.J. (1982) 'The participant-observer as a human being: Observations on the personal aspects of field work,' in R. Burgess (ed.) *Field Research: a Sourcebook and a Field Manual* (London: Allen & Unwin).

Garon, S. (1997) *Molding Japanese Lives: The State in Everyday Life*, Princeton: Princeton University Press.

Gelb, J. (1998) 'The equal employment opportunity law', *Yale Asia-Pacific Review* 1 (November): 44–66.

Gelb, J. and M.L. Palley (eds) (1994) *Women of Japan and Korea: Continuity and Change*, Philadelphia: Temple University Press.

Gellner, E. (1983) *Nations and Nationalism*, Oxford: Basil Blackwell.

Giamo, B. (1994) 'Order, disorder and the homeless in the United States and Japan,' *Doshisha American Research* 31: 1–19.

Gibney, F. (ed.) (1998) *Unlocking the Bureaucrat's Kingdom: Deregulation and the Japanese Economy*, Washington, D.C.: Brookings Institution Press.

Gill, T. (1999) 'Wage hunting at the margins of urban Japan,' in S. Day, E. Papataxiarchis, and M. Stewart (eds), *Lilies of the Field:*

Marginal People Who Live for the Moment (Boulder: Westview Press), pp. 119–36.

.... (forthcoming 2001) *Men of Uncertainty: The Social Organization of Day Laborers in Contemporary Japan*, Albany: State University of New York Press.

Goffman, E. (1961) *Asylums: Essays on the Social Situation of Mental Patients and Other Inmates*, New York: Anchor Books.

.... (1963) *Stigma: Notes on the Management of Spoiled Identity*, Englewood Cliffs: Prentice Hall.

Goldstein-Gidoni, O. (1997) *Packaged Japaneseness: Weddings, Business and Brides*, Honolulu: University of Hawai'i Press.

Gordon, A. (ed.) (1993) *Postwar Japan as History*, Berkeley: University of California Press.

Gottfried, H. and N. Hayashi-Kato (1998) 'Gendering work: deconstructing the narrative of the Japanese economic miracle,' *Work, Employment and Society* 12 (1): 25–41.

Hakuhōdō Seikatsu Sōgō Kenkyūsho [Hakuhōdō Lifestyle General Research Center] (1985) 'Bunshū no tanjō [The birth of the 'divided mass'], Tokyo: Nihon Keizai Shinbun-sha..

Hanayama K. (1988) *Sosen no kuyō. Kore dake shite ireba jubun.* [Memorial services for ancestors: this is all you need to know], Tokyo: Escargot Books.

Hani G. (1979) *Kyōiku no ronri – Monbushō haishi-ron* [The logic of education - the argument for abolishing the Ministry of Education], Tokyo: Diamond-sha.

Hannerz, U. (1986) 'Theory in anthropology: small is beautiful? The problem of complex cultures,' *Comparative Studies in Society and History* 28: 362–67.

.... (1989) 'Culture between center and periphery: toward a macroanthropology,' *Ethnos* 54: 200–16.

.... (1990) 'Cosmopolitans and locals in world culture,' *Theory, Culture and Society* 7 (2–3): 237–51.

.... (1992) *Cultural Complexity: Studies in the Social Organization of Meaning*, New York, Columbia University Press.

Hartcher, P. (1997) *The Ministry: The Inside Story of Japan's Ministry of Finance*, London: HarperCollins Business.

Hashimoto, S. and K. Takahashi (1994) *Nihonjin no ishiki no 20 nen* [Japanese consciousness over 20 years], Tokyo: NHK Hōsō

Bunka Kenkyūjo Yoron Chōsa-bu [NHK Broadcasting Culture Research Center, Public Opinion Survey Department].

Havens, T. (1974) *Farm and Nation in Modern Japan: Agrarian Nationalism, 1870–1940*, Princeton: Princeton University Press.

.... (1994) *Architects of Affluence: The Tsutsumi Family and the Seibu-Saison Enterprises in Twentieth-Century Japan*, Cambridge, Massachusetts: Council of East Asian Studies, Harvard University.

Hayashi, C. (1988) *Nihonjin no kokoro o hakaru* [Measuring the Japanese mind], Tokyo: Asahi Shinbun-sha.

Hayashi, C., S. Nishihira, and T. Suzuki (1965) *Zusetsu: nihonjin no kokuminsei*, [A diagrammatical chart: the national character of the Japanese], Tokyo: Shiseidō.

Hayashi, M. (ed.) (1993) *Zusetsu Dewa Sanzan Jinja 1400 nen* [A diagrammatical chart: 1,400 years of Dewa Sanzan Shrine], Haguro: Dewa Sanzan Jinja Shamusho [Dewa Sanzan Shrine Affairs Office].

Heitmeyer, W. *et al.* (1995) *Gewalt: Schattenseiten der Individualisierung bei Jugendlichen aus unterschiedlichen Milieus*, Weinheim, München: Juventa.

Hendry, J. (1995) *Understanding Japanese Society* (2nd edn), London: Routledge.

Herbert, W. (1992) '*Yakuza* – ausgegrenzte Subkultur oder integrierter Teil der japanischen Gesellschaft?' in E. Lokowandt (ed.) *Zentrum und Peripherie in Japan. Referate des 2. Japanologentages der OAG in Tokyo, 8./9. März 1990* (München: Iudicium), pp. 79–105.

.... (1996a) *Foreign Workers and Law Enforcement in Japan*, London: Routledge.

.... (1996b) 'Gewalt statt Harmonie? Zum Wertewandel in der Yakuza-Ethik,' in A. Schründer-Lenzen (ed.) *Harmonie und Konformität. Tradition und Krise japanischer Sozialisationsmuster* (München: Iudicium) pp. 210–23.

Herbert, W. and H.-J. Hippler (1991) 'Der Stand der Wertwandelsforschung am Ende der achtziger Jahre. "State-of-the-art" und Analyse der dokumentierten Forschungsergebnisse,' in M. Bockler *et al.* (eds), *Wertwandel und Werteforschung in den*

80er Jahren. Forschungs- und Literaturdokumentation 1980–1990 (Bonn: Informationszentrum Sozialwissenschaften), pp. vii–xxxix.

Higuchi, Y. (1993) 'Kōhyō deeta ni yoru kaiki bunseki kara mita Nihon kigyō to gaishikei kigyō no chigai' [On the difference between Japanese companies and foreign affiliated companies by regression analysis of published data], *Chōsa Kenkyū Hōkokusho* [Research Report] 48: 146–182.

Hikone Butsudan Jigyō Kyōdō Kumiai (ed) (1996) *Ōmi no teshigoto: Hikone butsudan* [Ōmi Craftsmanship: Hikone Buddhist Altars], Hikone: Hikone Butsudan Jigyō Kyōdō Kumiai.

Hikone Shiyakusho [Hikone City Office] (1987) *Hikone shishi* [History of Hikone], 3 vols., Hikone: Hikone Shiyakusho.

Hill, P. (2000) Japanese Organized Crime under the Bōryokudan Countermeasures Law, PhD dissertation, University of Stirling, Scottish Centre for Japanese Studies.

Hirasawa, Y. (1989) A Policy Study of the Evolution of Dōwa Education, EdD dissertation, Harvard University.

Hirschmeier, J. (1964) *The Origin of Entrepreneurship in Meiji Japan*, Cambridge, Massachusetts: Harvard University Press.

Hobsbawm, E. (1983) 'Introduction: inventing traditions,' in E. Hobsbawm and T. Ranger (eds) *The Invention of Tradition* (Cambridge: Cambridge University Press), pp. 1–14.

Hōmu Sōgō Kenkyūsho [General Research Center for Legal Affairs] (ed.) (1989) *Hanzai hakusho. Shōwa no keiji seisaku* [White Paper on crime: crime-fighting policy in the Shōwa era], Tokyo: Ōkurashō Insatsu-kyoku.

Hori, I. (1974) *Folk Religion in Japan: Continuity and Change*, Chicago: University of Chicago Press.

Horio, T. (1988) *Educational Thought and Ideology in Modern Japan: State Authority and Intellectual Freedom*, Tokyo: University of Tokyo Press.

Hoshino, K. (1980) 'Bōryokudan'in to ruihan,' [Gang members and repeat offenses] *Hanzai Shakaigaku Kenkyū* [Research on the Sociology of Crime] 5: 42–61.

Hosokawa, B. (1969) *Nisei: The Quiet Americans. The Story of a People*, New York: W. Morrow.

Huber, T.M. (1994) *Strategic Economy in Japan*, Boulder: Westview Press.

Hughes, E.C. (1960) 'Introduction: The place of field work in social science,' in B. Junker, *Field Work: An Introduction to the Social Sciences* (Chicago: University of Chicago Press).

Hulme, D. (1996) 'Temps catch on in Japan,'*Japan Times,* April 1, 1996 (*http://web3asia1.com.sg/timesnet/data/ab/docs/ab0964.html*).

Hunter, J. (ed.) (1993) *Japanese Women Working*, London: Routledge.

Huntington, S. (1996) *The Clash of Civilizations and the Remaking of World Order.* New York: Simon & Schuster.

Ichioka, Y. (1988) *The Issei: The World of the First Generation Japanese Immigrants, 1885–1924*, New York: Free Press.

Ieda, S. (1991) *Ierō kyabu: Narita o tobidatta onnatachi* [The yellow cab: women who flew away from Narita], Tokyo: Kōyū Shuppan.

Imamura, A.E. (ed.) (1996) *Re-Imaging Japanese Women*, Berkeley: University of California Press.

Inglehart, R. (1977) *The Silent Revolution: Changing Values and Political Styles among Western Publics*, Princeton: Princeton University Press.

.... (1990) *Culture Shift in Advanced Industrial Society*, Princeton: Princeton University Press.

Ino, K. (1992) 'Kenryoku to yakuza no rekishi,' [The history of the authorities and the *yakuza*] in Ishii, S. (ed.) *Yakuza to iu ikikata. Toshi no soko ni hisomu otokotachi no monogatari* [The *yakuza* way of life: tales of men lurking in the depths of the city] (Tokyo: JICC), pp. 258–71.

Ishihara, M. (1964) *Wako* [Japanese pirates], Tokyo: Yoshikawa Kōbunkan.

Ishii, S. (ed.) (1987) *Yakuza to iu ikikata. Toshi no soko ni hisomu otokotachi no monogatari* [The *yakuza* way of life: tales of men lurking in the depths of the city] Tokyo: JICC.

.... (1992) *Yakuza to iu ikikata. Kore ga shinogi ya!* [The *yakuza* way of life: This is a rip-off!], Tokyo: JICC.

Ishitoya, S. (1991) *Nihon o suteta Nihonijn* [The Japanese who abandoned Japan], Tokyo: Sōshisha.

Ivy, M. (1989) 'Critical texts, mass artifacts: the consumption of knowledge in postwar Japan,' in M. Miyoshi and H.D. Harootunian (eds), *Postmodernism and Japan* (Durham: Duke University Press), pp. 21–46.

Iwahashi O. (1998) '*Bōryokudan* crimes and countermeasures.' Paper presented at the Kobe Pre-Conference '98: 'Organized Crime and Organizational Crime: Frontiers in Research, Theory and Policy,' Kobe, 19–21 August 1998.

Iwai, H. (1963) *Byōri shūdan no kōzō. Oyabun kobun shūdan kenkyū* [The structure of a pathological grouping: research on paternalistic groups], Tokyo: Seishin Shobō.

Iwao, S. (1993) *The Japanese Woman: Traditional Image and Changing Reality*, Cambridge, Massachusetts: Harvard University Press.

Iyer, P. (1991) *The Lady and the Monk: Four Seasons in Kyoto*, New York: Vintage Books.

JAL Cabin Attendants' Union (1995) *Our View on Part-Time Cabin Crew*, (*http://www.bekkoame.ne.jp/jcau/part.html*).

Japan Insight (1999a) 'Marriage: The new division of labour,' (*http://jin.jcic.or.jp/insight/html..._new_division/the_new_division.html*).

.... (1999b) 'Discrimination against women,' (*http://jin.jcic.or.jp/insight/html/...rking/discrimination_against02/html*).

Japan Institute of Labour (1999) *Labour Situation in Japan*, Tokyo: Japan Institute of Labour.

Japan NGO Report Preparatory Committee (1999) *Japan NGO Alternative Report: Towards the Special Session of the UN General Assembly 'Women 2000: Gender Equity, Development, and* Peace,' Tokyo: Japan NGO Report Preparatory Committee.

Jarvie, I. C. (1982) 'The problem of ethical integrity in participant observation,' in R. Burgess (ed.), *Field Research: A Sourcebook and a Field Manual* (London: Allen & Unwin).

JETRO (1999) *White Paper on Foreign Direct Investment*, Tokyo: JETRO.

Jinnai, H. (1995) *Tokyo: A Spatial Anthropology*, Berkeley: California University Press.

Johnson, C. (1982) *MITI and the Japanese Miracle: The Growth of Industrial Policy, 1925–1975*, Stanford: Stanford University Press.

.... (1995) *Japan: Who governs? The Rise of the Developmental State*, New York: W.W. Norton.

Jolivet, M. (1997) *Japan: The Childless Society*, London: Routledge.

Ka, C.-M. (1995) *Japanese Colonialism in Taiwan: Land Tenure, Development and Dependency, 1895–1945*, Boulder: Westview Press.

Kamata S. (1994 [1971]) *Shinitaeta fūkei* [The extinct landscape], Tokyo: Diamond-sha.

Kaplan, D.E. and A. Dubro (1986) *Yakuza: The Explosive Account of Japan's Criminal Underworld,* Reading, Massachusetts: Addison-Wesley.

Kaplan, D.E. and A. Marshall (1996) *The Cult at the End of the World: The Incredible Story of Aum*, London: Arrow Books.

Kaplan, M., A. Kusano, I. Tsuji, and S. Hisamichi (1998) *Intergenerational Programs: Support for Children, Youth, and Elders in Japan*, Albany: State University of New York Press.

Karan, P.P. and K. Stapleton (eds) (1997) *The Japanese City*, Lexington: University of Kentucky Press.

Karatani, K., A. Asada, and J. Derrida (1984) 'Chō-shōhi shakai to chishikijin no yakuwari,' [The ultra-consumption society and the role of intellectuals] *Asahi Jaanaru*, May: 6–14.

Kashiwahara, Y. and K. Sonoda (eds) *Shapers of Japanese Buddhism*, Tokyo: Kosei.

Kato, J. (1995) *The Problem of Bureaucratic Rationality: Tax Politics in Japan*, Princeton: Princeton University Press.

Kato, T. and R. Steven (1993) *Is Japanese Management Post-Fordism?* Tokyo: Mado.

Katsura A. (1990) 'Sōsa jōhō izon no shūzai, hōdō kara dappi to bengoshi no sekimu,' [The escape from news-gathering and broadcasting that depends on police reports, and the responsibilities of lawyers] in Y. Narizawa (ed.) *Hanzai hōdō no genzai* [Crime reporting today], Tokyo: Nihon Hyōronsha, pp. 28–47.

Katz, R. (1998) *Japan, the System that Soured: The Rise and Fall of the Japanese Economic Miracle*, Armonk: M.E. Sharpe.

Kayashima, A. (1993) *American Democracy on Trial in Japan*, Tokyo: Otori Shobō.

Keene, D. (1998) *Dawn to the West. Japanese Literature of the Modern Era: Fiction*, New York: Columbia University Press.

Keidanren (1995) 'Re-evaluating the Japanese corporate system,' *Keidanren Review* (*http://www.keidanren.or.jp/english/journal/rev002*).

Keisatsuchō (ed.) (1978) *Keisatsu Hakusho. Keisatsu katsudō no genkyō* [Police White Paper: the present situation of police activities], Tokyo: Ōkurashō.

.... (1989) *Keisatsu Hakusho. Tokushū – Bōryokudan taisaku no genjō to kadai* [Police White Paper. Special Feature: Circumstances and themes of anti-*yakuza* policy], Tokyo: Ōkurashō.

.... (1991) *Keisatsu Hakusho. Tokushū – Yakubutsu mondai no genjō to kadai* [Police White Paper. Special Feature: Circumstances and themes of the drugs problem], Tokyo: Ōkurashō.

.... (1993) *Keisatsu Hakusho. Bōryokudan taisakuhō shikō l nen o furikaette.* [Police White Paper: Looking back at the first year of the Organized Crime Countermeasures Law], Tokyo: Ōkurashō.

.... (1997) *Keisatsu Hakusho. Kokusai terō jōsei to keisatsu no torikumi* [Police White Paper: The state of international terrorism and the police response] Tokyo: Ōkurashō.

Kelly, W.W. (1991) 'Directions in the anthropology of contemporary Japan,' *Annual Review of Anthropology* 20: 395–431.

Kenrick, D. M. (1990) *Where Communism Works: The Success of Competitive Communism in Japan*, Tokyo: Charles E. Tuttle.

Kidder, R. (1997) 'Disasters chronic and acute: issues in the study of environmental pollution in urban Japan,' in P.P. Karan and K. Stapleton (eds), *The Japanese City* (Lexington: University of Kentucky Press), pp. 156–75.

Kitagawa, J. (1966) *Religion in Japanese History*, New York: Columbia University Press.

Kitano, H. (1976) *Japanese Americans: The Evolution of a Subculture*, Englewood Cliffs: Prentice-Hall.

Kitazawa, H. (1988) 'Puro senshu ya geinōjin dake de wa bōryokudan to seizaikai no kōzō yuchaku,' [Structural collusion of professional sportsmen and showbiz entertainers with underworld gangs and the business world], *Uwasa no Shinsō* 3: 56–63.

Klages, H. (1984) *Wertorientierungen im Wandel. Rückblick Gegenwartsanalysen Prognosen*, Frankfurt am Main and New York: Campus Verlag.

.... (1988) *Wertedynamik. Über die Wandelbarkeit des Selbstverständlichen,* Zürich: Edition Interform.

Kluckhohn, C. (1962) 'Values and value-orientations in the theory of action: an exploration in definition and classification,' in T. Parsons and E.A. Shils (eds), *Toward a General Theory of Action: Theoretical Foundations for the Social Sciences* (New York: Harper & Row), pp. 388–433.

Kmieciak, P. (1976) *Wertstrukturen und Wertwandel in der Bundesrepublik Deutschland. Grundlagen einer interdisziplinaren empirischen Wertforschung mit einer Sekundaranalyse von Umfragedaten*, Göttingen: Schwartz.

Komai, H. (1995) *Migrant Workers in Japan*, London: Kegan Paul International.

Kondo, D.K. (1990) *Crafting Selves: Power, Gender, and Discourses of Identity in a Japanese Workplace*, Chicago: University of Chicago Press.

Konno, T. and Y. Fujisaki (1994) *Imin-shi: [I] Nanbei-hen* [The history of migration. Vol.1: South America], Tokyo: Shinsensha.

.... (1996) *Imin-shi: [II] Ajia Oseania-hen* [The history of migration. Vol.2: Asia and Oceania], Tokyo: Shinsensha.

Kriska, L.J. (1997) *The Accidental Office Lady*, Tokyo: Charles E. Tuttle.

Kurokawa, M. (1995) 'Working life and family life: Policies for their harmonization,' in *National Report: Japan, Working Life and Family Life: Policies for Their Harmonization* (1994 JIL Comparative Labor Law Seminar, Japan Institute of Labour, JIL Report 1995, no.4), pp. 65–80.

Labour Relations Bureau (2000*) Springtime Wage Increase* (*http://www.jil.go.jp/estasis/e0304.htm*).

Lam, A.C.L. (1992) *Women and Japanese Management: Discrimination and Reform*, London: Routledge.

Lebra, T. (1984) *Japanese Women: Constraint and Fulfillment*, Honolulu: University of Hawai'i Press.

Leupp, G.P. (1992) *Servants, Shophands and Laborers in the Cities of Tokugawa Japan*, Princeton: Princeton University Press.

Levi-Faur, D. (1997) 'Friedrich List and the political economy of the nation-state,' *Review of International Political Economy* 4(1): 154–78.

Levy, R.I. (1995) 'Emotions, knowing and culture,' in R.A. Shweder and R.A. LeVine (eds), *Culture Theory: Essays on Mind, Self and Emotion* (Cambridge: Cambridge University Press).

Lewis, C.C. (1995) *Educating Hearts and Minds: Reflections on Japanese Preschool and Elementary Education*, Cambridge: Cambridge University Press.

Linhart, S. and S. Früstück (eds) (1998) *The Culture of Japan as Seen Through Its Leisure*, Albany: State University of New York Press.

Lo, J. (1990) *Office Ladies and Factory Women*, Armonk: M.E. Sharpe.

Lutz, C.A. (1988) *Unnatural Emotions: Everyday Sentiments on a Micronesian Atoll and their Challenge to Western Theory*, Chicago: University of Chicago Press.

Lutz, C.A. and L. Abu-Lughod (eds) (1990) *Language and the Politics of the Emotions*, Cambridge: Cambridge University Press.

MacPherson, K.L. (ed.) (1998) *Asian Department Stores*, Honolulu: University of Hawai'i Press

Maffesoli, M. (1996) *The Time of the Tribes: The Decline of Individualism in Mass Society*, London: Sage.

Manabe, K. (1997) 'Kachikan no kenkyū no shiza: Sono sokutei hōhō to ryōiki o megutte' [The viewpoint of value research: methods and areas of measurement], Paper presented at the 48th Conference of the Kansai Sociological Association, Nagoya, May 25, 1997.

Management and Co-Ordination Agency (1996) *Survey on Service Industries*, Tokyo: Management and Co-Ordination Agency (*http://jin.jcic.or.jp/stat/stats/07IND66.html*).

.... (1999) *Annual Report on the Labor Force Survey*, Tokyo: Management and Coordination Agency.

Marcus, G.E. (1995) 'Ethnography in/of the world system: the emergence of multi-sited ethnography,' *Annual Review of Anthropology* 24: 95–117.

Marks, J. and R.T. Ames (eds) (1995) *Emotions in Asian Thought: A Dialogue in Comparative Philosophy*, Albany: State University of New York Press.

Marr, M.D. (1997) 'Maintaining autonomy: the plight of the American skid row and Japanese *yoseba*,' *Journal of Social Distress and the Homeless* 6(3): 229–50.

Marshall, B.K. (1994) *Learning to Be Modern: Japanese Political Discourse on Education,* Boulder: Westview Press.

Martinez, D.P. (ed.) (1998) *The Worlds of Japanese Popular Culture: Gender, Shifting Boundaries and Global Cultures*, Cambridge: Cambridge University Press.

Marx, G.T. (1993) 'Ironies of social control. Authorities as contributors to deviance through escalation, nonenforcement, and covert facilitation,' in H.M. Pontell (ed.), *Social Deviance. Readings in Theory and Research* (Englewood Cliffs: Prentice Hall), pp. 8–22

Matsuzawa, T. (1988) 'Street labor markets, day laborers, and the structure of oppression,' in G. McCormack and Y. Sugimoto (eds), *The Japanese Trajectory: Modernization and Beyond* (Cambridge: Cambridge University Press), pp. 147–64.

McCormack, G. and Y. Sugimoto (eds) (1988) *The Japanese Trajectory: Modernization and Beyond,* Cambridge: Cambridge University Press.

McCormack, G. (1996) *The Emptiness of Japanese Affluence*, Armonk: M.E. Sharpe.

McVeigh, B.J. (1997) *Life in a Japanese Women's College: Learning to be Ladylike*, London: Routledge.

.... (1998a) 'Linking state and self: how the Japanese state bureaucratizes subjectivity through "moral education",' *Anthropological Quarterly* 71 (3): 125–37.

.... (1998b) *The Nature of the Japanese State: Rationality and Rituality*, London: Routledge.

.... (under review) *Japan's Ministry of Education: Strategic Schooling and the Construction of Japanese Identity* (book manuscript).

Mestrovic, S. (1997) *Postemotional Society*, London: Sage.

Meyer, R. and W. Rüegg (1979) 'Wertforschung im systematischen internationalen Vergleich,' in H. Klages, and P. Kmieciak (eds), *Wertewandel und gesellschaftlicher Wandel* (Frankfurt am Main and New York: Campus Verlag), pp. 41–60.

Miller, D. (1994) *Modernity: An Ethnographic Approach*, Oxford: Berg.

Miller, R.A. (1982) *Japan's Modern Myth: The Language and Beyond*, New York: Weatherhill.

Mita, M. (1992) *The Social Psychology of Modern Japan*, London: Kegan Paul International.

MITI (1998) *White Paper on International Trade*, Tokyo: Ministry of International Trade and Industry (*http://www.miti.go.jp/report-e/g98WO42e.pdf*).

Miyake, H. (1989) 'Religious rituals in Shugendō,' *Japanese Journal of Religious Studies* 16 (2–3): 111–16.

.... (1996) 'Shugendō no rekishi to Mine-iri' [The history of mountain asceticism and the *Mine-iri* ritual] in H. Miyake, (ed.): *Mine-iri – Shugendō no honshitsu o motomete.* [The *Mine-iri* ritual: searching for the true essence of mountain asceticism], Yamagata: Chitose Gurūpu Kaihatsu Sentaa [Chitose Group Development Center].

Miyamoto, M. (1994) *Straitjacket Society: An Insider's Irreverent View of Bureaucratic* Japan, Tokyo: Kōdansha.

Miyata, N. (1996) *Kegare no minzokushi: sabetsu no bunkateki yōin* [The ethnology of ritual pollution: Cultural factors contributing to discrimination], Kyoto: Jinbun Sho'in.

Mizoguchi, A. (1992) 'Yamaguchi-gumi to bōryokudan shinpō' [The Yamaguchi Syndicate and the new organized crime law], in S. Ishii (ed.) *Yakuza to iu ikikata. Kore ga shinogi ya!* [The *yakuza* way of life: this is a rip-off!], Tokyo: JICC, pp. 246–57.

.... (1997) 'Jitsuroku: Takumi Masaru, "gokudō" o kaeta otoko'[Document: Takumi Masaru, the man who changed the *yakuza*], *Bungei Shunjū*, Nov. 1997: 290–302.

Mock, J. 1993. 'We have always lived under the castle: historical symbols and the maintenance of meaning,' in R. Rotenberg and G. McDonogh (eds), *The Cultural Meaning of Urban Space* (Westport: Bergin & Garvey), pp. 63–74.

Moeran, B. (1996a) 'In pursuit of perfection: the discourse of cars and transposition of signs in two advertising campaigns,' in J.W. Treat (ed.), *Contemporary Japan and Popular Culture* (London: Curzon), pp. 41–66.

.... (1996b) *A Japanese Advertising Agency: An Anthropology of Media and Markets*, London: Curzon Press.

.... (1997) *Folk Art Potters of Japan: Beyond an Anthropology of Aesthetics*, Richmond: Curzon.

Möhwald, U. (1995) 'Value patterns and value change in Germany and Japan (2): Pluralization of value patterns in Germany and Japan,' *Chūbu Daigaku Kokusai Kankei Gakubu Kiyō / The Journal of the College of International Studies, Chubu University*, 20 (March 1995): 91–131.

.... (1996) 'Japanische Einstellungen zur geschlechtlichen Egalität im Wandel,' in E. Janssen, U. Möhwald, and H.-D. Ölschleger (eds) *Gesellschaften im Umbruch? Aspekte des Wertewandels in Deutschland, Japan und Osteuropa* (Munich: Iudicium), pp. 179–207.

.... (1998) 'Kachikan ruikei ni tsuite' [On value types], *Chūbu Daigaku Kokusai Chiiki Kenkyūjo Kokusai Kenkyū* [International Studies, Chubu University Research Institute for International Studies], Vol. 14 (March 1998): 1–22.

Mori, H. (1997) *Immigration Policy and Foreign Workers in Japan*, Basingstoke: Macmillan.

Morley, P. (1999) *The Mountain is Moving: Japanese Women's Lives*, Vancouver: University of British Columbia Press.

Morris-Suzuki, T. (1994) *The Technological Transformation of Japan: From the Seventeenth to the Twenty-First Century*, Cambridge: Cambridge University Press.

Nagano T. (1992) '"Kokutei kyōshi-ka" o neratte iru no ka' (Are they aiming to make 'state teachers'?), in H. Sakamoto and H. Yamamoto (eds.), *Monbushō no kenkyū: kyōiku no jiyū to kenri o kangaeru* [research on the Ministry of Education: thinking on educational freedom and rights], Tokyo: San'ichi Shobō, pp. 195–218.

Nagatomo, S. (1992) *Attunement Through the Body*, Albany: State University of New York Press.

Nakae, T. (ed) (1977) *Gendai no butsudan, butsugu kōgei*, [Present-day craft production of Buddhist altars and altar fittings], Tokyo: Kamakura Shinsho.

Nakane, C. (1970) *Japanese Society*, Berkeley: University of California Press.

Nakano, M. (1996) 'New campaign to change an ineffective law: discrimination against women workers in Japan,' *Women's Asia 21: Voices from Japan* 2: 3–7.

Nakasone, Y. (1997) 'Re-examine fundamental education law,' *Daily Yomiuri*, April 21, p. 11.

Nakura, Y. (1997) Part-Time Workers in Japan, MA dissertation, University of Warwick.

Nakayama, T. (1930) *Nihon fujo-shi* [A History of Japanese women], Tokyo: Okayama Shoten.

Narizawa Y. (ed.) (1990) *Hanzai hōdō no genzai* [Crime reporting today], Tokyo: Nihon Hyōronsha.

Neary, I. (1989) *Political Protest and Social Control in Pre-War Japan: The Origins of Buraku Liberation*, Manchester: Manchester University Press.

.... (1997) 'Burakumin in contemporary Japan,' in M. Weiner (ed.), *Japan's Minorities: The Illusion of Homogeneity* (London: Routledge), pp. 79–107.

Nihon Hōsō Kyōkai Hōsō Yoron Chōsa-sho [NHK Broadcasting Public Opinion Survey] (1975) *Nihonjin no ishiki: NHK yoron chōsa* [The Mentality of the Japanese. NHK Opinion Survey], Tokyo: Shiseidō.

.... (1980) *Dai 2 Nihonjin no ishiki: NHK yoron chōsa* [The Mentality of the Japanese. NHK Opinion Survey 2], Tokyo: Shiseidō.

NHK Yoron Chōsa-bu (1991) *Gendai Nihon no ishiki kōzō* [The structure of consciousness in contemporary Japan], 3rd edition, Tokyo: Nihon Hōsō Shuppan Kyōkai.

.... (1998) *Gendai Nihon no ishiki kōzō* [The structure of consciousness in contemporary Japan], 4th edition, Tokyo: Nihon Hōsō Shuppan Kyōkai.

Ninomiya, S. (1933) 'An inquiry concerning the origin, development, and present situation of the Eta in relation to the history of social classes in Japan,' *Transactions of the Asiatic Society of Japan* 10: 47–154.

Nomura, H. (ed.) (1977) *Nihon no dentō butsudangyō* [The traditional Buddhist altar industry in Japan], Tokyo: Shōei Shuppan.

Ogasawara, Y. (1998) *Office Ladies and Salaried Men: Gender and Work in Japanese Companies*, Berkeley: University of California Press.

Oguma, E. (1995) *Tan'itsu minzoku shinwa no kigen: 'Nihonjin' no jigazō no keifu* [The Origin of the Myth of Ethnic Homogeneity: The Genealogy of 'Japanese' Self Images], Tokyo: Shin'yōsha.

Ogura E. (1996) 'Hikone butsudan no seiritsu,' in Hikone Butsudan Jigyō Kyōdō Kumiai, ed., *Ōmi no teshigoto: Hikone butsudan* [Ōmi craftsmanship: Hikone Buddhist altars], (Hikone: Hikone Butsudan Jigyō Kyōdō Kumiai). pp. 10–23.

Ohno, S. (1991) *'Hapon': Firipin Nikkeijin no nagai sengo* ['Hapon': The Long postwar period of ethnic Japanese in the Philippines], Tokyo: Dai-San Shokan.

.... (1997) *Kankō kōsu denai Firipin: rekishi to genzai; Nihon to no kankei-shi* [The Philippines away from the tourist route, history and present situation: the history of the Japanese connection], Tokyo: Kōbunken.

Okano, K. and M. Tsuchiya (1999) *Education in Contemporary Japan: Inequality and Diversity*, Cambridge: Cambridge University Press.

Okimoto, D. and T. Rohlen (eds) (1988) *Inside the Japanese System*, Stanford: Stanford University Press.

Ölschleger, D. *et al.* (1994) *Individualität und Egalität im gegenwärtigen Japan. Unterschungen zu Wertmustern in Bezug auf Familie und Arbeitswelt*, München: Iudicium.

Ölschleger, H.-D. and E. König, with B. Ölschleger (1997) *Japaner in der Neuen Welt: Eine teilannotierte Bibliographie von Werken zu japanischen Einwanderern in Nordamerika in Europäische Sprachen*, München: Iudicium.

Ooms, H. (1996) *Tokugawa Village Practice: Class, Status, Power, Law*, Berkeley: University of California Press.

Ortmanns, A. (1994) 'Rollenbilder im Wandel. Mann und Frau in japanischen Sozialkundebüchern von 1945 bis 1993,' *Japanstudien. Jahrbuch des Deutschen Instituts der Philipp-Franz-von-Siebold-Stiftung* 5: 281–309.

Osaka Jinken Rekishi Shiryōkan (1994) *Nihon no rekishi to jinken mondai* [Japanese history and human rights issues], Osaka: Kaihō Shuppansha.

Overholt, W. (1993) *China: The Next Economic Superpower*, London: Weidenfeld & Nicolson.

Part-Time Work Research Group to Consider Women's Working Life (1999) *Survey of Part-Time Workers*, Tokyo: Part-Time Work Research Group to Consider Women's Working Life.

Pascha, W. (1993) *Organisierte Kriminalität in Japan und Deutschland aus ökonomischer Sicht*, Duisburg: Universität – GH Duisburg.

Peak, L. (1991) *Learning to Go to School in Japan: The Transition from Home to Preschool Life*, Berkeley: University of California Press.

Picken, S.B. (1982) *Buddhism: Japan's Cultural Identity*, Tokyo: Kōdansha.

Pickering, J. (ed.) (1997) *The Authority of Experience: Essays on Buddhism and Psychology*, London: Curzon.

Plutshow, H. (1996) *Matsuri: The Festivals of Japan*, Folkestone: The Japan Library.

Price, J. (1967) 'A history of the outcaste: untouchability in Japan,' in G. DeVos and H. Wagatsuma (eds), *Japan's Invisible Race: Caste in Culture and Personality* (Berkeley: University of California Press).

Prus, R. (1996) *Symbolic Interaction and Ethnographic Research: Intersubjectivity and the Study of Human Lived Experience*, Albany: State University of New York Press.

Raz, A.E. (1999) *Riding the Black Ship: Japan and Tokyo Disneyland*, Cambridge, Massachusetts: Harvard University Asia Center.

Raz, J. (1992) 'Self-presentation and performance in the *yakuza* way of life. Fieldwork with a Japanese underworld group,' in R. Goodman and K. Refsing (eds.), *Ideology and Practice in Modern Japan* (London: Routledge), pp. 210–34.

.... (1996) *Yakuza no bunka jinruigaku. Ura kara mita Nihon* [The cultural anthropology of the *Yakuza*: Japan seen from its back door], Tokyo: Iwanami Shoten.

Reader, I. (1991) *Religion in Contemporary Japan*, London: Macmillan.

.... (1996) *A Poisonous Cocktail? Aum Shinrikyō's Path to Violence*, Copenhagen: Nordic Institute of Asian Studies.

Refsing, K. (1992) 'Japanese educational expansion, quality or equality,' in R. Goodman and K. Refsing (eds), *Ideology and Practice in Modern Japan* (London: Routledge), pp. 116–29.

Rengo White Paper (1999) *Invigorate Japan in All Aspects: Employment, Labor, Living and Economics*, Tokyo: JTUC Rengo.

Renshaw, J.R. (1999) *Kimono in the Boardroom*, Oxford: Oxford University Press.

Ritzer, G. (1996) *The McDonaldization of Society: An Investigation into the Changing Character of Contemporary Social Life*, Thousand Oaks: Pine Forge Press.

Roberson, J.E. (1998) *Japanese Working Class Lives: An Ethnographic Study of Factory Workers*, London: Routledge.

Roberts, G. (1994) *Staying on the Line: Blue-Collar Women in Contemporary Japan*, Honolulu: University of Hawai'i Press.

Rodinson, M. (1974) *Islam and Capitalism*, London: Penguin.

Rōdōshō Shokugyō Antei-kyoku [Ministry of Labor Employment Security Bureau] (1991) *Gendai wakamono no shokugyō ishiki: shokugyō ishiki no henka ni taiō suru tame ni.* [Work attitudes of modern youth: adapting to changing attitudes], Tokyo: Koyō Mondai Kenkyūkai [Research Group on Employment Problems].

Rohlen, T. (1974) *For Harmony and Strength: Japanese White-Collar Organization in Anthropological Perspective*, Berkeley: University of California Press.

.... (1976). 'Violence in Yoka High School: the implications for Japanese coalition politics of the confrontation between the Communist Party and the Buraku Liberation League,' *Asian Survey* 16(7): 682–99.

.... (1988) 'Permanent employment policies in times of recession,' in D. Okimoto and T. Rohlen (eds), *Inside the Japanese System* (Stanford: Stanford University Press), pp. 139–43.

Rohlen, T. and G. LeTendre (eds) (1998) *Teaching and Learning in Japan*, Cambridge: Cambridge University Press.

Rokeach, M. (1973) *The Nature of Human Values*, New York: The Free Press.

Rosenberger, N.R. (ed.) (1995) *Japanese Sense of Self*, Cambridge: Cambridge University Press.

Ryang, S. (1997) *North Koreans in Japan: Language Ideology and Identity*, Boulder: Westview Press.

Said, E.W. (1978) *Orientalism: Western Conceptions of the Orient.* London: Routledge & Kegan Paul.

Saiwai Chiku Kyōgikai [Saiwai Community Council] (1993) *Saiwai Chiku-kyō: 40 nen no ayumi* [Saiwai Community Council: 40 years of progress], Osaka: Dōwa Jigyō Sokushin

Saiwai Chiku Kyōgikai [Saiwai Community Council for the Promotion of Equality Projects].

Sakai, K. (1999) 'The situation of irregular employment in Japan,' Paper presented at Asia Working Women's Center Conference on Globalization and Women's Work in Asia, Tokyo, 13 December 1999.

Sakai, N. (1989) 'Modernity and its critique: the problem of universalism and particularism,' in M. Miyoshi and H.D. Harootunian (eds), *Postmodernism and Japan* (Durham: Duke University Press), pp. 93–122.

Sakakibara, E. (1993) *Bunmei toshite no Nihon-gata shihonshugi* [Japanese-style capitalism as civilization], Tokyo: Tōyō Keizai Shinpōsha.

Samuels, R. (1994) *'Rich Nation, Strong Army': National Security and the Technological Transformation of Japan*, Ithaca: Cornell University Press.

Sassen, S. (1991) *The Global City: New York, London, Tokyo,* Princeton: Princeton University Press.

Satō, M. (1993) *Shin-kaigai teijū jidai – Ōsutoraria no Nihonjin* [The new era of permanent residence abroad: Australia's Japanese], Tokyo: Shinchō-sha.

Schlesinger, J. (1997) *Shadow Shoguns: The Rise and Fall of Japan's Postwar Political Machine*, New York: Simon & Schuster.

Schmid, P. (1996) *Die Todesstrafe in Japan*, Hamburg: Deutsch-Japanische Juristenvereinigung.

Schoppa, L. (1991) *Education Reform in Japan: A Case of Immobilist Politics*, London: Routledge.

Sedgwick, M.W. (1999) 'Does Japanese management travel well in Asia? Managerial technology transfer at Japanese multinationals in Thailand,' in D. Encarnation (ed.), *Japanese Multinationals in Asia: Regional Operations in Comparative Perspective* (Oxford: Oxford University Press), pp. 163–79.

.... (2000) 'Japanese manufacturing in Thailand: an anthropology seeking efficient, standardized production,' in I. Reader and M. Soderberg (eds), *Japanese Influences and Presences in Asia* (Honolulu: University of Hawai'i Press), pp. 78–97.

Seimei Hoken Bunka Sentaa (ed.) (1987) *Dai 2-kai Nihonjin no seikatsu kachikan chōsa* [Second survey of the life values of the Japanese], Tokyo: Seimei Hoken Bunka Sentaa.

.... (ed.) (1988) *Jibunshugi no jidai. Nihonjin no atarashii seikatsu kachikan* [The era of 'self-ism': the new life values of the Japanese], Tokyo: Tōyō Keizai Shinpōsha.

.... (1992) *Nihonjin no seikatsu kachikan chōsa – 1991* [Survey of the life values of the Japanese, 1991], Tokyo: Seimei Hoken Bunka Sentaa.

.... (1993) *Samayoeru Nihonjin. Deeta de yomu seikatsu kachikan no henyō* [The wandering Japanese: changes in life values as seen in the data], Tokyo: Tōyō Keizai Shinpōsha.

Seimei Hoken Bunka Sentaa and Nomura Sōgō Kenkyūjo (ed.) (1980) *Nihonjin no seikatsu kachikan. Shōrai shakai tenbō no tame ni* [The life values of the Japanese: toward an outlook on the society of the future], Tokyo: Tōyō Keizai Shinpōsha.

Sellek, Y. (1997) 'Nikkeijin: the phenomenon of return migration,' in M. Weiner (ed.), *Japan's Minorities: The Illusion of Homogeneity* (London: Routledge), pp. 178–210.

Seymour, C. (1996) *Yakuza Diary: Doing Time in the Japanese Underworld*, New York: The Atlantic Monthly Press.

Shimada, H. (1994) *Japan's 'Guest Workers': Issues and Public Policies*, Tokyo: University of Tokyo Press.

Shimahara, N. (1971) *Burakumin: A Japanese Minority and Education*, The Hague: Martinus Nijhoff.

Shinotsuka, E. (1994) 'Women workers in Japan: past, present, future,' in J. Gelb and M. Palley (eds), *Women of Japan and Korea: Continuity and Change* (Philadelphia: Temple University Press), pp. 95–119.

Shire, K. (2000) 'Gendered organization and workplace culture in Japanese customer services.' *Social Science Japan Journal* 3 (1): 37–57.

Shūkan Tōyō Keizai ed. (1996) *Kaigai shinshutsu kigyō sōran – kunibetsu-hen '96.* [A general survey of enterprises active abroad: by country, 1996], Tokyo: Tōyō Keizai Shinpōsha.

Shweder R.A. and R.A. LeVine (eds) (1995) *Culture Theory: Essays on Mind, Self and Emotion,* Cambridge: Cambridge University Press.

Siddle, R. (1996) *Race, Resistance and the Ainu of Japan*, London: Routledge.

Sjoberg, G. (1967) *Ethics, Politics and Social Research*, London: Routledge & Kegan Paul.

Skov, L. and B. Moeran (eds) (1995) *Women, Media and Consumption in Japan*, Honolulu: University of Hawai'i Press.

Smith, R.J. (1974) *Ancestor Worship in Contemporary Japan*, Stanford, California: Stanford University Press.

Sōmuchō Gyōsei Kansatsu-kyoku [Management and Coordination Agency, Administrative Supervision Bureau] ed. (1995) *Zaigai hōjin no anzen/fukushi no genjō to kadai* [The present situation and concerns regarding the safety and welfare of Japanese nationals living abroad], Tokyo: Ōkurashō.

Sōmuchō (1995) *Tenkanki o mukaeta dōwa mondai: Heisei gonendo dōwa chiku jittai haakutō chōsa kekka no kaisetu* [A turning point in the equality problem: analysis of the results of the 1993 surveys to assess conditions in *dōwa* districts], Tokyo: Chūō Hōki Shuppan.

Stevens, C. (1997) *On the Margins of Japanese Society: Volunteers and the Welfare of the Urban Underclass*, London: Routledge.

Sugihara, S. (1997) *Between Incompetence and Culpability: Assessing the Diplomacy of Japan's Foreign Ministry from Pearl Harbor to Potsdam*, New York: University Press of America.

Sugimoto, Y. (1997) *An Introduction to Japanese Society*, Cambridge: Cambridge University Press.

.... (1999) 'Making sense of *nihonjinron*,' *Thesis Eleven* 57: 81–96.

Sugimoto, Y. and J. P. Arnason (eds) (1995) *Japanese Encounters with Postmodernity*, London: Kegan Paul International.

Sumitomo, K. and K. Itakura (1998) *Sabetsu to meishin: hisabetsu buraku no rekishi* [Discrimination and superstition: the history of *buraku* discrimination], Tokyo: Kasetsusha.

Tabb, W. (1995) *The Postwar Japanese System: Cultural Economy and Economic Transformation*, New York: Oxford University Press.

Taira, K. (1993) 'Dialectics of economic growth, national power, and distributive struggles,' in A. Gordon (ed.), *Postwar Japan as History* (Berkeley: University of California Press), pp. 167–86.

Takaki, R. (1994) *Issei and Nisei: The Settling of Japanese America*, New York: Chelsea House.

Tamanoi, M.A. (1998) *Under the Shadow of Nationalism: Politics and Poetics of Rural Japanese Women*, Honolulu: University of Hawai'i Press.

Tanaka, Y. (1988) 'Nuclear power and the labor movement,' in G. McCormack and Y. Sugimoto (eds), *The Japanese Trajectory: Modernization and Beyond* (Cambridge: Cambridge University Press), pp. 129–46.

Terry, E. (1998) 'Two years after the Kobe earthquake,' in F. Gibney (ed.), *Unlocking the Bureaucrat's Kingdom: Deregulation and the Japanese Economy* (Washington, D.C.: Brookings Institution Press), pp. 231–42.

Thompson, G. (ed.) (1998) *Economic Dynamism in the Asia-Pacific*, London: Routledge in association with the Open University.

Tipton, F.B. (1998) *The Rise of Asia: Economics, Society and Politics in Contemporary Asia*, Honolulu: University of Hawai'i Press.

Tobin, J.J. (ed.) (1992) *Remade in Japan: Everyday Life and Consumer Taste in a Changing Society*, New Haven: Yale University Press.

Togawa, A. (1950) *Haguro yamabushi to minkan shinkō* [Haguro mountain priests and private-sector promotion], Tsuruoka: Fumiya Shoten.

.... (1994) 'Haguro-san no shugyō' [Ascetic practices on Mount Haguro], in Miyake, Hitoshi (ed.): *Shugendō shugyō taikei* [The Structure of Mountain Ascetic Practice], Tokyo: Kokusho Kankō Kai [Association for Publishing National Literature], pp. 346–86.

Tōkei Sūri Kenkyūjo Kokuminsei Chōsa I'inkai [Institute of Mathematical Statistics, National Character Survey Committee] (ed.) (1961) *Nihonjin no kokuminsei.* [A study of the Japanese national character], Tokyo: Shiseidō.

.... (1970) *Dai 2 Nihonjin no kokuminsei.* [A study of the Japanese national character 2], Tokyo: Idemitsu Shoten.

.... (1975) *Dai 3 Nihonjin no kokuminsei.* [A study of the Japanese national character 3], Tokyo: Idemitsu Shoten.

.... (1982) *Dai 4 Nihonjin no kokuminsei.* [A study of the Japanese national character 4], Tokyo: Idemitsu Shoten.

.... (1992) *Dai 5 Nihonjin no kokuminsei.* [A study of the Japanese national character 5], Tokyo: Idemitsu Shoten.

.... (1994) *Kokuminsei no kenkyū, dai 9-kai zenkoku chōsa* [Research on the national character: The ninth national survey], Tokyo: Tōkei Sūri Kenkyūjo.

Traphagen, J. (2000) *Taming Oblivion: Aging Bodies and the Fear of Senility in Japan*, Albany: State University of New York Press.

Treat, J.W. (ed.) (1996) *Contemporary Japan and Popular Culture*, Richmond: Curzon Press.

Tu, W.M. (ed.) (1996) *Confucian Traditions in East Asian Modernity*, Cambridge, Massachusetts: Harvard University Press.

Turner, B.S. (1984) *The Body and Society: Explorations in Social Theory*, Oxford: Blackwell.

Turner, C.L. (1995) *Japanese Workers in Protest: An Ethnography of Consciousness and Experience*, Berkeley: University of California Press.

Uchida, J. (1990) 'Keizai shakai no henka to bōryokudan no henshitsu: tenkanki o mukaeta bōryoku taisaku,' [Socioeconomic change and the changing nature of the *yakuza*: anti-gang policy at a turning point], *Keisatsugaku Ronshū* [Papers on Police Studies], 43/6: 36–51.

Uchida, T. (1998) 'Discussion: the future of women in the workplace,' *Women's Asia 21: Voices from Japan* 4: 2–14.

Umi no Mukō de Kurashite Mireba Program Staff, *et al.* eds (1996a) *Umi no Mukō de Kurashite Mireba* [How about living abroad?] (Part 1), Tokyo: Futabasha.

.... (1996b) *Umi no Mukō de Kurashite Mireba* [How about living abroad?] (Part 2), Tokyo: Futabasha.

Upham, F. (1987) *Law and Social Change in Postwar Japan*, Cambridge, Massachusetts: Harvard University Press.

van Wolferen, K. (1989) *The Enigma of Japanese Power*, New York: Alfred A. Knopf.

Ventura, R. (1992) *Underground in Japan*, London: Jonathan Cape.

Wakisaka, A. (1997) 'Women at work,' in M. Sako and H. Sato (eds), *Japanese Labour and Management in Transition: Diversity, Flexibility and Participation* (London: Routledge), pp. 131–50.

Wallerstein, Immanuel (1974) *The Modern World System: Capitalist Agriculture and the Origins of the European World-Economy in the Sixteenth Century*, New York: Academic Press.

Ward, K. (ed.) (1990) *Women Workers and Global Restructuring*, Ithaca: ILR Press, School of Industrial and Labor Relations, Cornell University.

Waswo, A. (1996) *Modern Japanese Society 1868–1994*, Oxford: Oxford University Press.

Watanabe, T. (1999) 'Buraku-shi no tenkan' [Turning points in Buraku history], *Gendai Shisō* [Contemporary Thought] 27(2).

Watanuki J. (1986): 'Kachi tairitsu no keizoku to hen'yō' [Continuity and change in value cleavage], in J. Watanuki *et al.*, *Nihonjin no Senkyō Kōdō* [The Voting Behavior of the Japanese], Tokyo: University of Tokyo Press, pp. 38–53.

Watson, J.L. (ed.) (1997) *Golden Arches East: McDonald's in East Asia*, Stanford: Stanford University Press.

Wawrytko, S.A. (1995) 'The murky mirror: women and sexual ethics as reflected in Japanese Cinema,' in C.W.H. Fu and S. Heine (eds), *Japan in Traditional and Postmodern Perspectives* (Albany: State University of New York Press), pp. 121–68.

Weber, M. (1987) *The Protestant Ethic and the Spirit of Capitalism*, London: Unwin.

Weiner, M. (1994) *Race and Migration in Imperial Japan*, London: Routledge.

Weiner, M. (ed.) (1997) *Japan's Minorities: The Illusion of Homogeneity*, London: Routledge.

White, M. (1994) *Material Child: Coming of Age in Japan and America*, Berkeley: University of California Press.

Whittaker, D.H. (1990) ' The end of Japanese-style employment,' *Work, Employment and Society* 4 (3): 321–47.

.... (1997) *Small Firms in the Japanese Economy*, Cambridge: Cambridge University Press.

Wood, C. (1993) *The Bubble Economy: The Japanese Economic Collapse*, Tokyo: Charles E. Tuttle.

.... (1994) *The End of Japan Inc., and How the New Japan Will Look*, New York: Simon & Schuster.

Woodall, B. (1996) *Japan Under Construction: Corruption, Politics, and Public Works*, Berkeley: University of California Press.

Worm, H. (1988) 'Das organisierte Verbrechen in Japan – einige Daten und Aspekte,' in M. Pohl (ed.), *Japan 1987/88. Politik und Wirtschaft* (Hamburg: Institut für Asienkunde), pp. 68–93

Yamada, M. *et al.* (eds) (1994) *Godaime Yamaguchi-gumi ga yuku* [The Yamaguchi Syndicate under its Fifth Leader], Tokyo: Futaba-sha.

Yamaguchi, M. (1990) 'Nyūsu kachi handan kijun no kenshō,' [A survey of the standards used to make news judgments], in Y. Narizawa (ed.), *Hanzai hōdō no genzai* [Crime Reporting Today], (Tokyo: Nihon Hyōronsha), pp. 94–115.

Yamamoto H. (1992) 'Monbushō wa donna tokoro ka' ['What kind of place is the Ministry of Education?'], in H. Sakamoto and H. Yamamoto (eds) *Monbushō no kenkyū: kyōiku no jiyu to kenri o kangaeru* [Research on the Ministry of Education: Thoughts on Educational Freedom and Rights], Tokyo: San'ichi Shobō, pp. 26–49.

Yamamoto, S. (1985) *Hataraite tabi-shita Osutoraria: waakingu horidee taiken-ki* [I Have Worked and Travelled in Australia: Record of a Working Holiday], Tokyo: Acorns International.

Yamashita, S. (1999) *Bari – kankō jinruigaku no ressun* [Bali: what can we learn from the anthropology of tourism?], Tokyo: University of Tokyo Press.

Yamazaki, T. (1999) *Sandakan Brothel No.8*, Armonk: M.E. Sharpe.

Yanagihara, K. (1994) *'Zaigai' Nihonjin* [Japanese who 'live abroad'], Tokyo: Shōbunsha.

Yazaki, T. (1973) 'The history of urbanization in Japan,' in A. Southall (ed.) *Urban Anthropology* (New York: Oxford University, Press), pp. 139–61.

Yoneyama, L. (1999) *Hiroshima Traces: Time, Space, and the Dialectics of Memory*, Berkeley: University of California Press.

Yoshino, K. (1992) *Cultural Nationalism in Contemporary Japan: A Sociological Inquiry*, London: Routledge.

.... (1997) *Bunka nashonarizumu no shakaigaku* [The sociology of cultural nationalism], Nagoya: Nagoya University Press.

Young, L. (1998) *Japan's Total Empire: Manchuria and the Culture of Wartime Imperialism*, Berkeley: University of California Press.

Yuasa, Y. (1987) *The Body: Toward an Eastern Mind-Body Theory*, Albany: State University of New York Press.

List of Contributors

BEFU, Harumi: Emeritus Professor of Anthropology, Stanford University.

BISHOP, Beverley: a former Lecturer at Shiga University, currently completing a doctorate at the Political Economy Research Centre, Sheffield University.

CLAMMER, John: Professor of Comparative Cultures, Sophia University.

DAVIS, John: currently completing a doctorate in the Department of Social and Cultural Anthropology at Stanford University

EADES, Carla: an independent researcher and former part-time Lecturer at Shiga University and Shiga Prefectural University in Hikone.

EADES, Jerry: Professor of Asia Pacific Studies, Ritsumeikan Asia Pacific University.

GILL, Tom: Associate Professor, Institute of Social Studies, University of Tokyo.

HERBERT, Wolfgang: Professor at Tokushima University.

McVEIGH, Brian: Associate Professor at Toyo Gakuen University.

MÖHWALD, Ulrich: Professor of Sociology, College of International Studies, Chubu University.

NISHIYAMA, Yuriko: an independent researcher, translator, and teacher of English in Hikone.

RIESSLAND, Andreas: Visiting Lecturer, Keio University.

SEDGWICK, Mitchell: Senior Research Fellow in Cross-Cultural Studies, Oxford Brookes University.

YANASE, Hiroko: an independent researcher, translator, and teacher of English in Hikone.

Index